MW01484364

Gotham City

14 MILES

14 Essays on Why the 1960s Batman TV Series Matters

Gotham City

14 MILES

14 ESSAYS ON WHY THE 1960S BATMAN TV SERIES MATTERS

edited by

Jim Beard

SEQUART RESEARCH & LITERACY ORGANIZATION   EDWARDSVILLE, ILLINOIS

Gotham City 14 Miles: 14 Essays on Why the 1960s Batman TV Series Matters
Edited by Jim Beard

Copyright © 2010 by the respective authors. Batman and related characters are trademarks of DC Comics © 2010.

Revised first edition, November 2011, ISBN 978-1-466-33305-5. First edition, December 2010.

All rights reserved by the author. Except for brief excerpts used for review or scholarly purposes, no part of this book may be reproduced in any manner whatsoever, including electronic, without express written consent of the author.

Cover by M. Mrakota Orsman; please visit mirthquake.net. Design by Julian Darius. Interior art is © the respective copyright owners.

The author wishes to thank to John Stacks, Bob Furmanek, and Trevor Kimball for help tracking many of these interior images down. The author further wishes to thank the members and moderators of the 1966 Batman Message Board for facts, friendship, and fun.

Published by Sequart Research & Literacy Organization. Edited by Jim Beard, with thanks to Julian Darius, Mike Phillips, Cody Walker, and Matthew Elmslie.

For more information about other titles in this series, visit Sequart.org/books.

Contents

"Giant Lighted Lucite Map of Gotham City": An Introduction

by Jim Beard

A Beard family urban legend tells of my sister, then six years old, innocently asking my parents why was it that, if the Batcave was only 14 miles away, we couldn't just drive out and visit it.

My sister mistook Gotham City for our hometown and believed the magical Batcave to lie just outside the city limits. She obviously also believed Batman and Robin to be real, just like Santa Claus. I was, alas, only nine months old when *Batman* premiered on 12 January 1966, but by June 1967, the series also had its powerful bat-hooks in me. At that time, my mother made this annotation in my baby book: "14 mos. Dances to record 'Batman.'"

I was a believer. The show introduced me to the Caped Crusader before meeting him in print, making me into the comic-book fan I am today. Since then, I've heard a multitude of stories about kids' literal belief in *Batman* and what it meant – and still means – to them. You probably have one of your own or know someone who does.

Imagine how kids of the mid-1960s saw *Batman*: nothing before had been so colorful, so crazy, so in-your-face. The TV series did far more to put children in Robin's place than the actual comics ever did. Kids often felt as if they could

Special Aptitudes

Age

14 mos. dances to record "Batman".

In his baby book, Jim Beard's mother notes in summer 1966 the earliest sign of his fascination with Batman.

Christmas 1966 with the Beards.   Note the coveted Switch 'N Go Batman Batmobile Set.

find the Batcave on their own, ride with their hero to police headquarters, and learn what super-criminal was perpetrating what crime spree this time.

For two seasons, the series burned like a Batcave Bunsen burner, hot and steady, then flickered to a slow heat in the final season before being extinguished forever. Maybe it was a blessing that its televised life was cut so short: can you imagine how much more flak it would receive today if it had continued?

Yes, adults' perceptions of the show usually differ from those of children, especially those who didn't grow up with the series or were already adults when it originally aired. It's become almost a traditional American value to put *Batman* down – a knee-jerk reaction that might seem funny or clever but that's also painful to those who honestly believe in the show's worth. I distinctly remember the sense of hurt and unreality the first time I heard someone putting down *Batman*'s bat-fights as "totally fake." I was dumbfounded. Fake? To me they were what they were: an integral slice of the show that you accepted as part of the whole.

Any show that so clearly divides opinions needs to be fully reassessed. *Batman* has become legendary and continues to serve as an inspiration to creative types around the world, yet it also still ends up as the butt of jokes and clichés. That dichotomy fascinates me, both as a Batman fan and as a student of pop culture. I have my own perspective on the series, but I also believe that time hasn't been too kind to memories of *Batman*. The show needs to be laid out and examined thoroughly for both its merits and its faults. You may love it or hate it, and I get that – but *why*?

Yet over the years, there have only been a handful of other books concerning the show, which is amazing for such a landmark of pop culture. At the front of the line must stand Joel Eisner's *The Official Batman Batbook*, first published in 1986 and the first quantification of the show's scope and detail. Then there are the three volumes of James van Hise's *Batmania*, which aimed itself solidly at the series's fans. Lastly comes the Holy Trinity of Bat-autobiographies: Adam West's indispensable *Back to the Batcave* (1994), Burt Ward's *Boy Wonder: My Life in Tights* (1995), and Yvonne Craig's *From Ballet to the Batcave and Beyond* (2000). Other than a few magazine spotlights and the like, that's about it for the show that once held the entire country spellbound twice a week.

When I pitched *Gotham City 14 Miles* to the fine folks at Sequart, I tried to boil my theme down to one simple question: "Why does this show matter?" To wit: why is it still fondly remembered though also soundly reviled? Why is it cited as an inspiration to artists and musicians and filmmakers and writers, yet also used as an example of what *not* to do in today's comics and films? Why have the finer details and nuances of the show's stories, design, and performances been either forgotten or never truly appreciated at all?

Overall, why isn't *Batman* '66 being seriously discussed?

In the third-season episode "I'll be a Mummy's Uncle," we learn that the secret Batcave below stately Wayne Manor is surrounded by a shield of nigh-impregnable "Batanium," which King Tut tries to break through. Both *Batman* fandom and the show's haters seem ensconced in Batanium – firm in their beliefs and perceptions, unwilling to allow the shield to come down and allow new thought or opinion to strike their foundations. Perhaps this book can help smash through those barriers – and expose a few myths and clichés along the way.

I wanted *Gotham City 14 Miles* to be as fun and eclectic as the TV series itself and set out to create a cadre of essayists who could make that vision a reality. In no way did we want this book to be merely a celebration of *Batman*; anyway, the best way to celebrate the show is probably to take it seriously. And a *Batman* "lovefest" would probably end up being fairly boring after the first few essays. No, what the show required most was critical dissection and examination, with an eye towards its weight and worth, not simply to be maintained as a monument to its admirers. Most contributors do appreciate *Batman*, which in part attracted them to write about the show, but they argue their case rationally, elevating the critical discourse surrounding the show, and felt free to admit the show's failings too. Their diversity, ranging from seasoned professionals to talented newcomers, from comics scholars to comics creators, offers a treasure trove of varied perspectives and insight.

The themes and topics addressed were carefully chosen with this in mind. Our aim was to be as diverse in the topics addressed as in the essayists addressing them, amassing a body of perspectives on important subjects.

At the time of this writing, *Batman* '66 has never been officially issued for home viewing, whether on VHS, DVD, Blu-Ray, or stone tablet. The point of this book is not to rail against that particularly pig-headed injustice (what, they can crack the human genome but they can't negotiate the rights to *Batman*?). But it's all the more important, given this unavailability, to shine a light on this important artifact of American pop culture – and to begin its critical reexamination.

In such a critical reappraisal, both adherents and naysayers give a little to find common ground. This book is for both alike. It's a starting point, laying the groundwork for further critical discussion. You don't have to love the show to enjoy the essays here; you just have to be willing to explore this important but rarely explored topic.

14 miles, 14 essays: atomic batteries to power, turbines to speed – and enjoy your trip!

Jim Beard's Bat-obsession comes full circle, as he sits in the Batmobile at the 2010 C2E2 convention.

Bats in their Belfries: The Proliferation of "Batmania"

by Robert Greenberger

America entered the second half of the 1960s with its head swimming from political and social change. The shock of John F. Kennedy's assassination was just wearing off when, just before Christmas 1965, the Soviet Union started shipping rockets to North Vietnam, spurring Lyndon Johnson to push deeper into Vietnam. In the final weeks of 1965, Americans rejoiced at the first controlled rendezvous between space capsules, *Gemini 6* and *Gemini 7*, giving America the edge in the space race. After meeting for years, the Second Vatican Council concluded its substantial changes to Catholicism. America's baby boom generation ended; 1965 saw 1.2% population growth, the lowest since 1945. The Beat Generation, hallmark of the 1950s, had given way to the Hippie Generation. Hairstyles grew longer and clothing more colorful. Rather than be concerned with poetry and far-out thoughts, teenagers were starting to demand social change.

Advances in technology were also changing popular culture. Sony introduced the Betamax video recorder in 1965. But probably no such change was more dramatic than the the arrival of large color TVs. While NBC and CBS were slow to convert their primetime programming to color, ABC made the loudest noise about its full-color shows (although NBC was the first network to go all-color, at the end of 1966).

TV seasons were also getting shorter. The number of primetime episodes per season had peaked at 39, allowing 13 weeks for repeats or specials, meaning almost year-round original programming. Rising costs and a larger inventory of filmed programming allowed the networks to cut back, so that the 1965-1966 season averaged about 30 episodes per show. And while replacement series arrived with regularity between October and April, the networks never really ballyhooed their mid-season replacements because they denoted failure.

With ABC struggling with falling ratings and executives stumped over how to attract an audience, Harve Bennett, the company's director of West Coast development, began to think a cartoon show might be the way to go, aping the success of the compentition's animated fare. (Bennett would go on to develop a number of pop-culture icons, including shows such as *The Six Million Dollar Man*, and produced the most successful of the 1980s Star Trek films.) So they could license something assured of success, Bennett and ABC commissioned a survey of characters then popular with kids. The number one result: the Man of Steel.

In the spring of 1965, ABC executives approached National Periodicals (which would become DC Comics) to negotiate the rights to make a Superman show. But Broadway was already developing the musical *It's a Bird, It's a Plane, It's Superman*, which kept the Man of Steel off-limits. ABC settled for the lesser-known and poorer-selling Batman, who ranked third on the survey (behind Dick Tracy, who had already been optioned by NBC) but who was enjoying a creative rejuvenation by this time under the editorial guidance of Julius Schwartz.

What Bennett didn't realize at the time – but his colleague Yale Udoff, ABC's director of late-night programming, did – was that Batman was poised for resurgence. The seeds for Batmania had already been planted, though no one at ABC knew what they were about to unleash.

Throughout 1965, Columbia Pictures had been roadshowing an edited version of the 1940s *Batman* serial, collapsing the 15 chapters into a lengthy feature film. The movie also played at Hugh Hefner's Playboy Mansion, where Udoff saw it and was enchanted. As *Time* magazine reported in November,

> In a college town, who today outdraws *Dr. Strangelove*, outclocks *Gone With the Wind*, and breaks all known records for popcorn sales? It's not a

bird or a plane but, of all things, *Batman*. The 1939 comic-strip creation of Bob Kane, which Columbia Pictures filmed in 1943 as a 15-episode serial, has now been spliced, end to end, to produce a 248-minute marathon of fist fights, zombies[,] and ravenous alligators. Last week[,] it was packing the house at an off-campus theater near the University of Illinois, and Columbia plans similar orgies in 20 major cities.

As *Time* concluded, "Offered one Columbia executive: 'Comic-book heroes are the only heroes we have nowadays.' Said one Batfan: 'It's pop art.' Says another: 'Where else can you get entertained for four hours for a buck and a quarter?'" There it was: Batman was pop art, and ABC was poised to unleash that very thing into every living room in America.

Bennet and Udoff recommended a Batman series, but Edgar Sherick, ABC's programming chief, thought they were nuts. Sherick's number two, Douglas Cramer (who would later embrace pop culture by producing *Wonder Woman* for ABC in the 1970s), also chimed in. ABC ultimately decided to buy the rights and determined that an animated Batman series was ideal for their 7:30 PM timeslot (then network-controlled primetime). The network saw the show being done in a straight fashion and assigned 20th Century-Fox's TV division to produce the series for ABC.

In those days, while all TV was considered suitable for every demographic, the earlier slots (7:30 to 9 PM) were aimed towards children and families, while later hours offered slightly more adult fare. In the earlier hours, animated shows mixed with live-action ones; in 1964, families could enjoy *The Flintstones* and *Jonny Quest* or live-action sitcoms like *The Munsters* and *My Favorite Martian*. A year later, it was much the same with *Shindig* and *Flipper* rounding things out. Putting dramatic fare at 7:30 began as counter-programming with *Twelve O'Clock High*, *Combat*, and *Rawhide*.

Fox turned the series over to producer William Dozier, and Cramer took Dozier to lunch to discuss the concept. The producer later recounted to *TV Guide*, "ABC had bought the concept without any idea what to do with it." Having been offered the series based on a character he was unfamiliar with, Dozier purchased comics to read *en route* to a meeting in New York. In *The Official Batman Batbook*, he told Joel Eisner, "At first, I thought they were crazy. I really thought they were crazy, if they were going to try to put this on TV. Then I had just the simple idea of overdoing it, of making it so square and so serious that adults would find it amusing." This would play into the camp trend that had been bubbling around the periphery of pop culture at the time.

Fox's William Self suggested Dozier offer the pilot to Eric Ambler, a mystery novelist who also wrote for TV's *Checkmate* and *Epitaph for a Spy*. After Ambler rejected Dozier's offer, the producer selected Lorenzo Semple, Jr. to write the pilot for what had by then evolved into a live-action series. The two men had worked together in the past, and the producer figured the writer had just the right sensibility for the subject matter. Semple also claimed to have been the one who decided to play things ultra-serious and therefore push the show into camp, making it play to both kids and adults.

ABC penciled the show in for the fall 1966 season and let it quietly percolate throughout the summer of 1965. The first actor cast was Alan Napier as Alfred the butler. It wasn't until late summer that Adam West and Burt Ward did their screen tests. The general public first heard about the impending series in the 15 September *Wall Street Journal*. Comic fans first caught wind of the news that same month, when co-creator Bob Kane tipped off Biljo White's *Batmania* fanzine.

But ABC's fall line-up proved such a disaster that the network scrambled to prepare a handful of mid-season replacements and, needing a fresh start, dubbed these replacements as the network's "Second Season." *The Adventures of Ozzie and Harriet* had ended its long run, replaced on Wednesday nights by *Shindig*, a twice-weekly half-hour broadcast which also aired Thursday nights. A pop-music show, *Shindig* capitalized on the nation's renewed fascination, in the wake of Beatlemania, with Top 40 music. But *Shindig* was hemorrhaging viewers.

As its replacement, ABC turned to *Batman*, moving the show's debut to 12 January 1966, half a season earlier than planned. In mid-October, the Associated Press reported that *Shindig* had been cancelled, with both its Wednesday and Thursday evening slots going to the adventures of the Caped Crusader and the Boy Wonder.

The pilot was shot about a week after the series was moved earlier on the schedule. Based on *Batman* #171 and featuring Frank Gorshin's Riddler, the pilot tested poorly because audiences had no idea what they were watching (camp was an alien concept for primetime) and whether or not it was to be taken seriously – panicky news for the network, which had already committed to 13 episodes. Fox rushed into full-scale production, shooting the second episode in early November, racing the clock given the impending holiday shutdown and mid-January air date.

Nervous, ABC cranked up the publicity machine, and you had to be in a coma not to know that Batman was coming to TV in the New Year. Batman headlined the network's "Second Season" initiative and appeared prominently in advertisements, which besieged viewers all through the holidays.[1] The 28 January 1966 issue of *Time* explained,

> *Batman* would have attracted nobody but preschoolers were it not for ABC's ingenious promotion efforts. Skywriters emblazoned BATMAN is COMING in the heavens above the Rose Bowl game. Every hour on the hour, TV announcements bleated the imminent arrival of the Caped Crusader. Hordes of people who recalled Bob Kane's comicbook [sic] creation as well as the 1943 movie serial pushed their toddlers out of the way to get a good look at the TV set.

In the end, everyone watched. And came back Thursday to see how a drugged Batman and kidnapped Robin could apprehend the diabolical Prince of Puzzlers. Then they talked about it. They everyone and their friends came back to watch the following week.

When *Batman* debuted that fateful winter, its Wednesday timeslot competition was *Lost in Space* on CBS and *The Virginian* on NBC, while Thursdays also offered *The Munsters* or *Daniel Boone*. Audiences of any age had seen nothing like *Batman*. It was the four-color comic book brought to vivid life. This effect was enhanced when Dozier had National Periodical letterer Ira Schnapp create a set of comic-book sound effects to be superimposed over the fight scenes, helping to transform the hero from printed page to TV screen.

Critics weren't sure what to make of the show, particularly because it didn't seem to fit with the sitcoms, dramas, and animated shows usually offered at that time. Most critics tried to analyze the show as either straight drama or sitcom, without pausing to grasp that the show was unique. As a result, mixed reviews were the only downside to the debut.

---

[1] Some of the promotional material seems as overdone as the show itself. It described West as a "talented actor with the rugged ability of a natural athlete... [who could] heroically scale the sides of buildings, battling arch criminals in hand-to-hand combat, and in other situations where superb athletic skill is necessary." To further cement West's role as an action hero, the material stated that he was "personable, and tall, with a gladiator's virile physique, a warm voice, expressive eyes, and a conversational style." Generations later, after the body-building fad redefined Hollywood hunks, West is more likely to be known for his paunch.

A full-page ad for ABC's "Second Season," headlined by *Batman*. From *TV Guide*, 8-14 January 1966 issue. Copyright © Greenway Productions, DC Comics, and 20th Century-Fox.

The ratings, though, were beyond anything the network could have expected. Trendex, the era's version of overnight Nielsen ratings, showed that the debut episode had an astonishing 49% sampling in the top 50 TV markets. The concluding episode the following evening added ten percentage points. The marketing had worked, and the show was a monster hit. *Lost in Space* and *The Virginian* never knew what hit them.

Even better, they grew as winter turned to spring. During the season which ended in May, *Batman*'s Wednesday installment was rated the number 10 program, while the second part on Thursday notched the number five slot.

A more detailed study from Nielsen, covering the two-week period in January that featured the first four episodes, showed the Wednesday night edition in ninth place with the Thursday conclusion in eighth. This single series moved the network up two ratings points, unheard of back in those days. For the week of 13 February, Thursday's *Batman* was America's number one series, with the Wednesday opener taking fifth.[2] ABC's audience share jumped 10% in a single month, leading viewers to sample other fare, bolstering the network's profits. The company's "Second Season" strategy had paid off in spades, producing a show more successful than any of the new fall offerings.

Clearly, the series was a smash success for all concerned, and it changed the cast's lives. "The Saturday morning after the show premiered," Adam West wrote in *Back to the Batcave*,

> I drove to Big Bear with my kids for some skiing. In my ski clothes and goggles, my wool cap pulled down low to protect me from the cold, I got out of the car in a tiny place named Fawnskin. As I crossed the road to the general store, I heard people behind me yelling excitedly, "Batman! Batman!"

This crystallized for the actor that his life had changed forever. He continued,

> I would find this phenomenon repeated over and over through the years, and to this day. Fans never simply want to shake my hand or get an autograph, they want to talk about what Batman meant to them, how it made them feel secure and happy in a time of chaos and war. Don Adams has people ask him to sign their shoes, and Bob Denver will always get a "Yo, Gilligan!" from fans. But from the very start, Batman touched the child in viewers and that has always made for a very special bond with the people I meet.

---

[2] Then, as now, weekday ratings typically increased as the weekend approached, and this was true for *Batman* too – even if that meant more people watched the Dynamic Duo escape from deathtraps than get into them.

Overnight, America could not get enough of the Dynamic Duo. Suddenly, people were sprinkled their conversations with "Holy This" and "Holy That." Children donned towels and fought crime on the playground, chanting Neil Hefti's theme music. As Michael Eury noted in *The Batcave Companion*, the show

> instantly struck a chord with American viewers, and mushroomed overnight across the demographic spectrum. Kids were mesmerized by its colorful characters and frenetic action, but annoyed or bewildered as their parents chortled at the show. High schoolers formed local chapters of Batman Clubs. College students congregated in TV rooms and dorms for twice-weekly *Batman* viewing parties.

"In fact," West wrote,

> Batmania grew the second week as the Penguin proved as big a draw as the Riddler. Everyone was talking or writing about us, wanting an interview, trying to understand and explain the appeal, raving about the innovative camerawork – tilted angles for the bad guys – or the lavish sets or Neil Hefti's catchy jazz score.

The 28 January issue of *Time* profiled Dozier and his creation, noting,

> The real joker is that Batman has already hit the top ten in the ratings, and the spin-offs have begun. Discothèques have kicked off a new dance, the "batusi," and five recordings of the *Batman* theme song have already been rushed to stores, along with a single called "Batman and Robin." There is even every expectation that grown men will be showing up at Andy Warhol's next party dressed like the Batman.

The "batusi" was so successful that it has yet to fade away, and the show even affected hairstyles, as gels and hairsprays allowed women to sport bat-tipped 'dos.

Quickly, TV and social critics lumped *Batman* with the camp craze sweeping the nation by this point in the decade. England's Museum of Broadcast Communication summed up the series's appeal this way:

> *Batman* incorporated the expressive art and fashion of the period in its sets and costumes. It also relied excessively on technological gadgetry transforming the show into a parody of contemporary life. It was this self-reflexive parody-camp of the comic character that boosted the ratings of the program to the top ten during its first season. The show was not to be taken seriously. The acting was intentionally overdone and the situations extremely contrived.

Susan Sontag made the idea of camp mainstream in her 1964 essay "Notes on Camp" for *Partisan Review*, which created a literary sensation. According to the 1967 book *Fads, Follies and the Delusions of the American People*, Sontag first declared Batman "low camp" in 1965, when he was just a long-running comic-book character.   Author Paul Sann's chapter "Batman: Galahad in a Cape" noted that, once the series aired, *The New York Times* upgraded him to "high camp" as the "twin viruses of pop art and camp" collided.   Newspapers picked up on the oddity and played a role in the Caped Crusader's elevation from super-hero to pop-culture icon.

In the 2 May 1966 *Saturday Evening Post*, John Skow offered a more cynical view, writing that Batman had become

> an obligatory topic in every conversation, a factor in the cravings of every department-store executive, a dull-day column lightener for every editorialist, the theme of every junior-high-school dance, and a pass word for every adult who[,] for reasons praiseworthy or contemptible[,] wished to slip past the sentries of the young. Now Batmania spreads throughout the nation. The climate of foolishness produces winds of idiocy. Federal Communications Commission Chairman E. William Henry, who knows better, appeared at a Washington benefit recently wearing a Batman suit. At the University of Connecticut, Jimmy Juliano rigged himself out as Batman, persuaded his roommate to approximate Robin, and capered about the campus.   University officials revealed themselves as Batfinks when they proclaimed that the capering must not recur. [...] A topless Batwoman was inevitable. In San Francisco, bare-topped *frugistes* are as common as Chinese waiters, and a girl without a gimmick is just a thorax in the crowd.

"Why did Batman work so well as a property in 1966 and not before?" Chip Kidd asked in his *Batman Collected*.

> Perhaps because the very weaknesses that rendered him useless during the Second World War made him perfect for the Vietnam era. So many people wanted to escape that war – by any means possible. Escape to psychedelia, escape to drugs, escape to Canada, escape to Batman. And what an escape they got. While bearing less resemblance than ever to his somber 1939 image, the Batman on TV in 1966 transported the viewer in the fashion of the best popular art: children were thrilled to take it at face value, while their parents delighted in its irony and sarcasm, and *everybody* loved the way it looked.

The media quickly dubbed the craze "Batmania," since nothing like it had been seen since the Beatles arrived on *The Ed Sullivan Show* a scant two years previous. Manufacturers, having been caught unprepared for the pop quartet's impact on America, were equally fast to latch on to the new fad, and products started appearing with lightning speed.

Kidd's book covers Batman merchandise from 1939 through today, but a disproportionate number of pages are devoted to the sheer volume of Batman-branded merchandise from the '60s. In an ad for Zepel Batman Jackets, Robin complains, "Gosh Batman, it's a crime the way everyone is cashing in on our popularity." "Right Boy Wonder!" his partner admits. "But in a society characterized by the competition of individuals who search freely for their interests in the interaction of economic relationships, what can you expect?!!!"

Quite true, but parents could never have imagined the previously unparalleled volume of treats, party favors, toys, games, crafts, books, records, and electronics. Back in the '50s, during the height of the *Adventures of Superman* TV series, there wasn't this much product bearing the "S" shield, and the best Davy Crockett could offer was a coonskin cap.

In fact, the overnight success of the *Batman* series helped rewrite the rules of modern-day mass merchandising and licensing. The 11 March issue of *Time* noted,

> The Batboom is V-RROOMing onto the retail stage just in the nick of time; after a $40 million splurge, the sale of James Bond 007 products is tailing off. Gimbels of Philadelphia, the first store to carry Batman T shirts, sold out its shipment of 360 in a day, ordered 2,400 more. Sales of all kinds of Batman merchandise would be still bigger except that manufacturers mistimed the impact, have fallen as far as six weeks behind in deliveries. "I've seen maybe 50 items in hand samples," complains Charles Lucas, Chicago-based buyer for 495 Walgreen [sic] drugstores. "But we've only got about ten in our stores." The Batmania delights no one so much as Licensing Corp. of America, which holds the licensing rights to the TV-comic-strip hero (as well as to 007). Since *Batman* went on TV in January, LCA has signed up 53 major companies for Batman products, and 45 other contracts are being negotiated. The licensees make every kind of item to which a Batman insignia can be stuck, sewn[,] or stapled. Colgate-Palmolive is marketing Batbath bubble soap. Hallmark is bringing out Batman greeting cards. Toy companies, including Mattel, Ideal, Louis Marx[,] and Remco, are turning out Batman toys. There are Batmasks, Batcapes, Batkites, Batbuttons, Batpuppets[,] and Batguns as well as jackets, pajamas, towels, quilts, wallets, bathing suits, lunch boxes and pencil cases with Batman insignia on them.

National Periodicals was clearly caught unprepared, as the packaging artwork bore little resemblance to the sleek Carmine Infantino-style then gracing the comics. Instead, they used whatever clip art could be found, so there was a lot of images by Dick Sprang and Sheldon Moldoff, some of it mixed and matched, so styles from different eras were cobbled together for the packaging. Quality control was non-existent, so colors and styles were wrong, while some of the product choices made little sense. The quality of the manufacturing also varied wildly, with the vast majority being disposable.

Still, less than two months after the debut, *Time* reported in their 11 March 1966 issue,

> The four-to-twelve age set continues to marvel while Batman and his protégé, Robin the Boy Wonder, rout such Gotham City scoundrels as the Penguin and the Mad Hatter. Teen-agers and the college crowd still consider it sophisticated to snigger at Batman's wildly exaggerated plots and cliché-cluttered dialogue. As a result of the show's high ratings, merchants are anticipating a $50 million sale this year of Batman toys, clothes[,] and other accessories.

This figure proved conservative: the *Toronto Telegram* reported that in the first year, the craze generated $75 million in licensing revenues.

It should be noted that Licensing Corp. of America was a sister operation to National Periodicals, and at the time they were a publicly-traded company. Its success sent the stock soaring, reaching a new high of $45 the week of 13 March 1966, setting the stage for the 1968 sale of the company to Steven Ross's company Kinney, the first steps into what became Time-Warner.

National Periodicals also had to contend with illegal knockoffs which threatened to crowd the official product off the shelves, and in April they took out ads warning about licensing infringements. By late June, they were forced to sue to protect the rights. A story in the 23 June 1966 *New York Times* said the company "filed suit yesterday charging five large merchandising organizations here with selling merchandise that has not been properly licensed."

Not that licensing was any guarantee of quality – or even being on the up and up. Shea Stadium, home to the New York Mets, played host on 25 June 1966 to a licensed "Batman Concert." 20,000 people attended. The event featured Adam West and Frank Gorshin, with performances from the Young Rascals, the Detroit Sound, the Batusi Girls, Jr. Walker and the All-Stars, the Temptations, the Chiffons, Shades of Blue, and Skitch Henderson and his orchestra. The coverage in *The New York Times* began with, "Holy cacophony! Shea Stadium was pretty much of a disaster area yesterday afternoon, until the Caped Crusader came from out of left field (literally) to give the paying customers a semblance of their money's worth." But when creditors were not paid, New York Licenses Commissioner Joel J. Tyler opened an investigation.

Batman had barely debuted when the pop duo Jan & Dean released *Meet Batman* with the Dynamic Duo on the cover. It reached #66 on the *Billboard* Hot 100 list. Hefti's catchy "Batman Theme" was released as a single and hit as high as #35. A version by the Marketts did better, cracking the Top 20 at #17. It

Trade advertisement warning against unlicensed use of Batman & Co. From *Toys and Novelties* (1966).

has since been covered through the years by the Who, the Kinks, and virtually every surf band on Earth. Dickie Goodman released the novelty record *Batman & His Grandmother*, featuring a Batman story with samples from other pop hits of the era (known as "break-in" style); it hit #70.

Adam West parlayed his newfound fame and cut a single, "Miranda," with lyrics mentioning wearing a mask. It never gained much chart traction.

Ward became a teen heartthrob, battling Bobby Sherman and Donny Osmond for coverage in *Tiger Beat*. Ward cannily parlayed his instant popularity into a single, recorded in June 1966 and released 14 November. The lyrics were crafted, using actual fan mail, by Ward in association with music legend Frank Zappa. "Robin the Boy Wonder" featured lyrics such as,

> Oh, Boy Wonder, I'm making a gum wrapper chain to symbolize my love for you. It's going to be as long as I am tall, and I'm 5 foot 10 inches in stocking feet. Please, Boy Wonder, *please*, come next Saturday and sleep for a week or two. I will feed you breakfast in bed, I will make your bed for you, and I like you so much that I want you to spend the whole summer with me.

Radio stations in Chicago briefly played the single until they decided the lyrics were too suggestive.

Within months, the show was affecting its youngest viewers in unexpected ways. *The New York Times* first reported that Frances B. Marsh, director of the Norwood Parish School in Chevy Chase, Maryland, saw how hyped up her students were on Thursdays and Fridays after watching the weekly adventure. Some were worn out from having trouble falling asleep after all that adrenaline-pumping action so close to bedtime. Her dilemma, echoed by other educators, became a recurring theme in media reports for the rest of the year.

Social scientists and commentators fell over themselves trying to explain the show's instant appeal. Psychologist Eda LeShan said, "To adults the whole thing is a delicious joke; from the safety of their maturity, they look back with amusement on the hero of their youth. Children, on the other hand, particularly younger children, take the whole thing very seriously. For them, the experience can be very confusing." On the other hand, Duke University's Dr. David Singer noted adults were "tuning in to laugh at themselves because the super-hero they had turned to in the 1940s out of their own childhood insecurities had now become so ridiculous."

The show reached international fame as other countries clamored to air the show. The U.S.S.R.'s media outlet, *Pravda*, even chimed in. On 30 April, *The New York Times* reported, "Batman ran into the Communist newspaper *Pravda* yesterday and – POW! – the collision was earthshaking. The Soviet organ accused the Caped Crusader of brainwashing Americans to become 'willing murderers in the Vietnam jungle.'" "Batman is nothing more than a glorified FBI agent," *Pravda* complained, "a capitalist murderer who kills his enemies beautifully, effectively and with taste, so that shoulder blades crack loudly and scalps break like cantaloupes." Of course, Batman hadn't killed anyone on screen or in print since the villainous Monk back in 1939. On 12 September 1966, United Press International reported, "The Soviet satire magazine *Krokodil* today unmasked Batman and Robin and said they looked 'like idealized representatives of the F.B.I.'"

As the show began to air in England, the children there also donned towels and blankets for capes, and in August a young boy died while playing Batman. According to Reuters, "TV chiefs issued a warning to millions of youngsters today after an inquest on a boy who died while imitating his masked and cloaked hero, Batman."

Meanwhile, the show enjoyed summer reruns in America, fueling excitement for the early-August release of *Batman*, the feature film based on the series that was rushed into production seemingly minutes after the first season wrapped. Once principal photography ended in May, the post-production process was pushed into a narrow two-month window.

While the film didn't play to the same enthusiasm as the weekly series, it kept Batman and Robin in the forefront of people's minds. As a result, when 43 children were scheduled to receive Junior Good Citizens Awards in New York's Central Park in late August, word that the Dynamic Duo would also be appearing meant nearly 7000 kids turned up and overran the mall.

The Pittsburgh Steelers altered their football uniforms for fall 1966 to a black and yellow design clearly inspired by the TV series. These uniforms lasted until 1968, when they were replaced with those still in use.

Perhaps for the only time in history, comic-book sales skyrocketed as a direct result of a media tie-in. According to its published annual sales, *Batman* sold an average of 453,745 copies per month, ranking ninth in 1965. A year later, it took the top slot with average sales of 898,470 copies per issue, a peak which the title has never matched.

From 1966 through 1972, even the *Batman* comic strip was revived, initially written by former editor Whitney Ellsworth and illustrated by long-time Schwartz stablehand Joe Giella.

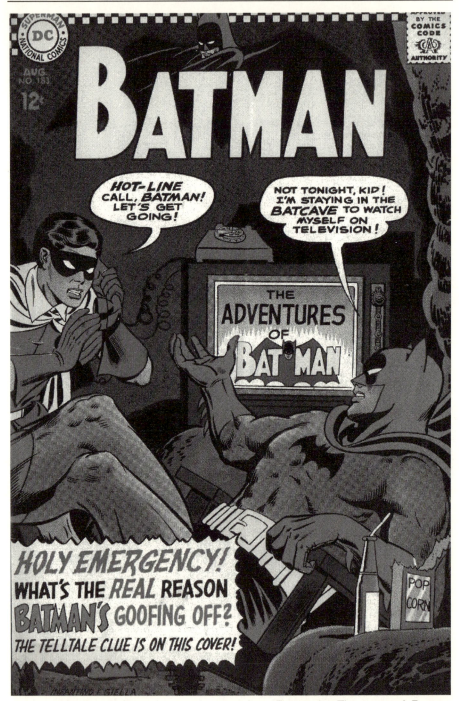

Not even the Caped Crusader was immune from Batmania. The cover of *Batman* #183 (Aug 1966). Art by Carmine Infantino and Joe Giella. Copyright © DC Comics.

The show also influenced saturday-morning fare, already evolving from Hanna-Barbera's animal antics. It had already begun to ape what was hot among adults, starting with spies in the James Bond mold but, by mid-decade, also heavily featuring super-heroes. In 1965, there were just one or two super-heroic shows, such as *Underdog*, but in 1966, as *Batman* hit the screens, Filmation was introducing an animated Superman for the first time since the 1940s. The fall 1966 season also featured *Cool McCool*, a spy series conceived by Bob Kane, and his influence was felt elsewhere. *The Lone Ranger* returned to TV, and shows like *Frankenstein Jr. and the Impossibles* debuted. Despite being a 30-foot tall robot, Frankenstein Jr. still wore a black mask to protect his identity. *Space Ghost*, designed by celebrated comics creator Alex Toth, also arrived that fall and blended science fiction with super-heroics.

Primetime, too, was not entirely immune from Batmania. Both CBS and NBC launched competing super-hero shows, and both networks decided that *Batman*'s success meant that all super-heroes had to be played for laughs. In the hopes of replicating *Batman*'s Second-Season smash debut, CBS gave the world *Mr. Terrific* as a mid-season replacement on 9 January 1967. Not at all based on the DC Comics character of the same name, this was a sitcom starring Stephen Strimpell as an insignificant nebbish who gained powers from pills (a variation on Captain America's super-soldier formula). Assigned missions by the federal government, in the form of the deadpan John McGiver, Stanley Beamish popped a pill and for 60 minutes became Hourman – er, make that Mister Terrific. The show was neither clever nor funny and lasted just the half season.

On the exact same evening, NBC debuted *Captain Nice*, a more clever take on super-heroics. Unlike the competition, they intentionally made a satire of the genre with creator Buck Henry, who had a hit with the network's *Get Smart*. Starring William Daniels, the show was about a scientist who developed a formula that gave him super-powers, but he was shoved into heroics by his domineering mother, and he retained his insecurities, including a fear of heights. Although smarter, this too lasted just the half season, ending on 28 August, the same night as *Mr. Terrific*'s final broadcast.

Dozier, though, decided to take things in the other direction and revived radio's Green Hornet as a serious half-hour crime drama. It gave the world Al Hirt's remarkable theme performance and Bruce Lee as Kato but was a one-season wonder that made no impact on audiences. Even a March 1967 appearance by the Green Hornet on *Batman* didn't help, as the two different

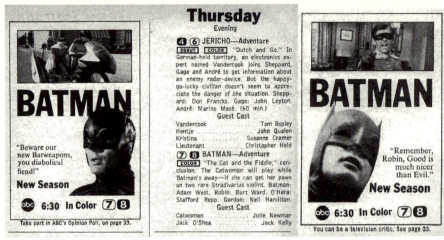

Two quarter-page ads from *TV Guide*'s Fall 1966 preview issue, the first of which appeared beside the listing for the episode "The Cat and the Fiddle."

tones could not be mixed well, especially with one of the sillier foes, Colonel Gumm, played wonderfully by Roger C. Carmel.

Dozier also tried his hand at a *Wonder Woman* series, filming a short segment to tantalize the network into buying the sitcom. Based on the clip now found on YouTube, ABC wisely declined.

Unlike Beatlemania, the Batman frenzy burned out in relatively quick fashion. Maybe it was too much too soon, or maybe the serious issues of the day – from rising drug use to the Vietnam War – made the show seem too frivolous. Either way, by 1968 the show was done.

In fact, the weakening began as early as the opening of the second season, in the fall of 1966. Ratings were off from the spring, and critics were noticing that adults seemed to have had their fill. "Some commentators feel that the show became too self-consciously campy," Les Daniels opined in *Batman: The Complete History*. "Or that new villains created to accommodate visiting stars were somehow substandard (although Victor Buono as King Tut and Vincent Price were certainly up to snuff). Perhaps the novelty of a show that was admittedly silly had simply worn off." By 29 September 1967, *The New York Times* wrote, "Nothing is deader than yesteryear's fad, or so at least moan merchants who have been stuck with unsalable stocks of yo-yos, Davy Crockett hats[,] and Batman costumes."

Dozier and his team tried to sustain the hip factor with a plethora of high-profile celebrities who either popped out of windows during the obligatory Bat-climb or played villains who got sillier as they drifted from the show's comic-book roots. Prophetically, he told *Saturday Evening Post* writer John Skow, "*Batman* will fade, of course. We won't keep all the adults we have now."

For the third season, premiering in fall 1967, ABC hedged its bets by cutting the show down to once a week but asked DC to come up with a new female character. Carmine Infantino had been added as the comics' art director, so he and editor Schwartz created Batgirl, who debuted in *Detective Comics* #359 (Jan 1967). She was prominently featured in several stories before Yvonne Craig debuted, playing Batgirl with sexy verve.

But the writing was on the wall. In 1968, The *Toronto Telegram* noted, "At its peak, *Batman* attracted 55 percent of the viewing audience, a surprising two-thirds of it adult. Now, adult viewers have dwindled to 10 percent." A story in *The Columbia Missourian* in January 1968 reported,

> Word comes from the show's producer that the program will be discontinued because of a loss of adult viewers, who had made up much of the audiences. Holy ratings, Batman! Batman and Robin had quite a following. Pre-empting of their programs by big news events would bring thousands of protests from their loyal viewers. So, as the narrator would say: 'Will this be the end of Batman or will Robin come to save the day? Did the Batmobile zip off into the sunset, or did it merely throw a rod? "Tune in next week for an exciting rerun."

The anticipated news broke on 14 February 1968, when the Associated Press announced "*Batman*'s TV Spot Going to *Second Hundred Years*," a gentle sitcom starring Arthur O'Connell and not aimed at kids. *Batman* aired for the final time exactly one month later, an early exit for a primetime season.

NBC offered to pick up the show, but 20th Century-Fox's TV division struck the sets the week before, making a revival too expensive.

Even during the show's decline, it continued to influence TV programming. By fall 1967, super-heroes conquered Saturday morning as ABC countered CBS's DC heroes (which now boasted Superman paired for an hour with Aquaman) with the Fantastic Four and Spider-Man, which also reflected Marvel's growing popularity. There was *Birdman and the Galaxy Trio*, *Moby Dick and the Mighty Mightor*, and, believe it or not, *Super President*. For fall 1968, as America adjusted to life beyond Batman, Saturday morning continued to mine comic books: Archie and the gang from Riverdale demonstrated a shift from heroes to comic books in general, while the Dynamic Duo also arrived in animation for one season.

The rise of Batmania helped comics sales, but its ebb hurt them too. As ratings declined, fans started to complain about Batman appearing in too many

In a metafictional turn, *Batman* comments on its own increased sales – and cleverly manages to point readers to other DC titles in the process. The cover of *Batman* #199 (Feb 1968).   Art by Carmine Infantino and Murphy Anderson. Copyright © DC Comics.

comics, a fact Schwartz acknowledged by printing the complaints in the letter columns. In 1967, sales of *Batman* stayed in the number one spot, but average per-issue sales declined gently to 805,700. In 1968, the year the show left primetime, the title slid to third place, with average sales of 533,450. The following year, Marvel's *Amazing Spider-Man* eclipsed the Dark Knight for the first time, as *Batman* slid to ninth place; its 355,782 average copies were less than the title sold prior the show's debut, four years earlier.

By fall 1968, *Batman* was off the air and destined for TV syndication, where it has been playing ever since, perpetuating the common beliefs that comic books were strictly for kids. Newspapers, which began writing headlines using the sound effects Dozier appropriated from the comics, have never stopped using "Biff!" and "Pow!" to alert readers to something about comics. This continued even in the 1980s, when mass media woke up to the knowledge that comics were no longer just for kids (if they ever were), often undercutting the point.

The Batman TV show got one last gasp in 1972. A public service advertisement called "Equal Pay" featured TV's Dick Gautier (from 1967's *Mr. Terrific*) as a hero alongside Burt Ward and Yvonne Craig.

Of course, Batman, having been thrust onto the world stage by Batmania, has remained there ever since. While the show ran in syndication and the mania died down, Batman continued to be seen every Saturday morning on ABC's *Super Friends* and, in 1977, regained his own half-hour animated show on CBS. This new show, poorly written and animated, substituted fighting (strictly verboten by Standards and Practices) with the antics of Bat-Mite and incompetent criminals. It did, though, reunite West and Ward to provide the voices. In the late 1970s, they donned their costumes once more, joined by Frank Gorshin, still lithe as the Riddler, in two absurdly bad specials for NBC, live-action adaptations of the *Super Friends* concept.

In the summer of 1980, DC Comics announced that rights for a Batman feature film had been sold, and in 1989 it finally was released. The teaser poster consisted only of the Bat-symbol, a testament to Batman's continued strength in public consciousness. The trailer provided the first glimpse of how director Tim Burton envisioned Gotham City – no longer a barely disguised Los Angeles but a unique city in its own right, owing much to Frank Miller's *The Dark Knight Returns*. The film, much darker than the TV series, garnered excellent reviews and was also among the first features to set a record for hitting $100 million in box office receipts in record time – a mere 10 days. A second wave of Batmania swept the country, this time with more sophisticated and better quality-controlled merchandise flooding the market. Among the items released were facsimiles of the 1960s Topps Cards, bringing them to a new generation. Meanwhile, the 1960s show and movie found new life in syndication. This new wave lasted longer than the original TV series and led to the celebrated animated version, which reminded people that sophisticated and well-done fare can be offered to younger viewers without talking down to them.

The movies, though, continued to deteriorate in quality, with director Joel Schumacher, who replaced Burton after two films, ultimately blaming Warner Bros. for forcing him to make his two films more accessible and riper for merchandising. By the fourth film, 1997's *Batman and Robin*, the movies' absurdity had grown to the point where it rivaled the TV series in camp. It also drove the franchise deep into the ground, causing it to hibernate for nearly a decade before being resurrected by Christopher Nolan.

During all this time, Adam West, still making show appearances in and out of costume, reportedly volunteered to appear in the films as Thomas Wayne (though West denies this) even while dismissing the movie's darker mentality. West and many of his supporting performers did the convention circuit, reliving those brief, bright glory years. West, Ward, and Yvonne Craig all penned memoirs heavily discussing their time in the Batcave. Craig summed up the difference in the two generations of Batmania in her memoir, *From Ballet to the Batcave and Beyond*:

> What most people forget is that when the '60s TV series came out, there were lots of die-hard *Batman* fans who had come to love the comics from the '40s (which were dark), and really resented the "camp" attitude we had taken! Now it's the baby boomers who are disgruntled that the movies aren't closer to the shows they came to love.

Kurt Kuersteiner, writing for *The Wrapper Magazine* in 2004, observed:

> Thirty years after the first *Batman* TV program was produced, Batman is still big. It spun off several cartoon series for TV, fuels the ongoing comic book franchise, and inspired four different modern motion pictures with stars ranging from Jack Nicholson, Danny DeVito, Michelle Pfeiffer, Christopher Walken, Jim Carey, Tommy Lee Jones, Uma Thurman, and Arnold Schwarzenegger.

> Meanwhile, Adam West and Burt Ward have continued to give speeches about their glory days as the Caped Crusaders. On one such occasion, Burt Ward was displaying his old costume at a Harvard speech. It was valued at half a million dollars. A questioner asked 'When is a costume not a

costume?   When it's stolen!'   The lights went out and the costume vanished.   Ward received photos in the mail of various students wearing the cape.   It was eventually returned.   The leader of the gang of thieves turned out not to be the Riddler or the Joker, but rather, another clown prince of crime: the then editor of the *Harvard Lampoon* and future late night NBC talk show host, Conan O'Brien. Holy Celebrity Larceny!

Batmania might have been short-lived, but it never completely died.

The 1960s Batman TV Series from Comics to Screen

by Peter Sanderson

In his autobiography, *Man of Two Worlds*, legendary Batman comics editor Julius Schwartz wrote that, in the early 1960s,

> a gentleman about to take an airplane flight had nothing to read, and he happened to pick up an issue that I [Schwartz] had edited. He enjoyed the Batman story and particularly enjoyed the villain of the piece, who was the Riddler. The stories, characters, and ideas excited him, and he tracked down another previous issue that featured the Joker. The gentleman's name was William Dozier, and he set in motion the deals that brought about the *Batman* TV show, with himself as producer.[1]

That particular Riddler story, the first to feature the character in two decades, was "Remarkable Ruse of the Riddler" in *Batman* #171 (May 1965), which would serve as the basis for the first two-part episode of the *Batman* TV series.

This is a charming anecdote, but it is not entirely true, although Schwartz apparently believed it was. In his book *DC Comics: Sixty Years of the World's Favorite Comic Book Heroes*, author Les Daniels notes that "Dozier always maintained he was reading *Batman* while flying across the country because ABC

---

[1] Schwartz, Julius, with Thomsen, Brian M. *Man of Two Worlds*. Harper Entertainment, 2000. P. 123.

had already acquired rights to the character."[2] DC Comics (then still officially known as National Periodical Publications) had indeed already made a deal for a *Batman* TV series with the ABC TV network, which had outsourced the project to Twentieth Century Fox, which in turn assigned it to Dozier's Greenway Productions. Did Dozier pick up *Batman* #171 at an airport newsstand? Or is it more likely that DC Comics had provided him – or ABC or Fox – with a batch of *Batman* comics from the last few years as reference material? Now that Dozier, Schwartz, and Lorenzo Semple, Jr. (the show's "executive script consultant" and initial head writer) have passed away, it is probably impossible to determine exactly how many *Batman* comics the creators of the 1960s TV series actually read. But we certainly can identify some of them, since during the first season, the show adapted specific stories from the comics.

Which specific comics Dozier and others read becomes important when one understand that, when the TV series went into production in 1965, the two Batman comics, *Batman* and *Detective Comics*, had only recently undergone a major creative transition. Only two years before, they had sunk to their nadir and were reportedly on the edge of cancellation, leading to a dramatic change of direction. What's curious here is that before that point, Batman had been much sillier. In other words, exactly at the same time a campy Batman appeared on TV, his comics were getting more serious.

The man who usually gets the blame for the silly period of Batman comics is Jack Schiff, who edited Batman from 1943 to early 1964. Beginning in 1957, the comics began to infuse science-fiction elements into what traditionally had been a noir series dealing with urban crime.[3] In "Batman's Super-Enemy" (*Detective Comics* #250, Dec 1957), Batman and Robin contend against John Stannar, a criminal who had found extraterrestrial weaponry. Two months later, in *Batman* #113 (Feb 1958), Batman journeys to another planet in "Batman – The Superman of Planet X!" For the next half decade, extraterrestrial aliens and space travel were frequent elements in Batman

---

[2] Daniels, Les. *DC Comics: Sixty Years of the World's Favorite Comic Book Heroes*. Bulfinch Press, 1999. P. 138.

[3] As far back as 1944, the character Professor Carter Nichols had been sending Bruce Wayne and Dick Grayson back into past centuries, where they would then have adventures as Batman and Robin, encountering Robin Hood, the Three Musketeers, and Marco Polo, among others. Nichols stories continued into the early '60s, by which point Batman and Robin were battling aliens on some of their trips into the past.

stories. One recurring nemesis of the late 1950s and early '60s was Doctor X, a costumed scientist who created Double X, a super-powerful energy duplicate of himself (starting in *Detective* #261, Nov 1958). In the early '60s, the shape-shifting Clayface became another frequent nemesis, starting with *Detective Comics* #398 (Dec 1961).

Even Batman himself seemed "alien" at times during the late '50s and early '60s. He wore a succession of brightly colored costumes in "The Rainbow Batman" (*Detective* #241, Mar 1957). On other occasions, Batman underwent literal transformations, perhaps most notoriously into the striped superhuman called "The Zebra Batman," (in *Detective* #275, Jan 1960). He was also turned into a merman, a giant, an invisible man, a mummy, and even a baby!

In the 1950s, Batman even acquired an entire "Batman Family" of supporting characters, in apparent imitation of the "Superman Family." Kathy Kane, the original Batwoman, debuted in *Detective* #233 (July 1956).[4] She was eventually joined by her niece, Betty Kane, the original Bat-Girl, in *Batman* #139 (Apr 1961). Batman even had a dog, Ace the Bathound, who wore a mask into battle and first appeared in *Batman* #92 (June 1955, three months after Krypto the Superdog had debuted in the Superboy story in *Adventure Comics* #210, Mar 1955).

Whereas Superman was repeatedly pestered by Mr. Mxyzptlk, a magical imp from the Fifth Dimension, Batman had his own magical imp with which to contend. Mr. Mxyzptlk was Superman's enemy, but Bat-Mite, who first appeared in *Detective* #267 (May 1959) was a mere nuisance who proclaimed himself to be Batman's "greatest fan."

In other words, the Batman comics of the late '50s and early '60s had become radically different from the dark crime melodrama the series had been when it debuted in 1939. Though editor Jack Schiff has long been blamed for all of this, it wasn't really his decision and had a lot to do with shifting tastes. The super-hero genre, though immensely popular when it originated in the late 1930s and the World War II years, had faded in the late 1940s. By the early 1950s, only three super-heroes still retained their own regular titles: Superman, Batman, and Wonder Woman. Other genres, including science fiction, became more popular in comics. DC's editorial director in the 1950s,

---

[4] Batwoman actually preceded the introduction of Supergirl in 1959. Perhaps Batwoman was inspired by previous female counterparts of male super-heroes, like Hawkgirl, Bulletgirl, and Mary Marvel.

Irwin Donenfeld, reportedly instructed his editors to slant their stories towards science fiction, including space travel and aliens (though Donenfeld himself later claimed he could not remember doing so).[5] From interviewing DC writers and artists of the period, comics historian Ken Gale has theorized that *Superman* editor Mort Weisinger pressured Schiff into making these changes to *Batman*: "Mort's rather fiery personality, so I'm told, completely overwhelmed Jack's more introverted personality[,] and he convinced Jack to put more sci[-]fi (meaning that in the pejorative b-movie sense) into Batman."[6] Indeed, by the end of Schiff's editorial reign, the series did seem to resemble the 1960s Weisinger *Superman* with its aliens and "Superman Family." Whoever issued the orders, Schiff reportedly knew this was the wrong direction for Batman, but he had no choice in the matter.[7]

But in the latter half of the '50s, another paradigm shift came to comics. Starting with 1956's landmark *Showcase* #4, introducing Barry Allen as the "Silver Age" Flash, editor Julius Schwartz presided over the reinvention of the super-hero genre. Together with collaborators such as writers John Broome and Gardner Fox and artists Carmine Infantino and Gil Kane, Schwartz reimagined '40s super-hero concepts for a new generation, including the Flash, Green Lantern, Hawkman, the Atom, and the Justice League of America (based on the earlier Justice Society). Science fiction was Schwartz's first love: before becoming an editor at DC, he had been the first literary agent to specialize in science fiction. And he successfully integrated science-fiction elements, still popular on their own, into these revived super-heroes. In direct response to the commercial success of Schwartz's *Justice League* that Stan Lee and Jack Kirby created the Fantastic Four, thereby launching Marvel's further reinvention of the super-hero genre.

Jack Schiff, however, had no real feel for science fiction, and those elements when used in Batman comics were often dreadful. To his credit, Schiff reintroduced some super-villains into the Batman titles, like the Penguin and Catwoman, but he also introduced such uninspired creations as Kite-Man

---

[5] As noted in Les Daniels's *Batman: The Complete History* (Chronicle Books, 1999).
[6] "The Wrongly Maligned Jack Schiff."
http://www.comicbookradioshow.com/schiff.html.
[7] In the 1983 *Overstreet Price Guide*, Schiff said that "I was having disagreements with the management about the 'monster craze' everybody was into. I fought the introduction into *Batman* and *Superman* of this trend, but I was pressured into using them."

and Mr. Polka Dot. The artwork, by Sheldon Moldoff (ghosting for Bob Kane), was stuck in the style of the Batman comics of the '40s, whereas Schwartz and Stan Lee were employing artists whose work had a more dynamic, contemporary look. Furthermore, Schwartz and Lee were aiming at older, more intelligent, and discerning (if still adolescent) readers, whereas Schiff's Batman stories often seemed mediocre, juvenile, and silly. One could say they were unintentionally campy.

Sales bore out Schiff's failure to appeal to the new generation of comics readers who embraced Schwartz and Lee's comics. From 1960 to 1962, sales fell on *Batman* from 492,000 to 410,000 and on *Detective* from 314,000 to 265,000.[8] DC's management had to take drastic action.

According to Les Daniels, "Although it seems inconceivable in retrospect, Bob Kane has said 'They were planning to kill Batman off altogether.'" Julius Schwartz told Daniels, "I wouldn't say they were going to kill it, but it certainly was being discussed."[9] Instead of cancellation, DC reassigned Schiff to be editor of Schwartz's two science-fiction comics, *Mystery in Space* and *Strange Adventures*. Schwartz was given the task of editing Batman in the hope that he could reinvent them the way he had other classic DC super-heroes.

Schwartz hated being forced to give up editing his beloved science-fiction series to take over *Batman* and *Detective*, and it appears that he initially knew little – and perhaps cared less – about Batman, despite the character's appearances in Schwartz's *Justice League*. In his autobiography, he recounts how writer John Broome "more or less seemed to have shared the same lack of excitement for Bob Kane's creation as I did."[10] That, Schwartz wrote, was why he and Broome notoriously blundered in that story by showing Batman using a gun, something that was utterly uncharacteristic for the character.[11]

The new editor took over the Batman titles with *Detective Comics* #327 (May 1964) and *Batman* #164 (June 1964). To write Batman, Schwartz assigned

---

[8] Today, of course, comics companies would be thrilled to have sales that were this high. But comic books were still a mass medium in the early 1960s, sold on newsstands everywhere, rather than appealing to a niche market in comic shops as they do today.

[9] Daniels, Les. *Batman: The Complete History*.

[10] *Man of Two Worlds*, p. 115.

[11] Or at least it had been since *Batman* #1 in 1940, when he machine-gunned some of Professor Hugo Strange's henchmen!

his two main scribes, John Broome and Gardner Fox.[12] One of Silver Age's greatest artists, Carmine Infantino, became the regular Batman cover artist and drew Batman in alternating issues of *Detective*. Sheldon Moldoff continued ghosting for Bob Kane in the other stories, but he now drew them in a more realistic, modern style.

Schwartz dubbed his remodeling of Batman the "New Look." To mark his takeover, Schwartz added the yellow oval around the bat-insignia on Batman's chest.

He succeeded brilliantly in bringing Batman up to the level of his other DC series, treating the material with seriousness and intelligence. The "New Look" issues may now seem dated by today's standards, but they were an essential intermediate step towards the truly adult and sophisticated work on Batman that Schwartz would edit in the 1970s.

Far from recognizing the serious potential of the Batman comics, Dozier and Semple regarded them as juvenile material ripe for affectionate satire. Dozier and Semple each claimed credit for the idea of doing *Batman* as deadpan comedy. The ironic humor would theoretically go over the heads of kids, who would take the show seriously, but would be appreciated by adults.

Dozier and Semple could easily have turned to Schiff's earlier, sillier science-fiction storylines for their comedic purposes, so why didn't they? If it was DC that supplied them with comics for reference, the company would probably have promoted the recent Schwartz-edited material. But instead, the TV series adapted stories from the Schiff era. Some of these had recently been reprinted in the comics, but others (like the only False-Face story) had not been. So Dozier must have had access to a number of Batman stories before the "New Look." It is possible that DC actively discouraged Dozier from using discarded elements from the comics, like Bat-Hound (although one should note how quickly DC gave in, when Dozier insisted on resurrecting Alfred, whom Schwartz had killed off). Perhaps Dozier and Semple, like Schwartz, felt that aliens, space travel, magic, and time travel were out of place in *Batman*, too silly even for the deadpan super-hero spoof they intended. Or did Dozier and Semple simply think that extraterrestrial monsters, super-powered beings, and period settings would be too expensive? Though the TV show did utilize science fiction (as in Mr. Freeze's condition or the dehydration weapon in the 1966 movie), it drew

---

[12] Fox had written some of the earliest Batman stories, and is credited with conceiving the batarangs and Batman's first flying vehicle, the Bat-Gyro.

the line by not adapting Schwartz's more science-fiction-oriented "New Look" Batman stories and characters, like the Outsider and Blockbuster.

For whatever reason, it is the Schwartz revision of Batman in the comics that served as the basis for the *Batman* TV show. Except for Alfred, Dozier did not use elements from the Schiff era that Schwartz had specifically rejected.

Although its admirers may balk at admitting it, Schwartz's "New Look" Batman could sometimes unintentionally make Batman look as silly as the TV show. For example, in "Remarkable Ruse of the Riddler" (mentioned at the start of this essay), Batman and Robin attend the Gotham City Police Athletic League's annual picnic and relax while sitting beneath "a shady tree," something today's grim avenger would never do. In "The Joker's Last Laugh!" (*Detective* #332, Oct 1964), the Joker uses loco weed to send Batman and Robin into uncontrollable laughing fits.[13]

Nonetheless, it appears that Schwartz did soon undertake a serious analysis of the Batman comics and devised specific goals for revamping them. Schwartz stated that,

> By my estimation, the Batman in the years prior to my tenure had strayed away from the original roots of the character. Batman was regarded as the world's greatest detective, so I decided that he should return to his dark-mystery roots. Likewise, he was also a great escape artist so I decided to bring back the trap motifs that Bill Finger had done so well during the early years.[14]

Dozier disregarded Schwartz and Fox's love of mysteries. But Schwartz's focus on Batman's escape artistry may have been a major influence on the *Batman* TV show's format. During its initial two seasons, Batman ran twice a week, with the Wednesday episode ending with a cliffhanger that typically put Batman, Robin, or both into a deathtrap. "Tune in tomorrow," the narrator (Dozier himself) would command, "same Bat-Time, same Bat-Channel." The heroes would free themselves in the Thursday episode. The TV series even adapted one of the stories Schwartz had built around a deathtrap, "Batman's Inescapable Doom Trap" (*Detective* #346, Dec 1965), for the early "Zelda the Great" story arc.

But while the deathtraps seem to have come from Schwartz, the cliffhanger format was probably Dozier's homage to the movie serials of the '30s and '40s,

---

[13] Perhaps this scene inspired the Riddler's use of laughing gas in the second episode of the TV series.

[14] *Man of Two Worlds*, p.116.

which had been part of his generation's childhood.[15] Batman and Robin had starred in two such serials in 1943 and 1949 for Columbia Pictures, and the serials may have been one of the inspirations for the *Batman* TV series. *Playboy* founder and comics enthusiast Hugh Hefner was a fan of the Columbia *Batman* serials, and according to Bob Kane, "One of the ABC executives was at the Playboy Mansion in Chicago when they were running 15 chapters together." Kane continued, "The Bunnies and Hugh and his friends were laughing and screaming and hissing the villains. It was very campy." Kane also claimed he gave Dozier the idea for the cliffhangers.[16] Ironically, Schwartz did not do continued stories and cliffhangers in the "New Look" issues, although characters like Blockbuster and the Outsider would be carried over into subsequent adventures. Continued stories were rarities in the DC Comics of the '60s.

The TV show also adopted Aunt Harriet, a Schwartz invention. Schwartz pointed out that when he took over Batman, "DC had already taken a lot of heat from Dr. Fredric Wertham with his book *Seduction of the Innocent*," which claimed "how 'unnatural' the living arrangements were at Wayne Manor – what he construed as basically a household of three unmarried males" – Bruce Wayne, his ward Dick Grayson, and their butler Alfred.[17] Schwartz came up with a strategy to counter such homophobic charges:

> So I decided to bring a woman into the household, a spinster aunt of Dick "Robin" Grayson, who could possibly be seen as a sort of chaperoning den mother. Her name was Aunt Harriet – taken from the old Hoagy Carmichael song "Rockin' Chair," where he talks about his old Aunt Harriet, wherever she may be – and to provide the excuse for this, I decided that I would have Alfred the butler killed off.[18]

In retrospect, Schwartz admitted that "I probably could have brought a woman into the mix some other way – a marriage, a sister, another ward, or something – but, honestly, the first idea that crossed my mind was to kill off Alfred."[19] And so Schwartz killed the butler in "Gotham Gang Line-Up" (*Detective* #328, June 1964), written by Bill Finger.

---

[15] Earlier in the 1960s, Jay Ward's *Rocky and Bullwinkle* cartoons used cliffhangers to end episodes.
[16] Daniels, *DC Comics*, p. 138.
[17] *Man of Two Worlds*, p. 119.
[18] *Man of Two Worlds*, p. 120.
[19] *Man of Two Worlds*, p. 120.

But why? Perhaps one reason was Schwartz's admitted unfamiliarity with past Batman history. He had developed no affection for the character and probably had read relatively few of his past appearances at that point. Perhaps Schwartz had not seen the potential for Alfred to be Batman's confidante and primarily saw him as a housekeeper, a role that Aunt Harriet could fill equally well. Since Schwartz refers to Wertham picturing Wayne Manor as a household of three unmarried males, perhaps (consciously or unconsciously) Schwartz felt that he was reducing the likelihood of charges of homosexual subtexts by getting rid of the most expendable of those three unmarried males.

Schwartz's confidence that he had solved this supposed problem now seems rather naïve. He had actually set up a situation in which an adult male and his young ward were hiding their secret lives from the sole woman in their household![20] And just why is the comics' Aunt Harriet a "spinster" with no apparent interest in men? Schwartz unwittingly made the living arrangements at Wayne Manor more ambiguous. But the early 1960s were a more innocent time in popular culture.

In adopting Aunt Harriet, the TV show gave her a last name, calling "Mrs. Cooper," and the comics belatedly followed the show's lead, identifying her "Mrs. Cooper" name and her status as a widow in *Detective* #373 (Mar 1968). So she wasn't the unmarried "spinster" that Schwartz had originally intended after all. The TV series even gave her a suitor – though because he was played by Liberace, he wasn't exactly credible.

Though Schwartz treated Aunt Harriet seriously, Dozier and his collaborators seized upon the comedic potential of an older woman blissfully unaware that she was sharing a home with two costumed super-heroes. They cast actress Madge Blake, who had made a specialty of portraying rather silly middle-aged women. Schwartz's version of Aunt Harriet did not seem all that old and was actually rather intelligent, but Blake's Aunt Harriet seemed taken in by Bruce and Dick's most transparent ruses to conceal their dual identities.

Schwartz could also have easily settled the questions of Batman's sexual orientation by giving him a real girlfriend (as opposed to "playboy" Bruce Wayne's transitory female companions). Yet despite Schwartz's concern about Wertham, the early "New Look" Batman is remarkably free of women. Policewoman Patricia Powell was introduced in *Batman* #165 (Aug 1964),

---

[20] One could even see the TV show's Bat-Poles as sort of Freudian closet that Bruce and Dick enter to become Batman and Robin.

seemingly as a potential love interest for Batman, but that relationship went nowhere. Mystery author Kaye Daye was a member of the Mystery Analysts of Gotham City, a group that made repeated appearances in "New Look" stories (starting in *Batman* #164, June 1964), but hers was a minor role. Schwartz never used Catwoman until after the TV series debuted, though he did introduce Poison Ivy (co-created with writer Robert Kanigher and artist Sheldon Moldoff) in *Batman* #181 (June 1966). But Batman's attraction to Poison Ivy is treated with horror. Schiff's later years had considerably more positive female presence, through the roles of the original Batwoman and Bat-Girl were clearly meant as potential love interests for Batman and Robin, respectively. Schiff also used reporter Vicki Vale, though she was then portrayed as a knockoff of the '50s Lois Lane, a snoop out to uncover the hero's true identity. Schwartz banished all three characters without explanation. Until the introduction of the new Batgirl in *Detective* #359 (Jan 1967), there was no comparably strong female presence in Schwartz's '60s Batman comics. This is especially strange considering the strong female characters in Schwartz's other Silver Age comics, ranging from Hawkman's wife and partner Hawkgirl to Sue Dibny, wife of the Elongated Man, star of *Detective*'s back-up strip. Perhaps Schwartz and his writers sensed that Batman was "married" to his mission, so giving him a steady love interest was irrelevant. Not until the '70s did Schwartz's comics feature strong romantic interests for Batman (in the persons of Talia, co-created by Denny O'Neil and Bob Brown, and Silver St. Cloud, co-created by Steve Englehart and Walter Simonson).

In contrast, Dozier made certain there was a significant — and sexually appealing — female character in each episode of TV's *Batman*, in some cases even starring as the "special guest villain" like Julie Newmar's Catwoman and Anne Baxter's Zelda the Great. The leading female character is usually the male villain's moll (like the aptly named Molly, played by Jill St. John, in the initial two-parter). Not until the 1966 *Batman* feature film does Dozier's Batman fall in love — with an unmasked Catwoman. (The casting of Lee Meriwether as Catwoman in the movie probably prevents most people from noticing the major plot hole that would have been blatant had Julie Newmar been available to play the part: unless we are to assume that the movie is set before the TV series, Batman already knows what Catwoman looks like unmasked!)

Dozier may have liked Aunt Harriet, but Schwartz noted in his autobiography that "Dozier decided that there were a few changes that I had made that he wasn't too thrilled with. Foremost of all, Dozier insisted that

Alfred be part of the ongoing TV continuity, and so he contacted DC and told them to bring the butler back."[21] This is hardly the sole case of DC (or Marvel) changing their comics to bring them in line supposedly more popular movie or TV adaptations. But in this case, Dozier was more perceptive about Alfred's potential value than Schwartz had been. Indeed, following Frank Miller's influential reinterpretation of Alfred in *Batman: The Dark Knight Returns* (1986) into Batman's sardonically witty, indispensable confidante, aide, and father figure, many Batman comics readers might find it inexplicable that Schwartz had ever killed off Alfred. Alfred, portrayed by veteran character actor Alan Napier, was in the *Batman* TV series from its start in 1966, and by that summer, Alfred was back in the comics as well. As Schwartz explained in his autobiography, he had been running stories about a mysterious, unseen mastermind named the Outsider who knew Batman's dual identity. So, "by brainstorming it with Gardner Fox, we worked out a way to reveal that the Outsider was really Alfred the butler," his mind and body having been distorted by a strange, scientific experiment.[22] Alfred, restored to his true self, returned to the comics in "Inside Story of the Outsider!" (*Detective* #356, Oct 1966).

In the comics, following Alfred's apparent death, Bruce Wayne established a charitable organization in his memory called the Alfred Foundation. Since its version of Alfred had never died, the TV series renamed it the Wayne Foundation. After Alfred's return, the comics changed the name as well.

The white-haired Napier makes Alfred look more elderly than the balding, middle-aged Alfred of the comics. Originally in the comics, Alfred did not start working for Bruce Wayne until after Wayne had become Batman. Napier's older Alfred might have inspired Frank Miller to revise Alfred's history in *Batman: The Dark Knight Returns*, making Alfred the Wayne butler during Bruce's childhood, an idea that has been adopted not only in the main Batman comics continuity but also in the Batman movies.

Traditionally in the comics, when Police Commissioner Gordon wanted to talk to Batman, he would shine the Batsignal into the sky. Schwartz must have thought this was too time-consuming a means of communication, since he quickly introduced "Batman's Hot-Line," a private telephone link between Batman and Gordon's office. The hotline was apparently named after President John F. Kennedy's famed "hot-line" phone connection with Soviet Premier

---

[21] *Man of Two Worlds*, p. 124.
[22] *Man of Two Worlds*, p. 124

Nikita Khrushchev. The *Batman* TV series renamed Batman's hotline as the Batphone, and each two-parter early on had an iconic scene in which Gordon phones Batman, who answers the Batphone out of costume.[23]

The *Batman* TV show rarely employed the Batsignal; ironically, in subsequent film and TV adaptations, the Batsignal has supplanted the hotline.

Schwartz said, "I just couldn't believe that [Bruce Wayne would] be going down into the Batcave on a winding staircase, so I had an elevator installed, an automatic secret garage door entrance / exit for the Batcave, and I also souped up the Batmobile."[24] Schwartz's changes to the Batcave and Batmobile seem to have inspired the classic TV sequence of the Batmobile zooming out of the Batcave's concealed entrance. Would the TV show have come up with the Bat-Poles had Schwartz not substituted the elevator for the staircase to the Batcave? Maybe Dozier saw the Bat-Poles as taking the elevator idea a (comedic) step further.[25]

Schwartz asserts that "I also decided to bring back some of Bill Finger's great villains that had been neglected in recent years." These included the Joker and the Riddler. In fact, the Joker had never been missing too long from Batman comics, and Schiff had recently revived the Penguin in *Batman* #155 (May 1963) and the Mad Hatter in *Batman* #161 (Feb 1964). In the early years of the "New Look," Schwartz actually de-emphasized the use of costumed super-villains. Perhaps Schwartz was again reacting against the excesses of the later years of Schiff's editorship on Batman comics, with its new, poorly-conceived costumed villains like Mr. Polka Dot. Although costumed villains abounded in another of Schwartz's series, *The Flash*, in the "New Look" Batman comics he seemed to prefer to pit Batman and Robin against non-costumed opponents. Adversaries like Johnny Witts ("The Man Who was One Step Ahead of Batman") and the Getaway Genius were simply men in business suits.

Schwartz did use Batman's most popular and notorious adversary, the Joker, but only sparingly; he turned up in "The Joker's Last Laugh" (*Detective* #332, Oct 1964) and "The Joker's Comedy Capers" (*Detective* #341, July 1965). Before the TV show's debut, Batman's second-most frequent adversary to date, the Penguin, made only one "New Look" appearance in "Partners in Plunder"

---

[23] One of the show's subtlest jokes is that Gordon never realizes that Bruce and Batman sound exactly alike.

[24] *Man of Two Worlds*, p.117.

[25] The show also makes it explicit that Alfred uses an elevator to descend to the Batcave.

(*Batman* #169, Feb 1965). Significantly, although the Joker and Penguin dress in distinctive manners, neither wears a costume in the same sense that Batman does.

The exception to the rule is a villain whom Schwartz rescued from obscurity. The Riddler debuted in *Detective* #140 (Oct 1948), returned in *Detective* #142 (Dec 1948), and had not been seen since – until Schwartz, writer Gardner Fox, and artist Sheldon Moldoff (ghosting for Bob Kane) brought him back in "Remarkable Ruse of the Riddler" (*Batman* #171, May 1965). Garbed in green tights covered with question marks, the Riddler is unmistakably a super-villain.

It is this story that very loosely serves as the basis for the first two episodes of the *Batman* TV show, "Hi Diddle Riddle" and "Smack in the Middle." Acknowledging the character's long absence from the comics, Fox's story has Edward Nigma, the Riddler, being released from a lengthy prison term and attempting to persuade Batman and Robin (who do not initially recognize him!) that he has reformed. First, he assists them in capturing a notorious gang called the Molehill Mob. That gang made its way into the TV adaptation as well, in which they work for the Riddler.

At one point in Fox's story, Batman and Robin find the Riddler pointing what appears to be a gun at an art dealer. Batman overpowers the Riddler, only to learn that the Riddler was being given the valuable jeweled Cross of the North as part of an inheritance. The "gun" turns out to be a cigarette lighter, and the Riddler had already sent Batman a riddle that could have alerted him to that fact.

Writer Lorenzo Semple, Jr. not only included this incident in "Hi Diddle Riddle" but gave it a dramatic twist. In the comics, the Riddler is trying to persuade Batman that he has reformed in order to conceal his master plan for a major robbery. Hence, the Riddler graciously excuses Batman for leaping to the wrong conclusion about the "gun." But in the TV show, the Riddler has Batman charged with false arrest as part of a plan to destroy Batman's crime-fighting career by forcing him to unmask in court. Later in the episode, Batman is surreptitiously drugged, causing him to act in public as if he were drunk. Again, the Riddler is attempting to discredit his nemesis.

For comedic reasons, Semple was showing what might happen in the real world to a super-hero in similar circumstances. Aside from the comedic tone, this is not that different from what Stan Lee and his collaborators were doing in the early Marvel Comics of the 1960s. One could easily imagine Spider-Man, who is frequently at odds with the law, making a mistake and being charged with false arrest.

Though Fox's Riddler has not reformed, he does not seem particularly evil or dangerous. In fact, he seems like the quiet sort of fellow who would be temperamentally attracted to spending his life working with puzzles.

Consider how different the Riddler is on TV. Instead of a quiet genius emerging from forced retirement, the first two episodes turn him into a long and active adversary of Batman, one fully capable of killing him. Much of the difference comes from Frank Gorshin's indelible performance as the Riddler. Although he wears a version of the comic-book costume, Gorshin's Riddler also appears in a green suit and bowler hat with question-mark motifs. Especially when he wears that suit, Gorshin seems like James Cagney as a super-villain, projecting a gangster's menace and toughness. At times, Gorshin's Riddler seems very cerebral, slowly working out his ideas, visibly savoring them. But famously, Gorshin's Riddler can instantly shift into manic expressions of glee, accompanied by his memorable, high-pitched, giggling laugh. Arguably, Gorshin's Riddler seems more like a dangerous comic trickster than the TV show's Joker.

The TV show's second two-parter, writer Lorenzo Semple, Jr.'s "Fine Feathered Finks / The Penguin's a Jinx," was fairly closely based on "Partners in Plunder" from *Batman* #169, written by France Herron and ghosted by Sheldon Moldoff. (The title of the comics story is even quoted in the episode.) In Herron's story, the Penguin is suffering from the super-villain version of writer's block, unable to think up a scheme worthy of himself. Then he has a brilliant idea: he will invent a random series of clues, letting Batman figure out what crime he supposedly intends. Schwartz and Herron seemed to be slyly poking fun at a standard trope of Batman stories in which super-villains taunt Batman with clues to their intended crimes, which he inevitably figures out. It seems odd for the TV show to parody a trope that may have been new to most viewers (although, of course, they had already met the Riddler, its foremost practitioner), but Semple presumably recognized Herron's satiric intent. And the TV adaptation is surprisingly faithful. In the comics, the Penguin ends up stealing a jeweled meteorite; in the TV version, the Penguin instead kidnaps a beauty queen, but the jeweled meteorite is nonetheless given a passing mention.[26]

---

[26] This is another example of how the TV show added women to the Batman

Some of what may seem like silliness in the TV version – the free umbrellas that give off sparks, the gigantic umbrella on a Gotham street, the "Penguin-magnet" that attracts Batman's utility belt – actually comes from the comics story. In the comic, the Penguin attempts to escape by riding a "jet-umbrella"; the TV show does not use this, perhaps for budgetary reasons, but the Penguin's flying umbrellas turned up later in the 1966 feature film.

Arguably, the comic makes Batman look more foolish than the TV version. On TV, Batman figures out the Penguin has bugged one of his trick umbrellas to eavesdrop on him and Robin as they try to deduce his plan. (It's lucky that Batman and Robin never refer to each other by their real names while the Penguin is listening!) In the comics, Batman and Robin never catch on to the fact that they effectively plan the villain's meteorite theft.

Again, the biggest difference between the comics and the TV adaptation lies in the performance of the "special guest villain." Burgess Meredith's iconic Penguin was not only the most frequent villain on the show but its most formidable. In the comics, the Penguin had traditionally seemed chubby and outwardly harmless. Even in "Partners," when the Penguin has his brainstorm, he does a silly little dance of joy. In contrast, Meredith always projected a sinister cunning. He's short but not fat, and he does not seem out of place in the fight scenes. He may quack and waddle, but he is believably menacing.

The most faithful of the TV adaptations is "The Joker is Wild / Batman Gets Riled," written by Robert Dozier (William's son). It is based on "The Joker's Utility Belt," written by David V. Reed from *Batman* #73 (Oct-Nov 1952), which had recently been reprinted in the "80-page giant" *Batman* #176 (Dec 1965). The TV version follows the comics story almost exactly and sometimes elaborates upon it. In the comic, the Joker robs a performance of the opera *Pagliacci*; on TV, the Joker impersonates the clown who is the leading character. In both versions, the Joker adopts his own trick-filled version of Batman's utility belt. This was a good vehicle not only for introducing the Joker to the TV audience but also to acquaint them further with Batman's utility belt.

Even though subsequent writers and actors have attempted different interpretations of the Riddler and Penguin, Gorshin's and Meredith's versions have probably proved the most enduring and powerful. The same cannot be said for Cesar Romero's Joker; rather than reinterpret the character, Romero hewed all too closely to the Joker of the '50s and '60s comics, who was indeed

comics' virtually all-male milieu.

the "Clown Prince of Crime." The TV show's Joker, however eccentric, is not insane, and although he would happily dispose of Batman and Robin, he is no serial killer. Even artist Carmine Infantino's visual interpretation of the Joker in '60s comics made him seem more macabre than Romero's jolly Joker. Considering the evolution of the Joker into a genuinely murderous madman in comics, animation, and film from the '70s onward, Romero's comparatively tame Joker, while likable and amusing, seems thoroughly dated.

"Instant Freeze / Rats Like Cheese," written by Max Hodge, was inspired by "The Ice Crimes of Mr. Zero" from *Batman* #151 (February 1959), which had also recently been reprinted in the "80-page giant" *Batman* #176 (Dec 1965). Though the TV episodes had a different plot, they were not only true to the comics' villain but improved upon him. For one thing, the TV show gave the comics' Mr. Zero the stronger name Mr. Freeze, which the comics quickly adopted. In the comic, due to an accident with a freezing solution, Mr. Zero could only survive at a temperature of zero degrees (Fahrenheit, presumably); on TV, Mr. Freeze could exist only at 50 degrees below zero, a temperature that would soon prove fatal to anyone else. The TV show adopted the ideas of Mr. Freeze's refrigerated suit and his freeze ray gun, while making both look far more ominous than they had in the comics. In the comics, Mr. Zero had a refrigerated lair where he would relax, wearing a dressing gown and ascot. This proved to be the key to his characterization on the TV series, which hired George Sanders, with his archetypal aristocratic persona, for the part. Unlike the actors who followed him in the role on the show, Sanders effectively underplayed the character. Although his episodes have their share of camp (including Batman's bat-thermal underwear), Sanders plays the role straight and proves memorable.

"Zelda the Great / A Death Worse Than Fate" hews closely to "Batman's Inescapable Doom Trap," written by John Broome, from *Detective* #346 (Dec 1965), with one major change. In the comics version, a male magician named Carnado steals $10,000 each year to pay an inventor named Eivol Ekdal for devising his latest trap for his escape act onstage. Just as the Penguin in "Partners in Plunder" induced Batman to plan his crime, Ekdal and Carnado lure Batman into their "inescapable doom trap" to learn how to escape it. The TV show uses the same basic plot but substitutes female magician Zelda the Great, played by Anne Baxter, for Carnado. She not only proves to be a more sympathetic character, who ultimately helps save the lives of Batman and Robin, but she also adds sex appeal to the show.

"The Thirteenth Hat / Batman Stands Pat," written by Charles Hoffman, seems based on two different comics stories which deal with the second Mad Hatter. Introduced in *Batman* #49 (Oct-Nov 1948), the original Hatter looked like Sir John Tenniel's portrait of the Lewis Carroll character. Years later, the comics introduced a second Mad Hatter, a fanatical hat collector with a prominent red mustache, who was determined to get his clutches on Batman's cowl ("The Mad Hatter of Gotham City," *Detective* #230, April 1956, which had been reprinted in 1964's *Batman Annual* #3). At one point, he even exposes Batman's cowl to radiation to get him to take it off. This Hatter returned in "The New Crimes of the Mad Hatter" in *Batman* #161 (Feb 1964), in which he patterns his crimes on the occupations (and hats) of the jurors who sent him to prison. These stories seem to have inspired the plot of "The Thirteenth Hat," in which the Hatter abducts the jurors (and their hats) and poses as a sculptor to try to persuade Batman to remove his cowl. (The Hatter used the radiation trick when he returned in the second season.)   David Wayne's mannered characterization of the Hatter is his own invention, and the "super-instant mesmerizer" device in his hat is the show's creation. This portrayal didn't prove overly influential, however; it is the original Tenniel-style Hatter who currently appears in the comics.

Considering how many more prominent Batman villains (like Two-Face) did not appear in the 1960s TV series, it's odd that the show not only used but even found the obscure False Face, who appeared in writer Bill Finger's "The Menace of False Face" (*Batman* #113, Feb 1958). The TV episodes "True or False Face / Holy Rat Race" by writer Stephen Kandel do not use the comics' plot but only the idea of a quick change artist. Is it possible that the real inspiration was the shape-changing villain Clayface, who had appeared many times in the Schiff comics?

The TV show's most important infusion of estrogen into the nearly all-male world of early 1960s Batman came with the introduction of Catwoman in "The Purr-Fect Crime / Better Luck Next Time." Strange as it now seems, Schwartz did not introduce Catwoman into his "New Look" comics until after she had appeared on the TV series; indeed, her last new story had appeared in *Detective* #211 in September 1954! Perhaps Dozier discovered her in the newspaper strip continuity that was reprinted in the "80-page giant" *Batman* #176 (along with the Mr. Zero and "Joker's Utility Belt" stories).

These two episodes, written by Stanley Ralph Ross and Lee Orgel, are not based on any specific comics story, but the writers were clearly familiar with traditional Catwoman tropes, including her cat-themed crimes, her "nine lives," and her sexual tension with Batman.   Nonetheless, the show revised Catwoman's image more radically than that of any other member of Batman's rogues gallery.   Though always intended to be a sultry beauty, a film noir anti-heroine transplanted into the super-hero genre, the comics' Catwoman had remained stuck in the '40s. Her traditional costume, with its billowing skirts, concealing rather than revealing her form, seemed old-fashioned for the mid-1960s.   By casting the sensual and slyly witty actress Julie Newmar as Catwoman and costuming her in a skintight black body suit, the show's producers not only brought Catwoman up to date but gave her a new sexual charge that was surprising for a show with a large child audience.   When Catwoman returned in the comics, she was costumed in a variety of skintight outfits, following the TV show's lead (e.g. *Batman* #197, Dec 1967).   Although the '40s costume would return in the comics at times, the Newmar Catwoman costume is surely the forebear of Catwoman's bodysuits in the comics from the 1980s on, not to mention Michelle Pfeiffer's Catwoman outfit in *Batman Returns*.

Oddly, "Death in Slow Motion / The Riddler's False Notion," written by Dick Carr, is based on John Broome's "The Joker's Comedy Capers" (*Detective* #341, July 1965). In that story, the Joker, disguised as director B. C. De Nil (an allusion to Cecil B. DeMille), enters a millionaire's contest to create a new silent comedy film.   Thus, the Joker has himself filmed committing a series of crimes while impersonating a series of classic comedians, luring Batman and Robin into the action.   Again, the comics story features comedy (like a pompous bank president being hit in the face with a pie) that is not unlike the TV show's silliness. So one can see why the producers picked this episode to adapt. But why make it a Riddler story?   Furthermore, the plot is revised so that the Riddler impersonates only one silent clown, Charlie Chaplin as the Tramp. Perhaps this was to take advantage of Gorshin's skills as an impressionist; he could act Chaplin's Tramp better than Romero presumably could.   Giving Gorshin this story might also be the producers' acknowledgment that his manic, giggling Riddler was more Joker-like than the actor playing the actual Joker.

In the climax of "The Riddler's False Notion," the Riddler dresses up as a Western outlaw in order to rob the wealthy silent film collector Mr. Van Jones (played, in an admirable casting coup, by Francis X. Bushman, who portrayed the villainous Messala in the 1925 silent film *Ben-Hur*). Possibly, the Riddler's Western guise was inspired by the comics story "The Remarkable Ruse of the

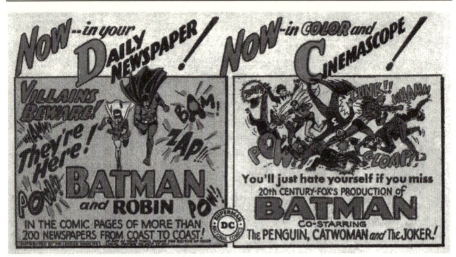

A DC house ad advertising Batman's revived comic strip alongside the 1966 movie, as it appeared in *Batman* #185 (Oct-Nov 1966) and *Detective Comics* #356 (Oct 1966). Copyright © DC Comics.

Riddler," in which he robs a party at a country-and-western club, saying, "Freeze, podners! This is a holdup!"

The show's first season was such an extraordinary hit that the comics understandably tried to take advantage of the fad. Batman prominently appeared on covers of *Justice League of America*, for example, and Schwartz began using super-villains more often in his *Batman* stories. The Riddler returned in *Batman* #179 (Mar 1966) to coincide with the show's debut, and the Joker and Penguin appeared later that year. Schwartz introduced new costumed villains, like Poison Ivy (in *Batman* #181, June 1966) and the Cluemaster (in *Detective* #351, May 1966), and revived another Golden Age menace, the Scarecrow (in *Batman* #189, Feb 1967).

With its second season, the *Batman* TV show virtually stopped adapting stories and adding characters from the comic books. It's odd that the show didn't bother to adapt the super-villains that Schwartz and his collaborators were busily inventing and reviving in the comics. (Poison Ivy certainly would have been a good showcase role for a guest actress. And what if horror legend Vincent Price had been cast as the Scarecrow instead of Egghead?) It is conceivable that the Archer, the villain in the second season's opening two-parter, was inspired by the Blue Bowman (from *Batman* #139, Apr 1961), an alternate guise of the villainous Signalman in the comics, but it seems more likely that the Archer was simply conceived as an evil version of Robin Hood. It has been hypothesized that Egghead was based on Barney Barrows, the genius criminal from "The Mental Giant of Gotham City!" (*Detective* #217, Mar 1955), but Barney had no egg fetish; more likely, Egghead is simply another in the long line of bald criminal masterminds in the super-hero genre.

Batman's co-creator, writer Bill Finger, co-wrote a two-parter in the second season, "The Clock King's Crazy Crimes / The Clock King Gets Crowned." (Perhaps it is another sign of the show's decline that its makers could no longer take the trouble to make their titles rhyme.) There was a DC costumed villain called the Clock King, but he was an adversary of Green Arrow. Was Finger aware of him? Did the TV show get special permission from DC Comics to use him? Or is the show's use of the name "Clock King" merely coincidental? It's possible that the show's Clock King was inspired by either the Clock (from *Detective* #265, Mar 1959) or the Clockmaster (from *Batman* #141, Aug 1961). Notably, the cliffhanger finds Batman and Robin trapped in a giant hourglass, echoing the giant props characteristic of Finger's stories in the comics. Finger's interests in high art may be the reason that the Clock King is out to steal surrealist paintings of melting clocks by Salvador Dali.

If there had been no *Batman* TV series in the 1960s, how often would the Riddler or Mr. Zero (a.k.a. Mr. Freeze) or the Mad Hatter – or even the Penguin or the Catwoman – have appeared in Batman comics in the following decades? How likely would it be that they would appear in animated series or live-action movies? These characters may principally owe their longevity in pop culture to their memorable portrayals on the 1960s TV show.

Since the camp approach had given Batman such extraordinary nationwide popularity, Schwartz and his collaborators seem to have attempted to try it out for themselves. "When the TV show was a success, I was asked to be campy," Schwartz once said, "and of course, when the show faded, so did the comic book."[27]

In a story by John Broome, *Batman* #188 (Dec 1966) introduces "The Eraser Who Tried to Rub Out Batman," a crook who wears a mask that, yes, makes his head look like the eraser on the end of a pencil.[28] At one point, a smiling Batman is surrounded by female fans who want his autograph. On the next page, Batman and Robin ascend the side of a building with their bat-ropes, a clear evocation of such scenes on the TV show. This is followed by a fight scene

---

[27] Daniels, Les, *DC Comics*, p. 141.

[28] Marvel had its own "Living Eraser" villain in *Tales to Astonish* #49 (Nov 1963), but this is probably coincidental.

This 1967 comic-book ad for the show was drawn (reportedly by George Tuska) to reflect the TV Batman costume (e.g. exposed eyes in cowl).   Copyright © DC Comics.

with big sound effects. Robin exclaims "Holy bonfire!" Next, Batman and Robin disguise themselves as an organ grinder and his monkey. The Eraser is revealed to be Bruce Wayne's old classmate named Lenny Fiasco. On first seeing a picture of Fiasco as the Eraser, Robin comments, "Boy, if that isn't camp – I don't know what is!"

And Schwartz and Broome didn't know what camp was – or at least had no feel for it. The jokes are uninspired, unsubtle, and unfunny. Worse, they get in the way of the story by making it too silly and stupid to be appreciated on a serious level. Only a few years before, Schwartz had reversed Batman comics' sales decline by ridding the series of the nonsense of the Schiff years and turning it towards the growing audience of intelligent young comics readers. No wonder his heart did not seem to be in catering to this new camp trend. He soon abandoned the experiment.

Producer William Dozier and writer Lorenzo Semple, Jr. sought to appeal both to children who would take Batman seriously and to adults who would react to the show's satiric subtexts. In the first season, they maintained a balance between the straight-faced and the self-parodic, and it was a huge hit. But from the start of the second season, that balance was lost. The show became broader and more obvious in its humor, and the Batman fad died as quickly as it had been born. Perhaps one of the reasons for the decline was that, after the first season, the show no longer adapted stories from the comics.

Without that grounding in a serious approach to super-hero stories, the writers lost themselves in increasingly uninspired and repetitive nonsense.

The show's producers actually collaborated with Schwartz in an effort to persuade ABC to renew the fading series for a third season. According to Schwartz, Dozier "asked if there was any way that we could add a young female as an ongoing cast member. I asked what kind of girl he had in mind, and as it turned out he had already worked out a possible scenario in his head whereby Commissioner Gordon had a daughter who decides to become Batgirl."[29]

Was Dozier unaware of Batwoman and the original Bat-Girl, whom he could have easily adapted into the TV series? Or did Dozier recognize that these were old-fashioned characters and realize that Schwartz and his collaborators could create a more contemporary sort of super-heroine? Whatever the case, Schwartz, Fox, and Infantino created Barbara Gordon, the new Batgirl, for "The Million Dollar Debut of Batgirl" (Detective #359, Jan 1967).[30] Barbara was like a cliché – the dowdy bespectacled librarian who proves to be a beauty. Not only did she take off her glasses and let down her hair but she also outfitted herself in a skin-tight black costume (not unlike Catwoman's) and went into combat. In her first comics story, Barbara dons her Batgirl costume to attend a masquerade ball but ends up battling the Golden Age super-villain Killer Moth and becoming a super-heroine.

The TV producers shot a seven-minute sequence with Yvonne Craig as Batgirl battling Killer Moth that persuaded ABC to renew Batman for a third season, although it would now run only once per week. Rather than use Killer Moth in the show, the producers used their strongest "guest villain," Burgess Meredith's Penguin, for the episode introducing Batgirl.

It should be noted how unusual a creation the new Batgirl was, both for comics and TV, in the 1960s. Action heroines who could physically fight as well as men were rarities in '60s popular culture. On TV, Batgirl was preceded only by Honey West, played by Anne Francis in the eponymous series from 1965 to 1966, and Mrs. Emma Peel, played by Diana Rigg on The Avengers from 1966 to 1968; both, like Batgirl, dressed for combat in black catsuits. Similar action heroines were almost wholly absent from the movies of the '60s. Of course, Wonder Woman had been in comics since the early '40s, but in the '60s, super-

---

[29] Man of Two Worlds, p. 124.

[30] The title might be a sly comment on Batgirl's importance to the fortunes of the TV show and related merchandising.

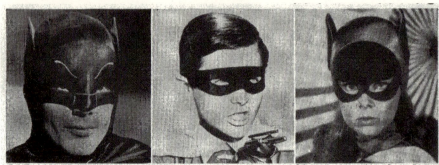

BATMAN, ROBIN AND BATGIRL on ABC TV THURSDAYS 7:30 PM-8:00PMest

A DC house ad advertising *Batman*'s third season, which appeared under a much larger ad for CBS's Saturday morning cartoons, then titled *The Superman / Aquaman Hour of Adventure*. The page is entitled "The Best of DC on TV," implicitly connecting the shows. From *Detective Comics* #369 (Nov 1967).

heroines like Marvel's Invisible Girl, Marvel Girl, Wasp, and Scarlet Witch avoided hand-to-hand combat. Batgirl was in the mode of Schwartz and Fox's Silver Age Hawkgirl, who flew into combat armed with weaponry, or the Golden Age heroine Black Canary (whom Schwartz had unsuccessfully attempted to revive in *The Brave and the Bold* in 1965).

Popular as Batgirl was, she could not halt the creative decline of the series, and the third season was its last.

Many comics fans in the 1960s resented the Batman TV series for mocking Batman and super-hero comics in general. A number of comics professionals, such as writer Denny O'Neil, artist Neal Adams, and editor Schwartz himself, likewise preferred a more serious treatment of the character. With sales plunging again, it was time to gamble with a new approach. Perhaps it was because there was such a strong reaction in the comics community against the Batman TV show that creators at DC Comics were able to take the series to the opposite pole. Having rescued, revitalized, and reimagined Batman in the early 1960s, Schwartz presided over a second reworking of Batman at the end of the decade. Under his guidance, O'Neil, Adams, and writer / artist Frank Robbins returned Batman to his roots, turning him back into the grim avenger of 1939 in a Gotham City that was a contemporary urban nightmare rather than a camp fantasy.

The most lasting influence of the TV show is that it provoked a counter-revolution, giving us the version of Batman and his world that has dominated comics since the '70s – and which, through animation and live-action films, has finally displaced the campy Batman in public consciousness.

DC Comics owns Aunt Harriet, but for over 30 years, she has been invisible in comics, as have all the characters created for the TV show. This seems rather odd. Julius Schwartz had introduced her as a substitute for Alfred, so once Alfred returned in the comics, Aunt Harriet had arguably become unnecessary. In *Detective* #356 (Oct 1966), in which Alfred returns, Aunt Harriet is assured in the final panel that she can stay on at Wayne Manor, but she rarely shows up afterwards, and her final appearance in the *Batman* comics canon to date is in *Batman Family* #4 (Mar-Apr 1975).

Perhaps the *Batman* TV show's depiction of Aunt Harriet as a foolishly and stereotypically oblivious old biddy has made her anathema to Batman writers in comics and animation since then. Again, Schwartz's version of Aunt Harriet in the comics was apparently younger and decidedly more intelligent. She even discovered the Batcave in *Detective* #351 (May 1966), though Bruce Wayne and Dick Grayson concocted evidence to convince her that they were Batman and Robin's friends, not the Caped Crusaders themselves. Neither the comics nor the TV version of Aunt Harriet seems a likely relative of members of a circus family like the Graysons. And why didn't she adopt Dick Grayson after his parents' deaths? Surely there is an untold story there.[31]

One way that comics professionals tip their hats to the '60s TV show is by making reference to characters created for the show. Characters and concepts that were created for the *Superman* radio show of the '40s (including Kryptonite) and the *Superman* TV show of the 1950s are owned by DC Comics. But DC's deal with Fox for the 1960s *Batman* TV series was different. Fox apparently co-owns characters created for that series, such as Chief O'Hara and various villains, including King Tut. Despite this, characters created for the show have managed to sneak into comics and animation over the years.

For example, writer Steve Englehart gave Chief O'Hara a cameo in "The Master Plan of Doctor Phosphorus" in *Detective Comics* #470 (June 1977), part of his legendary original "Dark Detective" storyline. The Chief's name is distinctly mentioned, but Walter Simonson draws him with his hand shielding his face, presumably to avoid trouble from the Fox lawyers.

In the story "What is a Door...?", the Riddler's origin story in *Secret Origins Special* #1 (1989), written by Neil Gaiman, the Riddler complains about how the world of Batman has grown grimmer and grittier since the good old days. "It

---

[31] But since Aunt Harriet has not appeared in comics since the 1970s, she arguably is not in continuity.

Writer Neil Gaiman fondly remembers the show in a story from *Secret Origins Special* #1 (Oct. 1989). Art by Bernie Mireault and Matt Wagner. Copyright © DC Comics.

was fun in the old days. There was the old cabal: Catwoman, Penguin and the Joker... We hung out together, down at the 'What a Way to Go-Go.' It was great!" In the second episode of the Batman TV show, "Smack in the Middle," Batman comments, "What a way to go-go" when the Riddler's moll Molly falls to her death. Moreover, the Riddler's reference to his "cabal" with the Catwoman, the Joker, and the Penguin may be Gaiman's allusion to the four villains teaming up in Fox's 1966 movie.

The Riddler continues, "There were all these guys you never see any more. King Tut. Egghead. Bookworm. Marsha, Queen of Diamonds. Where did they all go?" They went into oblivion, since DC Comics does not have the rights to use these villains created for the TV show. But Gaiman's point is that these villains reflected a more innocent time in the super-hero genre, when Batman's enemies were cunning and somewhat comical thieves rather than insane serial killers.

"You know what they call them now?" the Riddler soliloquizes. "Camp, kitsch, corny, dumb, stupid... Well, I loved them – they were part of my childhood." Here Gaiman clearly drops the mask of the character through which he is speaking. The Riddler was not a child in the '60s, but Neil Gaiman was, and he defends the show and the pleasures it gave him.

Egghead made a silent cameo appearance as one of Arkham Asylum's inmates in *Batman: Shadow of the Bat* #3-4 (Aug-Sept 1992), part of "The Last Arkham" storyline written by Alan Grant and drawn by Norm Breyfogle. It seems inappropriate for Egghead to be in an asylum since, despite his eccentric fixation on eggs, he was utterly rational on the TV series and certainly not insane.

The Jack Schiff Batman comics may be ready for critical reevaluation, suggesting that a sillier Batman has become once again tolerable. Dr. Carter Nichols, inventor of the time machine that transported Batman and Robin to different centuries during the Schiff era, appeared in the *Batman: The Brave and the Bold* episode "The Last Bat on Earth!" (2009) and in Grant Morrison's *Batman* #700 (Aug 2010) and *Batman: The Return of Bruce Wayne* #5 (Nov 2010). And Paul Dini, known for his work on *Batman: The Animated Series*, scripted a highly entertaining and inventive episode of *Batman: The Brave and the Bold*, entitled "Legend of the Dark Mite" (2009) and directed by Ben Jones, that co-starred Bat-Mite. Bat-Hound briefly appears in that episode, and it prominently features two Schiff-era villains, the Calendar Man (from *Detective* #259) and Cat-Man (from *Detective* #311, Jan 1963, Schiff's final year as editor).

Bat-Mite even briefly changes Batman's costume into that of the Zebra Batman – and tellingly, a version of the Adam West *Batman* outfit. There are giant apparitions of various classic Batman villains, including Mr. Freeze, who is instead called by his original name, Mr. Zero, and even Mr. Polka Dot!

In Gaiman's 1989 *Secret Origins Special* story, the Riddler bemoaned the fact that the dark, grim, and gritty treatment of Batman had displaced the brighter, cheerier version from the '60s. In contrast, Dini's teleplay asserts that there is more than one valid approach to the character, and it implies that the best of Schiff's Batman – and perhaps by extension the '60s TV Batman – represents one such viable approach. Similarly, Gaiman's "Whatever Happened to the Caped Crusader?" (in *Batman* #686 and *Detective* #852, both Apr 2009) also presents a multitude of different versions of Batman's life, reflecting different periods in the series' shared history, coexisting with each other and each equally valid.

Perhaps the most startling recent homage to the 1960s TV *Batman* was DC Comics' introduction of King Tut into the *Batman* comics, not in a cameo but in a starring role, over 40 years since he debuted on the TV show. Tut made his long-delayed comics debut in *Batman Confidential* #26 (Apr 2009), in a story written by Christina Weir and Nunzio DiFilippis. In an interview with Jeffrey Renaud for the website Comic Book Resources, Weir explained that "We had proposed the story idea with a new villain, the Sphinx, who would pose riddles Batman needed to answer." As a result, Batman would reluctantly team up with the Riddler, who is not pleased that another villain has plagiarized his *modus operandi*, to deal with the Sphinx's conundrums. The editor for the project was Mike Carlin, and Weir reported, "Mike thought it would be fun to do the same story with King Tut."[32]

But how, considering the legal questions involved? DeFilippis told CBR that "we worked from the concept of King Tut, a historic figure who clearly doesn't belong to DC or to Fox / the TV show. Because no one can hold a copyright on the boy King, we can build our own Tut, in a sense." As DeFilippis explained, he and Weir retained the basic concept from the TV series: "I want to assure the TV show fans that a lot of the central concept is intact, the central suspect" – who indeed proves to be King Tut – "is an Egyptologist who, due to a blow to the head, thinks he's the Boy King reborn." But they also had to make their Tut

---

[32] Renaud, Jeffrey. "At Last: Batman vs. King Tut." CBR News, Comic Book Resources, 12 Dec 2008.

different. In order to fit into the more somber world of today's Batman comics, he had to be a more serious character than the rather jolly, comical menace that Victor Buono played on TV. Furthermore, the new Tut could not have Buono's portly build. In part, that was because in Weir and DeFilippis's story there were various suspects, including the rather slim Riddler himself, who could be Tut. Of course, the new Tut also had to look different from Buono's for legal reasons. "So he needed a different physique," said DeFilippis, and the character ended up looking more like the statues of Egyptian pharaohs.

On the TV series, King Tut was a professor of Egyptology named William Omaha McElroy. In order to make the comics Tut sufficiently different from the TV version, Weir and DeFilippis gave the suspect who turns out to be Tut a different name. "So we named that character in honor of Victor Buono," DeFilippis told CBR. "His name is Victor Goodman. I'm half-Italian, so when I see Buono, I see 'good.'"

What made Victor Buono's King Tut memorable was that he was so endearingly funny. This new, rather humorless King Tut will probably not exert the same grip on readers' imaginations. But now that he has been introduced, like all other DC Comics characters, he will regularly be subject to reinterpretation by Weir and DeFilippis, as well as other writers.

Might other characters who were created for the *Batman* TV show in the 1960s someday reappear for more than brief, anonymous cameos? If DC Comics, Warner Bros., and 20th Century-Fox can ever resolve the issues over releasing the 1960s *Batman* for home viewing, wouldn't it be nice if as part of the agreement, DC gained the rights to the characters who originated on the show? (It's not as if Fox has been doing anything with them!) Then maybe we could see how Warner Animation would handle Egghead or the Bookworm in full-length stories, or how Chief O'Hara might fit into the Gotham City of the 21st century.

Even if that day never comes, we'll still have Catwoman, the Riddler, Batgirl, and all the other characters the show influenced – just as the comics, with all their contradictory tones, influenced the show.

Such a Character: A Dissection of Two Sub-Species of *Chiroptera homo sapiens*

by Jim Beard

Batman '66. You either love it or you hate it. Chances are, if you hate it, your reasons pretty much boil down to, "It's not Batman." It's a simplistic claim which deserves a simplistic retort: "Of course, it's Batman."

Far be it from me to come down on anyone who offers the above argument. I'm sure they're upstanding comic-book fans in their own right. But for those who enjoy the character of Batman as portrayed by Adam West, these complaints can be frustrating. Worse, they can also be insulting, as if to say that some Batman fans know the "true" character better than others. I often feel as if dismissing the TV show has become a knee-jerk reaction among fans, something done without fully understanding why. Perhaps some look no deeper than the bright colors and the widespread cliché of 1960s inanity.

What I'd like to offer here, rather than allegations of whose fandom is "purer," is a careful comparison of the comic-book Dark Knight with his cathode-ray-tube doppelganger. To do this, I'll first have to lay down a foundation from which to build my case, which I hope will be recognized as common ground among Bat-fans everywhere. Having done so, a careful, point-by-point examination of the two versions of the character will reveal that the

1960s TV Batman is simply one facet or face of the famous Caped Crusader. In fact, the evidence will show that not only is *Batman*'s Batman truly Batman, as much as any other, but that this Batman is worthy of our attention and study – and not our scorn.

Let's begin with the premise that that Batman's origin as first presented in *Detective Comics* #33 (Nov 1939) is the definitive accounting of the character and what he was intended to be. This is borne out by that story's particulars being present through every incarnation of Batman over 70 years. The story has also been used repeatedly to establish the character in reference works as Michael L. Fleisher's *The Encyclopedia of Comic Book Heroes, Vol. 1: Batman* (Collier, 1976) and Robert Greenberger's *The Essential Batman Encyclopedia* (Ballantine, 2008).

With those primal characteristics in mind, I'll then survey the first 11 Batman comic-book stories, published in *Detective Comics* #27-37 (May 1939 - Mar 1940). These stories present the Caped Crusader in his purest form, before the advent of Robin, the Boy Wonder. True, the TV series is very much a team effort between Batman and Robin, but for our purposes, it's necessary to narrow our focus to Batman himself. And everything that needs to be imparted about Batman is in those 11 stories. In fact, they're often pointed to by advocates for a darker Batman who see the TV show as untrue to the character.

While we're focusing on the earliest comics stories, it's also best to limit ourselves primarily to the first season of *Batman*, since it's widely considered to represent the show in its prime. The first season features a greater concentration of villains from the comic books and episodes based on actual published stories – not to mention that it was more popular with viewers at the time.

So what do we find when we compare the pure, unadulterated comic-book Batman with the TV Batman? There just isn't as much difference between the two as some (many?) would like to believe.

The Essential Batman

Using Batman's first origin story, both Fleisher and Greenberger offer a list of essential elements to define Batman. Their lists are almost identical. I've paraphrased them here, hoping to cut to the essence of their criteria:

1. Batman is Bruce Wayne.
2. Bruce Wayne's parents were murdered when he was a boy, inspiring him to become a crimefighter.

3. Bruce Wayne dresses in a bat costume and calls himself Batman to fight crime.
4. Batman's mental and physical powers are at the peak of human capability.
5. Batman is an inventor who has created many devices and vehicles to aid him in his crimefighting.

All else, say these scholars, is superfluous. Bat-chaff. Guano. The Batcave, Robin, Alfred, Commissioner Gordon, the villains, etc. – all go beyond these criteria, which are absolutely necessary for the character to "be" the Batman we have known since 1939.

Of course, there exist important details (or subcategories) within these listed items, such as the character's personality, his mission, and the kind of situations in which he often finds himself. I'll discuss these as we go, elaborating upon the above points but not straying beyond their boundaries.

So let's go down our laundry list of what makes Batman Batman.

Batman is Bruce Wayne. Just as in the very first Batman story, "Case of the Chemical Syndicate" (*Detective* #27), the TV Batman is secretly millionaire Bruce Wayne. In fact, the very first episode of *Batman* mirrors that first comic story by introducing us to Bruce *first*, then Batman soonafter. Bruce is as much in evidence in the TV series as he is in the first 11 printed tales – or perhaps even more so, since the millionaire doesn't appear as himself in every one of the comic stories.

Bruce's character is plainly drawn in both mediums: an orphaned millionaire with money and time to burn. In print, he's introduced as "disinterested in everything," but "Hi Diddle Riddle" reveals the TV Bruce to be an active philanthropist: his first act is to fund "anti-crime centers" in Gotham. Overall, the TV Wayne is barely distinguished from his dashing, cowled alter ego, whereas the comics depict him as for the most part maintaining a bored-with-life façade. In both media, Batman blithely uses his identity as Bruce as cover for covert missions, as seen in *Detective* #37 and in "Fine Feathered Finks" on TV.

In both his print and TV incarnations, Commissioner Gordon considers Bruce a friend, allowing him into his confidences and seeing him socially. Chief O'Hara, on the other hand, lets his disdain for Wayne show in "The Joker is Wild" and "A Death Worse than Fate," and his snide comments offer a rare glimpse at the public perception of the TV Bruce as a disaffected rich boy. Bruce seems to get along well with Gordon but is quick to question the

Commissioner's sanity in "The Curse of Tut," where he hangs up on the older man.

There's also a curious separation between Bruce Wayne and Batman in the series, almost as if they're two different people: strangely, Bruce constantly refers to Batman in the third person, and vice versa. In those first 11 comic tales, the millionaire is often shown changing into his action garb – a scene that is literally never witnessed on TV. (One assumes it was mandated that Adam West's hair must never be mussed by donning or removing his cowl on air.)

Both Bruce Waynes' concern for the citizens of Gotham is very much in evidence. "The Batman Wars against the Dirigible of Doom" (*Detective* #33) shows Bruce quick to aid the victims of the airship's assault on the skyscrapers, prefiguring his TV counterpart's almost-constant stream of philanthropy. On the show, the millionaire attends charity functions galore and even works to reform criminals: in the coda to "A Death Worse Than Fate," Bruce promises Zelda the Great a position at a children's hospital, once she serves out her prison term.

Bruce Wayne's parents were murdered when he was a boy, inspiring him to become a crimefighter. The print Batman conducts his adventures with an origin for six whole issues before his tragic tale appears in a tight, one-and-a-half-page prologue in *Detective* #33. Once it's over, his story of murdered parents and years of training is relegated to the background until 1948, when it's embellished and retold. Other than two poignant panels of a young Bruce crying over his dead parents, the early Batman is devoid of angst.

The angst that we now associate with the character is not present in 1939-40; it is, in fact, a product of the 1970s, extrapolated by writers who felt a need to give Bruce Wayne an inner darkness to match his original dark surroundings. (Even then, the 1970s were not fully given over to angst – Bob Haney and Jim Aparo's Batman of so many adventurous *The Brave and the Bold* tales is actually quite a good match for Adam West's interpretation.) The 1939-40 Batman is a straightforward hero surrounded by darkness but not dark inside, much as the TV Batman is a straightforward hero in exaggerated surroundings.

In his very first episode, the TV Batman wears his broken heart on his bat-sleeve, compared to his two-dimensional forebear. The murder of Bruce Wayne's parents is actually mentioned not once but twice in "Hi Diddle Riddle," and it figures into the plot when Bruce's career as Batman is endangered. Apparently, the show's producers had intentions – at least in the beginning – to make the horrible tragedy a part of their Batman's character, but the concept of death on *Batman* was ix-nayed immediately thereafter. The next storyline, "Fine Feathered Finks," mentions Bruce's "late father," and "The Bookworm Turns" includes a clock tower built "in memory of Bruce's father" – but these are the only real lingering nods to the Waynes' misfortune. The TV Batman had to make do on the lure of adventure alone – much like his print counterpart.

To be fair, there *is* a death in "Instant Freeze," but it's implied – though almost luridly so. And while we're at it, there are the two mobsters in "A Death Worse Than Fate" who Tommy gun each other, and, well, so much for that *Batman* urban legend.

(It's unclear in the TV series if Bruce's father is a medical doctor as he is in the later version of the comics origin. The millionaire consults his father's law books in "Hi Diddle Riddle," but that doesn't necessarily mean that the elder Wayne was a lawyer; doctors and the rich need to know the law too. Bruce also mentions an uncle in "Hi Diddle Riddle.")

Bruce Wayne dresses in a bat costume and calls himself Batman to fight crime. Though this concept is of course present in both comic and TV series, it's only in print that it achieves any real significance. The first 11 Batman tales are wonderful in showing off the sinister and foreboding look of the Dark Knight's costume. With its long, devilish ears, dark colors, and enveloping cape, it's pretty creepy. TV Batman – not so much. The show does little to play up the bat-motif as a disguise that promotes Batman as a "creature of the night," despite the infamous tagging of the word "bat" onto everything in sight, *ad infinitum*. And the less said over the lack of pointy ears and a cape that resembles batwings on Adam West the better...

Still, once in a while, someone on the show – perhaps Adam West? – remembers that Batman's silhouette is supposed to inspire fear in criminals, such as in "A Death Worse Than Fate," and the Dark Knight will hold up his somewhat limp bat-cape and project the "Shadow of the Bat."

I would be lax if I didn't mention one early nod in the TV show to the Caped Crusader's grim inspiration from a certain flying mammal. In the coda to "The Penguin's a Jinx," Commissioner Gordon regales some partygoers at Wayne Manor with the "origin of the bat-costume," telling them that Batman knew he needed a look that "strikes terror into a criminal's mind like the shape and shadow of a huge bat." How exactly Gordon came across this rather intimate detail of Batman's secret origin is not known, but it directly parallels the comics Batman.

It must be said, however, that rarely does a TV super-criminal show any sort of fear over Batman's appearance. No "superstitious cowardly lot" there.

One interesting note, concerning Bruce's operating as Batman, revolves around what I can only describe as newbie gaffes. The first 11 comic stories have several instances of blundering on his part, despite no mention of his being in the "early days" of his costumed career. Batman is "startled" in *Detective* #32 when taken by surprise, leaps impetuously at his foe there, and believes he's "going mad" in *Detective #33*. Furthermore, he quite astoundingly gets lost while driving and must stop to ask directions in *Detective #37* – this immediately after he's described as "already an almost legendary figure." The operative word there being "almost."

Fortunately for our purposes, the TV Batman is likewise guilty of neophyte mistakes. His first three episodes are rife with the kind of uncertainty that only a fledgling crimefighter would make: Batman's fooled not once but twice by the Riddler in "Hi Diddle Riddle," and it's Robin who smartly answers the bulk of the riddles. In "Fine Feathered Finks," he fails to successfully plant a listening device in the Penguin's lair (after being caught unaware by a device he himself would appreciate), and he admits he's failed in "The Penguin's a Jinx." But perhaps it's one of the Gotham Guardian's lowest moments when, in "Batman is Riled," our hero says that he "seems to be failing the public" and is ready to pack it in after a few tame taunts and boasts from the Joker.

Another peek into Batman's "learning curve" comes to us by way of the first Mr. Freeze episode, "Instant Freeze." It's a fascinating tale and one of my favorites, with a great performance by George Sanders as Freeze, the super-criminal created by Batman. That's right; I said Batman. It seems that in an early encounter – almost every villain in the show makes their debut sometime before we meet them on air – Batman bumped into some sort of solution that spilled on Freeze and denied him life above negative 50 degrees Fahrenheit. Alas, the Caped Crusader got better. Much better.

The print Batman operates almost exclusively at night in his early adventures, and here we come to one of the great divergences between the two incarnations of our hero in question. The TV Batman's comfortable in the bright sunlight of a typical Gotham day (forget the rainy streets as seen in the show's favorite stock footage of Los Angeles), but he *does* also run his crimefighting career at night on occasion. "The Penguin's a Jinx" and "Batman is Riled" come to mind on this score.

While we're on the subject of chasms that lie between the print and TV Caped Crusaders, I might as well get this out of the way: the comic-book Batman of the first 11 adventures is very much a vigilante wanted by the police, and his TV counterpart is the consummate "duly deputized agent of the law." The print Batman runs into trouble with the police right out of the starting gate, in *Detective* #27, and this status remains in place until after Robin's debut (specifically 1941's *Batman* #7). The TV Batman is practically on the GCPD payroll and renowned throughout town as an upstanding citizen – although a masked one. (Gothamites are prone to point out that their champion's identity is a secret one, over and over and over again.) The second-season episode "Batman's Anniversary" sheds little light on how long the Gotham Guardian's been working with the law, but it does imply that the arrangement between he and the police has been in place from the time that Batman begins.

Interestingly, Dawn Robbins, a visiting actress to the great metropolis, doesn't recognize the Dynamic Duo when they alight in her penthouse in "The Penguin's a Jinx." Her handler, a local, realizes that "not being from Gotham," she wouldn't know Batman and Robin. Another tip of the hat to Batman's newbie status, or simply a notation on the actresses' naiveté?

It's important to state for the record that, despite the emphasis some have placed on Adam West acting the clown, his Batman is in fact rather humorless. While he does indeed smile from time to time, the early comic-book Batman matches him smile for smile. In "The Case of the Chemical Syndicate," Batman snatches up information he needs to crack said case and, while sitting in his car, offers up a "grim smile." In several succeeding adventures, he smiles while he fights criminals, eventually delving into puns at the expense of his foes – and this was before Robin's notorious punning came along. In fact, the TV Batman never smiles while fighting nor cracks wise while cracking jaws. Most noticeable is that his infrequent smiles are delivered in brief fashion, almost in an embarrassed, tight, or shy manner. One might even categorize Adam West's expression behind his mask as a "grim smile."

Batman's mental and physical powers are at the peak of human capability. Both Batmans share a common bond in their mental and physical acuity, but when we focus on mental prowess, the TV Batman clocks in as the winner. The comic-book Dark Knight, in his first year of publication, can definitely think one step ahead of his adversaries, but he is also very, very much an *action* hero. With little preamble, the original Batman more often than not rushes headlong into situations with only the barest string of reason to guide him; thus, his entanglements with deadly dirigibles, giant apes, killer cults, vampires, and the common, garden-variety thug. There are definitely some sequences showing deductive work, but his legendary status as a great detective would only come with time – presumably, as he learns that half of his fantastic scrapes could have been avoided with a little bit of sound reasoning.

Where print Batman excels is in force of will. One incredible example of this is found in his bout with the Monk in *Detective* #31. Faced with the burning eyes of the red-robed vampire, our hero recognizes his foe's "uncanny powers," yet shrugs them off through "a tremendous effort of will."

The TV Batman is more of a sound thinker than an actual detective. Though often, his leaps of logic and feats of brain power come as fleet as hares in spring, he actually does do quite a bit of deduction, at least compared to his comic sire. Granted, much of it stems from his use of gadgets and bat-whatnots, but he manages to solve just about everything thrown his way. Obviously, the *Batman* scriptwriters didn't bother to put as much thought into the mental conundrums their Caped Crusader faced as, say, a mystery writer the caliber of Agatha Christie, but there's at least the *illusion* of deeper puzzles in the show. The TV Batman's definitely proud of his brain and espouses its use and upkeep at every turn – literally. Aside from his work as a detective, this Batman exhibits not only a great storehouse of important *and* trivial facts but also an eidetic memory. With total recall, Batman quotes police officers' names and badge numbers in "The Bookworm Turns," and he proves to be ahead of his time when his insights into the criminal mind sound like nothing less than today's profilers. The amount of deduction work in "Zelda the Great" is almost staggering.

In "While Gotham City Burns," there's a great moment where Batman must dredge a kernel of fact from deep within his mind. Not unlike his comic counterpart, he draws upon his force of will to comply. While spooky music plays in the soundtrack, we see our hero briefly put himself into what can only be described as a meditative state – years before such powers of concentration would be held in higher esteem.

It's not an accident that the producers and writers of *Batman* played up their star character's brain power. At that time, Batman was well-known as a detective, a hero without supernatural powers like Superman, and one that outwits his foes while thrashing them soundly. Bob Kane and Bill Finger's Batman, while definitely a cut above the crooks he chased, operated much like any other comic-book hero of the time: he's an all-around dashing figure, but not the mental giant he'd later become.

The print Batman is a physical marvel. Constantly leaping, swinging, and jumping his way through his adventures, he exhibits all the characteristics of the hyperactive. Most interestingly, the comic-book Batman of the first 11 stories frequently scales high walls with his silken cord – sound familiar? Almost 30 years later, it would become known as a "Bat-climb" and a major cliché of Adam West's Caped Crusader. Both versions are prone to use their Batarangs too, though the print Batman calls it a "Baterang." The first handful of *Batman* episodes show significant Batarang use, despite the then-crude special effects used to illustrate Batman's proficiency with the weapon. It's safe to say that both Batmen know how to use their fists, though the print Batman does so without the aid of a single garish, pop-art sound effect.

If we can look past all the jokes about Adam West's stomach, we can see that, while not as nimble as his comic counterpart, the TV Batman manages to run, jump, swing, and – yes – Bat-climb to good effect. Definitely a cut above and beyond his fellow Gothamites' capabilities.

And what would a discussion of the *Batman* TV show be without mention of all those dastardly deathtraps and confounding cliffhangers? It takes a few episodes for what will become known as the stereotypical Batman "great escapes" to find their final form – the first recognizable death-trap scenario with the Dynamic Duo in costumes arrives at the end of the 11th episode, "A Riddle a Day Keeps the Riddler Away" – but lasts to this day as a supremely memorable part of the show. It's important to point out that these traps call on both mental and physical prowess to solve and escape. The TV Batman's got that in spades.

As does the early print Batman, also. And boy, does *he* have traps and escapes that would make his TV successor green with envy. Seven out of the first 11 tales feature Batman in deathtraps and other ridiculously slippery situations: the Monk's dens of snakes and wolves, Dr. Kruger's death ray, and Hugo Strange's whipping rack, just to name a few. Kruger's tale (*Detective* #33) provides readers with an outlandish escape worthy of TV's overblown cliffhangers: Batman's shot and laid out for Kruger to disintegrate, but after the Dark Knight's seemingly turned into a "heap of ashes," we see one of Kruger's henchmen fleeing the scene and pulling off his mask – to reveal Bruce Wayne's slightly smiling face. What then follows is an explanation for the incredible escape that wouldn't have been too out-of-line issuing from Adam West's

One of Batman's earliest and most unbelievable deathtrap escapes, from *Detective Comics* #33 (1939). Art by Bob Kane and Sheldon Moldoff. Copyright © DC Comics.

mouth. In other words, implausible. The scene recalls a similar set-up in "Catwoman Goes to College," when the Caped Crusader escapes from a prison by fully exchanging identities with another – Alfred – and gets away with no one the wiser.

Batman is an inventor who creates many devices and vehicles to aid him in his crimefighting. Fleisher and Greenberger both figure this point into their criteria, but it's not explicitly stated in Batman's first origin. There, it's only said that he "becomes a master scientist." Regardless, the first 11 comic adventures are rife with Batman's crimefighting aids and even early attempts at specialized vehicles.

Much of the comic-book Batman's early technology was in the realm of possibility for the late 1930s, although his innovations in employing them can

An early example of Batman's inventiveness, from *Detective Comics* #29 (1939). Art by Bob Kane. Copyright © DC Comics.

be considered in the realm of the fantastic. The "Baterang" is indeed a riff on the Australian boomerang, and the "specially built high-powered auto" and utility belt only become incredible due to the settings and situations in which they are used. In his early tales, Batman's tech fits squarely in the pulp magazine tradition of which he is a product – i.e., nothing much more than what the 1930s and '40s were on the verge of utilizing in daily life.

The TV Batman, on the other hand, takes crimefighting technology and runs with it like his life depends upon it – and it often does. His prowess in the arena of innovation and technological speculation is unparalleled in TV fiction. It would be difficult to cover everything the Dynamic Duo uses in the first season of *Batman*, but suffice it to say that some of their devices have come to pass in our present day, while others still wait to be developed. *Batman*'s Batman is a consummate inventor and scientist – and engineer and chemist and radiologist and nuclear physicist and...

The comic-book Batman does gains one point on his TV progeny by introducing an aircraft – the Batgyro of *Detective* #31 – in his first year. The TV Batman doesn't unveil his Batcopter until his feature film, immediately following the first season of his show.

As we can see, *Batman* '66 accords with every aspect of what has made the character successful over several decades. The true differences between the comic and the TV show rest in their milieux – dark versus light. As the two-dimensional Bruce Wayne sits in his living room, in that first origin tale, he draws inspiration from an invasive bat to become a "creature of the night" – and he makes it so. Yet his TV counterpart heads out into the sun more often

Bruce had little time for his fiancée but plenty of time for his gadgets, including the Batgyro, in *Detective Comics* #31 (1939). Art by Bob Kane and Sheldon Moldoff. Copyright © DC Comics.

than not and is a creature of his brighter times, that idyllic 1960s of our collective delusion. Despite this difference of setting, the characters themselves remain close in their depiction.

Adam West's Batman

When Adam West first won the role of the Caped Crusader in 1965, he felt that he needed some sort of characterization in his Batman. "I wanted to try and figure out what kind of man we were dealing with here," he says in *Back to the Batcave*. He claims that he "loved" Batman comics as a child. (Born in 1928, he might very well have read the first 11 stories when they were new.) He soon realized, however, that the character was no longer the "two-fisted vampiric figure" of his youth but had become, in the mid-'60s, something of a James Bond type. West tells us that, after much research, he arrived at a short list of his own observations on what was necessary for the character:

1. Batman freely, and without hesitation, risks his life for the underdog.
2. His adventures… are set in the urban jungle, often among the downtrodden, which gives many of the tales a Dickensian flavor.
3. Batman is as plausible as a superhero can be.
4. Clothes help make the man…
5. Batman's a detective. He's got a good mind.
6. He's blessed… with the most memorable rogues' gallery this side of Dick Tracy.

West's list isn't too far afield, with a little squinting, from that of Fleisher and Greenberger. West attempted to bring insight to the character, translating this understanding onto the screen. Much like William Shatner and Leonard Nimoy are supremely enmeshed in the creation of Capt. Kirk and Mr. Spock, so too is Adam West in the crafting of the TV Batman.

It's worth touching upon West's early observations about the character, because he makes some good points that hold their own alongside Fleisher and Greenberger's lists as insights into Batman's power and personality.

Batman freely, and without hesitation, risks his life for the underdog. This might seem a no-brainer for a super-hero (let alone an everyday hero), but the 1939 comic-book Batman is not a very nice guy. Oh, he exhibits a bit of compassion for his fellow man, such as in *Detective* #30, where he shows some concern for an innocent old lady and takes time to help her, or several months later, in #36, where he soothes an abductee's jangled nerves. But overall, this Batman's a bit of a bastard – especially towards his foes.

In nine out of the first 11 print adventures, villains die. And in the majority of those cases, it's Batman who speeds them to their final and often gruesome reward. He punches them into vats of acid, throws them off buildings, breaks their necks, shoots them, or otherwise allows them to perish in various horrible ways. This is *justice* in the Golden Age of comics. Thank goodness none of the major Bat-villains are introduced in these early tales – we'd never have had them to enjoy today.

Yet the original Dark Knight fights for good. He loosens up a bit from time to time, perhaps if there's a female involved, but he's serious about his mission – and heaven help anyone who stands in his way.

The TV Batman's steadfast in his mission too. A straight-laced, sometimes even dour guy, his fight for what's right is written boldly across his primetime sagas. His concern for Gotham's citizens and the laws that bind them border on obsessive-compulsiveness. In "While Gotham City Burns," he states that his "duty is to the public," even to the detriment of Aunt Harriet and Alfred's own well-being. In "Hi Diddle Riddle," he champions "pedestrian safety." In "Fine Feathered Finks," when the Penguin's giant umbrella causes chaos in the streets, Batman's quick to warn bystanders to flee the scene, lest they become endangered.

But the TV Batman can be a bit of a bastard too. In the very first episode, after he threatens the villain's life over Robin's safety, he leaves the Riddler to seemingly die in the basement of the Moldavian embassy – not unlike his comic-book doppelganger. To underscore the point, he later claims his "only regret" in the case is the death of the Riddler's moll, Molly – not her boss's.

Batman frequently berates his adversaries with taunting labels like "fiend" or "devil."

But it is perhaps women for which the TV Batman may hold the greatest disdain. This Caped Crusader could very well be a misogynist.

Of course, Batman cannot form attachments to females due to his sworn duty to fight crime. For the most part, he maintains this choice throughout the TV series. At the coda of "Batman's Waterloo," the alluring Lisa Carson invites Bruce into her apartment, but he declines, telling her she'll make some man a fine wife but that he's "not that man." "The Wayne Foundation is my wife," he notes tellingly. But Lisa's kisses lure him inside anyway, as he smiles shyly – or is that slyly? – at us, the audience, and says, "Man cannot live by crimefighting alone."

But beyond these rare moments of warmth on the show, there are also moments of violence in the first season towards the "fairer sex" that may surprise those who think of the character in a rosier glow.

Molly is called a "poor, deluded child," though she's quite obviously a vibrant, vivacious woman. The Joker's moll Queenie is similarly labeled. The title character of "Zelda the Great" is given no leeway for her gender. Yet Batman later blurts out, "How can a *woman* stoop to such a trick?" once he learns Zelda's nefarious plan for Aunt Harriet. In "The Bookworm Turns," he promises "no harm" will come to Lydia Limpet but gasses her and hauls her off to the Batcave for an illegal and coercive hypnotism session. The beautiful Sherry Jackson, as Pauline in "The Riddler's False Notion," fares worse: Batman yells in her face, "By all that's holy I might do you violence!" and submits her to a chemical lie-detector against her will. How very pulp-ish of him. You'd think it was the roarin' '30s instead of the swingin' 60s.

In his defense, the TV Batman's muddled and mushy thoughts for Catwoman are well-documented – unless she's played by Eartha Kitt. And his touching remembrance of Molly, his wistful thoughts for Dawn Robbins in "The Penguin's a Jinx," and Zelda the Great prove that he also has a soft spot for the ladies.

The 1939 Batman actually has a fiancée, something few of his Golden Age compatriots can claim. I wonder exactly what creators Bob Kane and Bill Finger were thinking at the time, saddling their hero with the lovely but fairly commonplace Julie Madison in *Detective* #31, but they later rectified the situation by having Julie dump Bruce in 1941's *Detective* #49. The millionaire

Bruce Wayne (Adam West) succumbs to Miss Kitka (Lee Meriwether) at the latter's borrowed penthouse apartment. Publicity still from the 1966 *Batman* feature (signed by West). Copyright © Greenway Productions, DC Comics, and 20ᵗʰ Century-Fox.

barely blinks when he gets the news, and we assume he's probably pretty damn thrilled to be rid of this burden to his secret lifestyle.

His adventures... are set in the urban jungle, often among the downtrodden, which gives many of the tales a Dickensian flavor. I'm not sure how much of his work Charles Dickens would recognize in an average issue of Batman, but I get

The Dark Knight blithely leaves one girl to run off with another, in *Detective Comics* #32 (1939). Art by Bob Kane and Sheldon Moldoff. Copyright © DC Comics.

the gist of what Adam West is saying. Batman's very much a creature who lurks in and around skyscrapers, penthouses, and urban sprawl, and in his first 11 adventures, set predominantly in New York's Manhattan, rooftops are his haunt of choice. Yet in his first year, the print Batman takes a break from this urban setting to run off for a few issues to Hungary and Paris, while his TV counterpart goes three entire seasons and only leaves Gotham City once. Adam West's Caped Crusader isn't much the globetrotter, though that may owe more to budget restraints than a lack of interesting worldwide crime cases. But that's makes sense for the character. Throughout World War II, the comic-book Batman's adventures barely recognized the global conflict and kept their hero primarily on the home front. West said it best: Batman works better surrounded by brick and steel.

Batman is as plausible as a superhero can be. As one of the most human of all super-heroes, Batman's made his mark on pop culture as something we can all aspire to. For the most part. If our parents were murdered and we spent many of our formative years training to become the world's greatest detective and crimefighter, that is.

We've already talked about Batman's fallibility in his early tales and episodes, but it's worth bringing up the subject of injuries. We know, of course, that he can be shot, stabbed, beaten, and bruised. When he is, we feel this makes him more human, and, so the theory goes, we then identify with him. This idea is utilized in the original Batman's third adventure (*Detective* #29), wherein the Dark Knight is shot by Jabah, corpulent toady to the unfortunately-named Doctor Death, and our hero falls to the floor with a bleeding bullet wound. He shrugs it off fairly quickly, routs his foe, and (after changing back to Bruce) goes and sees his "family doctor." Despite the ease with which he dismisses his doctor's concern over how Bruce "shot himself," this would inaugurate 70 years' worth of injuries for Batman.

The TV Batman, while never taking a bullet or a shiv, has his fair share of headaches, including but not limited to being punched, bludgeoned, gassed, frozen, and squeezed. I'd like to think he's shown to be as human as his comic-book predecessor, but I can admit he seems a bit more implausible overall. But boy, does he ever like to talk about physical fitness.

Clothes help make the man... This seems like easy one. But can the costumes of both print and TV Batmans be considered the same? They're definitely the same outfit, with a few cosmetic differences mostly in color and cut, and both are recognizable as Batman's famous duds. But consider this: the look of the 1939 Batman is most likely as odd-looking to a young person today as Adam West's get-up. Again, it comes down to color and cut.

As the legend goes, Bob Kane supposedly intended Batman's costume to be grey and black. For highlights on the black parts, so as to not have large patches of black ink, he used the color blue. Eventually, the black mask, cape, boots, gloves, and trunks were interpreted as *being* blue. By the 1960s, Batman wore grey and blue, and that's the design the TV show's producers used – albeit an almost garish blue due to the satiny material used. But it's still the same costume as in 1939.

The major problem people have with the visual struck by Adam West in the Batman costume is not necessarily the clothes but the actor himself: somewhat paunchy in the middle, undeveloped in the chest and arms, and scrawny of leg. West may have made up for any sins of the costume had he been "built" to the standards of today's musclemen – or even those of the 1960s. But it's still Batman's costume – bat-ears, scalloped cape, and all.

He's blessed... with the most memorable rogues' gallery this side of Dick Tracy. That's absolutely true of the TV series Batman – but not so much of the original comic-book version. In the 1960s, TV screens ran wild with a circus procession of Bat-villains, but in 1939, readers were offered little more than pulp-inspired baddies. Regardless, a discussion of Batman's adversaries isn't germane to my topic, the Dark Knight's character – unless one is examining how he *reacts* to his foes.

Both Batmen look upon their respective opponents in much the same way: as people to be stopped in their selfish pursuits and then to be brought to justice.   Justice on TV meant prison and perhaps reformation followed by parole. In the comic pages of 1939, it usually meant death.

In "Batman's Waterloo," Adam West's Batman succinctly sums up his entire outlook on crime: "No man is above the law – or below it." In his first origin, the comic-book Batman clearly spells out his mission: "I swear by the spirits of my parents to avenge their deaths by spending the rest of my life warring on all criminals." To one, fighting crime is a war; to the other, it's a balancing of the social scale, rooted in the law.

As the actor behind the mask, Adam West's perception of Batman was important, and his list is instructive. So too was the perception of *Batman*'s producer, William Dozier, even though he had reportedly never read a Batman comic or had any knowledge of the character before producing the show. He told *The Official Batman Batbook* that his version of the Dark Knight "had to be played as though we were dropping a bomb on Hiroshima, with that kind of deadly seriousness." Dozier further elaborated that Batman "wasn't going to be Cary Grant, full of charm," but that West "just had to play a very square, hard-nosed guy..."

Equally, the Batman of 1939 is presented as straightforward as one could illustrate a super-hero, at the dawn of comic books. He's a steadfast guy in a dark world of crime and shadows. As I said before, Adam West's Batman is also an upright fellow but one who exists in a brighter, more cheerful world – albeit full of crime. The context might be different, but the two versions of the character are – for the most part – one and the same.

The Verdict

I don't mean to imply that *Batman* '66 is a literal adaptation of the 1939 comic-book character. It is instead an adaptation of the *spirit* of the character, and it hews closer to its source material than many people have, do, or will give it credit. For all its brightness, the TV Batman is in some ways, such as in his brainy solutions or his villains, arguably closer to what most identify as Batman than the 1939 printed version. For me, it all comes down to perception – and I've found that many people perceive the 1966 TV series in very odd and even unfair ways.

Often, people cannot see through the TV series's trappings to get to the heart of the matter: the character of Batman. They perceive the campiness of situations into which the character is thrust, rather than his approach, his problem-solving, his sense of justice, his means and motivations. It's a shame, really, because the show delivers much more than its bright surface. Just as the original comic-book stories are more complicated than their dark, pulpy flavor. *Batman* '66 has been unfairly saddled with and made to answer to the "relevance" the 1970s brought to the comics. What a crime.

Much of the misperception that the show's Batman diverges radically from the comics character stems from either a lack of knowledge of the hero or the simple regurgitation of the show's "legend" for campy comedy and hijinks. Flip attitudes toward the show's character began as early as the 11 March 1966 issue of *Life*, wherein a writer states with authority, "Batman is supposed to be cubical, of course..." Even West himself has spun his perception over the years. Although we've seen his more reverent take on the character in his 1994 *Back to the Batcave*, in that same 1966 *Life* piece, when asked his initial reaction to being offered the part, he responded *"Ecch!"*

We all have perceptions about the show, whether or not we've actually even seen the TV series. If you've never seen the show or haven't viewed it lately, your perceptions of its depiction of Batman just might be skewed. And not in a good way.

In the 1966 *Life* article, Adam West had hopes during the actual filming of the show that later viewers would find merit in *Batman*. "I want to do it well enough," he said, "that *Batman* buffs will watch reruns in a few years and say, 'Watch the bit he does here, isn't that great?'" Later, he opined in *Adam West Remembers Batman*,

> Batman has always been somewhat a product of the times, and he's evolved in many media. It's not a criticism of the contemporary dark persona of the character when I say I'm pleased that our Batman gave people a reason to smile and took them away from the cares of the real world for an hour each week.

And there's the crux of the issue: there's a Batman for everyone.

Both those first 11 comic adventures and the first season of *Batman* merit revisiting.   Both possess great character detail, and the personality and presence that exist in both remains strong, visionary, and compelling. Their tone may be different, but Batman remains recognizably Batman.

I believe I possess a power that some other fans do not, I'm sad to say: the ability to compartmentalize my love for Batman. Sure, I grew up with the 1966 *Batman* TV series, which introduced the character to me. I also grew up with the 1970s Batman cartoon and, of course, *Super Friends*. But I also grew up with lots of Batman comics. In the later '60s and in the '70s, DC Comics doled out reprints in regular fashion, and these provided an education into the history of not only Batman but of comic books as a whole. In your average "DC 100 Page Super Spectacular," a kid could be exposed to stories ranging from the 1930s to the 1970s, right next to one another, offering a treasure trove of characters, creators, and styles of storytelling. I came away with the idea that Batman, my favorite, had many faces and that all of them were the real deal. I had my particular favorites among them, sure, but I was able to accept all these Gotham Guardians into my heart and set them in their respective places in the character's history, as well as comics history generally.

In recent years, I've come to disagree with those who call Adam West the "real" or the "classic" Batman – he's just Batman. He's another face of Batman. Somehow, Bob Kane and Bill Finger, purposefully or not, designed a character in 1939 that allowed for interpretation while still retaining the core elements that make Batman memorable. That gives the character his character. You can't hurt the character of Batman unless you tear down and dispense with those elements that are part and parcel to his foundation. *Batman* '66 didn't throw the baby out with the bat-water; despite Dozier's cluelessness and West's supposed initial reluctance, they worked in tandem until they got it right.

1939 Batman, meet 1966 Batman. I call ye brothers.

Notes on Bat-Camp

by Timothy Callahan

The question arises: "Is the 1966 *Batman* TV show camp?" Does it live up to its reputation as a "camp classic?" Is it as "campy" as everyone seems to think? Does the use of so many quotation marks around my use of "camp" suggest that camp, in and of itself, is "campy?"

These are questions for the ages, but they demand answers, and that's why I'm here. But instead of answering the questions directly in a persuasive essay, or quoting from significant figures throughout human history in an attempt to justify my pre-determined conclusions, I will answer these questions in the form of 26 notes. Notes on *Batman*. Notes on the whole concept of camp.

These notes are for Susan Sontag.

1. Camp is not parody, even if exaggeration is used as the primary mode of parody. The exaggeration found in camp – what makes works of art or literature campy – exaggerates the artifice itself. It points out the inherent ridiculousness of what it is, and it does so in a showy yet straight-faced manor. Camp dares the audience to ask, "Is this for real?"

2. Though often used as a synonym for silly or frivolous, camp is neither. Camp is more substantial than that – even if it winks at the reader, the viewer, the participant, and hints that it doesn't take itself as seriously as it pretends to.

3. When she wrote her "Notes on Camp" in 1964 for *Partisan Review*, Susan Sontag didn't have the benefit of two major anchor pieces to determine what was and *wasn't* camp. She couldn't have predicted that Adam West, of the then-current film *Robinson Crusoe on Mars*, would don the garb of the

Caped Crusader two years later, and she couldn't have predicted that just over a decade later, a Jim Sharman movie musical would capture the essence of camp for an entire generation. Without *The Rocky Horror Picture Show* as a barometer for camp, it's no surprise that she was as loose with her definition as possible.

4. Sontag cites Tiffany lamps, *Swan Lake*, and "Lynn Ward's novel in woodcuts" as examples of "the canon of Camp," yet none of those things would be considered camp today. As time marches on, the camp of one era becomes the historical detritus of another. Some are forgotten, others remembered fondly, innocently. A select few become not "camp classics," but genuine classics. Their camp connotations drift away as they blend in with other historical relics. *The Merry Wives of Windsor* may well have been the height of camp, circa 1602. Today, it's just another Shakespeare play, one of many that don't rank among his best.

5. History can have another effect as well, if the work in question lingers from one era into the next.

Take TV's *The Price is Right*, for example. The sincerity of the contestants and the knowing smile of Bob Barker moved into the realm of camp sometime in the 1980s, long after the show had established itself as a straightforward slice of daytime entertainment. Now, in the hands of Drew Carey, it is too self-consciously camp, which makes it not-quite-camp-anymore. Barker's easy charm, while excitable housewives and soldiers on leave played Plinko, was replaced by the scornful chuckles of Carey, a comedian who plays the role of a character who knows it's all a joke.

Sincerity turns to camp which turns to post-camp irony, as the decades race by. It is not the thing itself which possesses the camp. It is its relation to the world around it.

6. Camp is, therefore, a mode of perception, though not a completely subjective one. It is a matter of taste, true, but each generation has commonalities of taste, even if unanimous agreement is impossible. Popular music is popular for many reasons, but one of which is the most painfully obvious: plenty of people simultaneously agree that it sounds good. Yet the Temptations of one generation become the C+C Music Factory of the next. Like popularity, camp is democratic.

7. The term "campy" can be dismissive, but camp does not mean bad, without merit, or trashy. Camp is celebratory, and its inherent joy can be misinterpreted as whimsy or fakery. But its primal concern is often fun.

8. So let's talk about the 1966 *Batman*, shall we?

Clearly, the performances of Adam West and Burt Ward provide much of the deadpan humor – or absurd, ridiculous humor – of the series, and the jaunty Nelson Riddle musical score creates just the right balance of liveliness and self-consciousness, but one man deserves the majority of the credit for giving *Batman* its tone: Lorenzo Semple, Jr.

Semple wrote the pilot and a handful of early episodes. And it was his take on the Batman universe that showed up on the small screen.

As Semple recounts in a 9 July 2008 article for *Variety*:

> It was a writer's hog heaven. I was sent four issues of the comic for plot ideas, each featuring one of the Big Four villains. The Joker seemed the best pilot choice, though I'm not sure why. I mailed Bill [Dozier] the script at Fox. He and his folks loved it. Then I flew back from Malaga to New York for a meeting with ABC, where Bill eloquently pitched the script and its high-camp POW!! BLAM!! WHAMMO!! style, those onscreen graphics already written in.

Semple seems to have no problem calling his pilot script "high-camp," but let's take a look at those early episodes and see what they reveal.

9. The opening two-parter, "Hi Diddle Riddle / Smack in the Middle," begins with a scene from the Moldavian embassy, and the tone of the series solidifies   immediately.   Robert   Butler's   direction   and   Sam   Levitt's cinematography establish the look that would dominate all the episodes that followed, but Semple's script provides the framework for a flamboyant, exaggerated tale of super-heroics.

The first scene features an exploding cake and a tiny pink and white parachute carrying a message from the Riddler.

As Sontag writes, "Camp sees everything in quotation marks. It's not a lamp, but a 'lamp'; not a woman, but a 'woman.' To perceive Camp in objects and persons is to understand Being-as-Playing-a-Role. It is the farthest extension, in sensibility, of the metaphor of life as theater."

Theatricality is the essence of *Batman*, from its very opening. Considering the mise-en-scene of *Batman*, it's surprising the exploding cake isn't labeled "exploding cake" the way everything else in Batman's world is clearly labeled.

10. Not only do West and Ward contribute to the theatricality with their line readings – West, smug and self-confident, even spouting the most on-the-nose dialogue; Ward, overly enthusiastic, as if shouting sincerity equals honesty of performance – but the supporting cast is equally in on the joke. Neil

Hamilton's Commissioner Gordon doesn't seem to come from the Stella Adler school in his soap-operatic delivery.

The daytime soap opera is surely the essence of camp. And though *Batman*'s low-rent theatrical flourishes don't share anything, visually, with *Days of Our Lives* or *General Hospital*, the supporting performances are often of the same standard. It's arch formality, it's artifice, swarming around knowingly-stilted lines of dialogue.

11. *Batman* is not parody. Not in the early episodes, at least. Later, it arguably evolves into self-parody. Cetainly, the repetition of its structure and the recursion of its clearly established rules (every episode is a two-parter with a guest villain, every episode has the same cues: the Bat-phone, the onomatopoeic fight scenes, the "Holy" declarations of observation) *lend* themselves to self-parody. Yet the series, as evidenced by the Semple-penned early episodes (the formative episodes, though the form came already molded into shape), isn't mocking comic-book super-heroics. It's playing them with sincerity. Arch sincerity, but not mockery.

12. It's certainly not satire, even though Semple, in his *Variety* piece, claims that he and producer William Dozier saw the series as a comedy, "hopefully appealing to kids as an absurdly jolly action piece and to grown-ups for its deadpan satire." The absurdly jolly action pieces are evident in every episode. The deadpan tone as well – particularly effective from Adam West, whose consistent deadpanery contrasts strongly with the over-the-top giggling, squawking, and Machiavellian hand-wringing of the guest villains.

But satire? No. To truly achieve satire, *Batman* would have to comment on social trends, on cultural problems. And though the series injects its own form of cultural relevance by drawing upon fashion trends of its era and by riffing on celebrity personas, it's never about anything other than its hermetically-sealed world.

13. Some of *Batman*'s hermetically-sealed theatricality, bearing no resemblance to anything in the real world: Bruce Wayne's Shakespeare bust, which pulls back to reveal the trigger for the secret entrance to the Batcave; the Batpoles, labeled "Bruce" and "Dick," even though you'd think the sharp minds of Batman and Robin could remember the difference between right and left; and the costumes, not just Adam West's – gray tights, eyebrow accentuated cowl, and silky cape – but also the fetishistic attention to detail in the super-villain garb. In the opening two-parter, the Riddler changes costume three times.

14.   Besides establishing the tone for *Batman*, Lorenzo Semple, Jr. also wrote a few well-regarded thrillers as well, including *The Parallax View* and *Three Days of the Condor*. But more importantly for our purposes, he wrote 1980's *Flash Gordon*.

Surely *Flash Gordon* has many of the same qualities as *Batman*: theatricality, gaudy set decoration, and music that amplifies the humor or undermines the seriousness.

Let's just admit it: *Flash Gordon* is camp.

15.   Let's just admit it: *Batman* is camp. Let's label it so, as neatly and clearly as every last item in the Batcave.

16.   Even if *Batman* doesn't capture all the qualities of pre-1966 camp, or provide a very narrow example of the broad swath of classic camp, the popularity of *Batman*, and its so-sure-of-itself-from-the-beginning, straightforwardly ridiculous tone, established it as the paragon of camp from that point forward.

17.   Let's celebrate that level of camp, shall we? Because *Batman*'s camp is transcendently fun. In the opening episode, Adam West's Batman gives us lines like, "Watch it, chum. Pedestrian safety," as Batman, improbably, pulls a Bat-suction cup hook from his belt, sticks it to the wall, and puts a human-sized slice of window bars on the hook. The slow pacing, the methodical process of cutting through a window and then keeping the window from falling on a citizen below – these are not things that would have come from the comic book. These are moments of camp that emerge from answering the question: "What would Batman and Robin really do, given this situation?" Not asking what they'd do if they were real, but asking what they would do considering their absurdly unreal existence.

18.   Frank Gorshin's Riddler laughs like Richard Widmark's Tommy Udo from 1947's *Kiss of Death*. This is not satire or parody. It's camp, and because Gorshin's performance has become such a cultural touchstone, it turns Widmark's performance to camp as well, retroactively.

19.   The opening episode also includes a scene involving a giant pickle jar filled with caviar. (You can tell, because it has a "caviar" label on it.) It's in the Molehill Mob hideout, and one of the thugs, all of whom work for the Riddler, says to Jill St. John's girlish femme fatale, "Watch them fish eggs, Molly. They're fulla calories. You'll blow up like a balloon."

20. Batman dances – does the Batusi – in the first episode, believe it or not, but not until he walks into the discotheque wearing his full costume, saying to the waiter, "I'll stand at the bar. I shouldn't wish to attract attention."

21. Robin couldn't get into the disco. He's underage and all, but when he discovers that Batman has stumbled into trouble, the Boy Wonder enables the helpfully-labeled "Anti-Theft" device on the Batmobile before getting shot by a tranquilizer dart from the nefariously giggling Riddler. The anti-theft device? Shoots fireworks. That's what keeps the Batmobile from getting stolen.

22. Yes, all of these things are campy. They define camp.

23. Here's something you don't see in the more recent, non-campy super-hero movies that have subsequently come out: super-heroes, in costume, talking on the telephone. Christopher Nolan and even Bryan Singer (who probably veers closer to camp than Nolan) avoid scenes with their costumed characters chatting to each other, phone receivers in hand. *Batman* is full of such scenes from the first episode onward.

24. Sontag's essay also addresses a potentially more controversial topic: the connection between camp and homosexuality. She writes, "The peculiar relation between Camp taste and homosexuality has to be explained. While it's not true that Camp taste is homosexual taste, there is no doubt a peculiar affinity and overlap." Sontag refers to a particular subset of homosexual style, of affectation, that we still see today in the films of John Waters or the celebrity punditry of Perez Hilton.

A kind of life-as-theater approach applies, Sontag suggests.

But the overtly "homosexual" overtones, or winking homosexuality, of *Batman* can't be ignored. I'm not talking about any implications about the relationship between Batman and Robin, nor between Bruce Wayne and his young ward. The series doesn't imply that at all.

Although, in the second part of the first Riddler two-parter, Robin is replaced by a female – Jill St. John's Molly, who dresses up in a Robin costume and puts on a mask that makes her look identical to Burt Ward. Identical. Because it is, in fact, Burt Ward playing the role but playing it in an exaggerated, effeminate manner.

That bit of faux-homosexuality, a man playing a woman playing a man, doesn't fool Batman. But it does seem to speak to a recognition that an aspect of traditional camp is the flamboyance of the homosexual stereotype.

It's a stereotype that someone like Oscar Wilde played up with his dandyism, with his cutting wit, with his aestheticism.

25.   47 episodes later, Semple wrote a two-parter about the villainous "Fingers" and his half-brother, Harry, both played by Liberace.

"The Devil's Fingers / The Dead Ringers" features a number of knowing winks at Liberace's public persona. Even though Liberace steadfastly denied his homosexuality and had won lawsuits against tabloids that had hinted at such things, the Semple screenplay for that two-part *Batman* episode plays up the "is-he-or-isn't-he?" jokes.

The entire plot for the two-parter hinges on ladies' man Chandell (a.k.a. Fingers, played by Liberace) and his attempted seduction of the chaste Aunt Harriet. At one point, Madge Blake's Aunt Harriet and Liberace's Chandell are inside his dressing room, sipping root beer from champagne glasses, arms intertwined.

Later, when he talks of his plans to marry Aunt Harriet and use their "joint bank account" to pay his gangster twin brother five million dollars in blackmail money, Chandell says (as he flaps his arms gracefully), "I'll cast off my criminal skin like a molting butterfly."

The best Liberace-is-actually-gay-and-everyone-knows-it-but-he-won't-admit-it joke appears near the end of the episode, when Aunt Harriet recounts the moment when Chandell kissed her hand. She's taken aback by the kiss because it wasn't what she expected. She says, enigmatically, "A girl can tell."

We later find out that she was referring to Chandell not actually being Chandell. He was replaced by his twin brother, Harry. But the joke implied something else entirely.

26.   Just in case there's any doubt that *Batman* qualifies as camp, the final image in "The Dead Ringers" shows Liberace's Chandell performing in prison. He's dressed in prison pinstripe, and so is his grand piano. Bold black and white stripes. Theatrical. Ridiculous. Artificial.

27.   Sontag writes, "Camp is the consistently aesthetic experience of the world. It incarnates a victory of 'style' over 'content,' 'aesthetics' over 'morality,' of irony over tragedy."

I'd agree with that statement.

But I would add, "it's also anything that's like the 1966 *Batman* TV show. Because that, my friends, is camp. Through and through."

Harry Chandell (Liberace) camps it up with Aunt Harriet (Madge Blake) in the second season's "The Devil's Fingers / The Dead Ringers" (1966). From William Dozier's archives. Copyright © Greenway Productions, DC Comics, and 20th Century-Fox.

Aunt Harriet's Film
Decency League

by Becky Beard

Batman is the first TV show I remember watching. I was two years old when it debuted in 1966, and my big brother, Skip, and I would eagerly plop down in front of the set. After having stripped to my underpants, I wrapped one of my father's belts around my waist and draped my favorite baby blanket over my shoulders for a cape. And after we saw the feature film, I asked Skip if Batman was real; he assured me that, yes, Batman was indeed real and that he was busy fighting crime to keep us safe.

What made *Batman* real to us? The actors. Kids don't know from producers, directors, gaffers, or key grips. It's what appears on camera that counts. And *Batman* boasted a half-century's worth of acting talent.

Celebrities of every ilk clamored to appear on the series, more than could be accommodated. Frank Sinatra, Elizabeth Taylor, Gregory Peck, and Yul Brynner were among the disappointed. Even United States Attorney General Robert F. Kennedy was turned away.

But what about those who made the cut?

The celebrated window cameos alone featured the likes of Jerry Lewis (who insisted on directing his own scene); Dick Clark; Sammy Davis, Jr.; Art Linkletter; Edward G. Robinson; Don Ho; Bruce Lee and Van Williams as the Green Hornet and Kato; Howard Duff as Det. Sgt. Sam Stone; Werner Klemperer as Colonel Klink; Andy Devine as Santa Claus; and Ted Cassidy as Lurch. (Cassidy's costars from *The Addams Family*, Carolyn Jones and John Astin, also appeared on the series: Jones as Marsha, Queen of Diamonds; Astin as the second of two actors to portray Riddler – the first being Frank Gorshin, Emmy-nominated for his work on the show.)

Other notables – both old-timers and up-and-comers – included Tony winner David Wayne, Oscar nominee Victor Buono, former child star Roddy McDowall, silent-screen legend Francis X. Bushman, comedienne Phyllis Diller, ecdysiast-turned-auteur Gypsy Rose Lee, fledgling thespian Teri Garr, and unfortunate hairdresser Jay Sebring, best remembered today as a victim (along with friend Sharon Tate) of cult leader Charles Manson's murderous associates.

With an article of this type there will always be a reader who thinks that the writer has overlooked such-and-such a favorite or that so-and-so should have been included. To properly document the show's numerous guest stars and their spider's web of pre-*Batman* connections would require a volume all its own. Instead, I have chosen to profile some of the personalities I think are most significant: those whose decades-long careers lent a credibility to the show that it might not otherwise have had and who, in turn, gained renewed visibility and a fresh generation of fans. As such, you won't see Frank Gorshin here, for example; as wonderful as he is in the show, he was a relative newcomer compared to thespians and vaudevillians like Tallulah Bankhead, Maurice Evans, and the raucous Rudy Valée.

So let's get started.

Alan William Napier-Clavering was born 7 January 1903 in Birmingham, England. Napier, a cousin of Neville Chamberlain (Prime Minister of the U.K., 1937-40), graduated from Clifton College and studied at the Royal Academy of Dramatic Art, later honing his craft on West End stages in the company of aspiring actors John Gielgud and Robert Morley. His film debut came in 1930 with *Caste*, but he had no great success on the screen until moving to America. Notable appearances after arriving in the states include the priest in Orson Welles's 1948 *Macbeth* (a character created by Welles for this bizarre reinterpretation of Shakespeare's tragedy), Cicero in 1953's *Julius Caesar*, and Sean Connery's father in Alfred Hitchcock's *Marnie* (1964). Napier was the first player cast for *Batman*, even before Adam West and Burt Ward. He'd never read comics before being hired and had no idea who Batman was. When his agent approached him with the part of Batman's butler, Napier found the notion ridiculous... until the money was mentioned. Alfred became Napier's

GOTHAM CITY CLASS OF 1966

TALLULAH BANKHEAD
ANNE BAXTER
MILTON BERLE

ART CARNEY
MAURICE EVANS
ZSA ZSA GABOR

LIBERACE
IDA LUPINO
BURGESS MEREDITH

ETHEL MERMAN
ALAN NAPIER
OTTO PREMINGER

VINCENT PRICE
CESAR ROMERO
GEORGE SANDERS

WALTER SLEZAK
RUDY VALLEE
SHELLEY WINTERS

One butler, 17 crooks – what a class act. Stills assembled and combined by M. Mrakota Orsman.   Copyright © Greenway Productions, DC Comics, and 20th Century-Fox.

best-known role. Alan Napier died of a stroke on 8 August 1988 in Santa Monica, California.

Oliver Burgess Meredith was born 16 November 1907 in Cleveland, Ohio. He made his Broadway debut in 1930 as Peter in *Romeo and Juliet* at Eva le Galliene's Civic Repertory Theatre. He continued acting with le Galliene's company and others, with performances in such notable productions as 1933's *Threepenny Opera*. During these years, Meredith became a favorite of playwright Maxwell Anderson, who created the role of Mio in *Winterset* for him; the show won the first-ever New York Drama Critics' Circle Award for Best Play. The 1936 film adaptation is often cited as Meredith's screen debut, but that actually came as an uncredited carny caller in Tod Browning's controversial *Freaks* (1932). Meredith starred opposite Lon Chaney, Jr. in the 1939 adaptation of John Steinbeck's *Of Mice and Men*; the film was nominated for four Oscars. After a stint with United States Army Air Forces in World War II, Meredith began adding directing and producing credits to his resume. Nor would the burgeoning medium of TV go unexploited; among his many guest spots were four episodes of *The Twilight Zone*, including the unforgettable "Time Enough at Last." "Buzz" (as he was known to be called) appeared in 20 installments of *Batman*. Burgess Meredith died 9 September 1997 in Malibu, California, suffering from Alzheimer's disease and melanoma; Adam West spoke at his memorial service.

Cesar Julio Romero, Jr. was born 15 February 1907 in New York City. His family was a prosperous one, but their fortunes fell with the collapse of the stock market on 29 October 1929. Fortunately, Romero was able to support the family as one half of a dance duo with heiress Lisbeth Higgins. When Romero made the move west, the family followed, and he lived with various relatives for the rest of his life. His screen debut came in 1933's *The Shadow Laughs*. His first significant role was playing Chris Jorgenson in 1934's *The Thin Man*, based on the novel by Dashiell Hammett; the film received four Oscar nominations and spawned five sequels. Romero's dark good looks enabled him to build a lengthy résumé playing an assortment of swarthy villains and Latin lovers. When World War II came along, he enlisted and (aboard the Coast Guard-manned assault transport U.S.S. Cavalier) saw action at Tinian and Saipan. He asked for no special treatment, winning the admiration of his shipmates. He worked as a winch operator and a powderman and, as occasion permitted, entertained his fellows. By the time of his discharge, he had made the rank of Chief Boatswain's Mate. "Butch" appeared in 19 installments of *Batman*. Cesar

Romero died of bronchitis and pneumonia on 1 January 1994 in Santa Monica, California.

George Henry Sanders, younger brother of actor Tom Conway (1904-1967), was born 3 July 1906 in St. Petersburg, Russia. The Russian Revolution forced the family to return to England, leaving their wealth behind them. Sanders worked at various jobs before a co-worker – Greer Garson – suggested he try show business. After arriving in Hollywood, Sanders played principal roles in B-movies and supporting roles in higher profile pictures. He made his uncredited film debut in 1929's *Strange Cargo*. He held starring roles in two film series, the Saint and the Falcon. When Sanders tired of playing Gay Lawrence, a.k.a. the Falcoln, he suggested his brother Tom as a replacement, so 1942's *The Falcon's Brother* killed off Sanders's character and introduced the character's brother, Tom (Conway). The only other film in which the two appeared together (again playing brothers) was 1956's *Death of a Scoundrel*, co-starring Sanders's second wife Zsa Zsa Gabor. (Sanders's fourth and final wife was Zsa Zsa's sister Magda; the marriage lasted six weeks.) He appeared in productions by Fritz Lang, Otto Preminger, and Cecil B. DeMille. The high point of his career was his portrayal of Addison DeWitt in *All About Eve*, for which he won the 1950 Academy Award for Best Supporting Actor. He made his TV debut in *The 20th Century-Fox Hour* (1955) and continued mixing TV and film work for the remainder of his life. "Never once did I get the feeling that he thought it was a comedown for him to be doing prime-time TV for $2,500 after a distinguished film career. Quite the contrary. I think the show's tone appealed very much to his own acerbic sense of humor," says Adam West in *Back to the Batcave*. West calls Sanders "icy and elegant," an apt description for the actor who played Mr. Freeze in the "Rats Like Cheese" and "Instant Freeze." In 1937, Sanders told friend David Niven that he intended to kill himself one day. He fulfilled his promise on 25 April 1972, overdosing on Nembutal in Castelldefels, Spain. His suicide note read, "Dear World, I am leaving because I am bored. I feel I have lived long enough. I am leaving you with your worries in this sweet cesspool. Good luck."

Anne Baxter was born 7 May 1923 in Michigan City, Indiana. Her father was a prominent executive with Seagrams Distillery; her mother was the daughter of famed architect Frank Lloyd Wright. Young Baxter attended the Brearley School, one of the country's most prestigious private institutions for girls. At the age of ten, she saw a play starring Helen Hayes and declared to her family that she intended to become an actor. By 13, she was working on Broadway. During these years, Baxter was tutored in the Stanislavski system of acting by the great Maria Ouspenskaya. At 16, Baxter tested for Mrs. DeWinter in Alfred Hitchcock's *Rebecca*. She didn't get the part, but she did get a seven-year contract with 20th Century-Fox. She was immediately lent to Metro-Goldwyn-Mayer for *20 Mule Team*, her first motion picture. Orson Welles cast her in his 1942 film *The Magnificent Ambersons*, and in 1947 she won a Best Actress in a Supporting Role Oscar for *The Razor's Edge*. Along with costar Bette Davis, Baxter was nominated for the Best Actress Oscar for 1950's *All About Eve*; neither won, but Baxter would go on to play the Davis role in *Applause*, a Broadway musical adaptation of the film. Baxter played two characters in *Batman*: Zelda in "Zelda the Great" and "A Death Worse Than Fate" and Olga (with Egghead) in "The Ogg and I," "How to Hatch a Dinosaur," and "The Ogg Couple." In his book *Back to the Batcave*, Adam West quips about Baxter's allure, "I understood, upon meeting her, why Chuck Heston and Yul Brynner fought so hard to win her in *The Ten Commandments*!" Anne Baxter died of a brain aneurysm on 12 December 1985 in New York City.

Arthur William Matthew Carney was born 4 November 1918 in Mount Vernon, New York. Despite being painfully shy, he won talent contests in grade school and high school. He began his professional career as a comic singer on Horace Heidt's *Pot o' Gold* radio program, making his uncredited screen debut in 1941 when the show became a feature film. Carney continued to be in demand as a voice actor because of his uncanny abilities as a mimic. World War II interrupted his career, and Carney took shrapnel at the Battle of Normandy, giving him a limp for the rest of his life. On TV's *Cavalcade of Stars* in 1950, Carney first teamed with Jackie Gleason. The pair had such good chemistry that Gleason recruited Carney to do additional sketches, including the domestic-comedy skits that later spun off into one of TV's all-time classics: *The Honeymooners*. Carney was nominated for a dozen Emmys, winning seven. In 1965, he originated the role of Felix Ungar, opposite Walter Matthau's Oscar Madison, in Neil Simon's *The Odd Couple*. On *Batman*, he appeared as Archer, a villain created for the "Shoot a Crooked Arrow" and "Walk the Straight & Narrow." Art Carney died of natural causes on 9 November 2003 in Chester, Connecticut.

Shirley Schrift was born 18 August 1920 in St. Louis, Missouri. Shortly after her birth, the family moved to Brooklyn, and by her late teens, she was working as a chorine and a vaudevillian. A few minor Broadway roles followed before her 1943 screen debut, under the name Shelley Winters, in *There's Something about a Soldier*. Her breakout role was as the ill-fated waitress Pat Kroll in

George Cukor's *A Double Life* (1947). She was nominated for an Oscar (Best Actress in a Leading Role) for 1951's *A Place in the Sun*. Winters was victimized by Robert Mitchum in Charles Laughton's 1955 masterpiece *The Night of the Hunter*, based on Davis Grubb's novel of the same name. She won Best Actress in a Supporting Role for 1959's *The Diary of Anne Frank*, later donating the statuette to the Anne Frank House museum in Amsterdam. She took home another Oscar for 1965's *A Patch of Blue*. On *Batman*, she appeared as a crime maven in "The Greatest Mother of Them All" and "Ma Parker." Shelley Winters, one-time roommate of Marilyn Monroe, died of heart failure on 14 January 2006 in Beverly Hills, California.

Walter Slezak was born 3 May 1902 in Vienna, Austria-Hungary. Son of heldentenor Leo, young Slezak studied medicine before being convinced to take a role in 1922's *Sodom und Gomorrha* by his friend – the film's director, Mihály Kertész (later Michael Curtiz). Slezak's first American film was 1942's *Once Upon a Honeymoon*, starring Cary Grant and Ginger Rogers. He memorably portrayed Willy in Alfred Hitchcock's 1944 suspense film *Lifeboat*. He won the 1955 Best Actor in a Musical Tony Award for *Fanny*. Slezak and wife Johanna "Kaasie" Van Rijn had three children, including Erika who (as of this writing) has won six Daytime Emmy Awards for her role on *One Life to Live*. He appeared as Clock King, a villain created for "The Clock King's Crazy Crimes," and "The King Gets Crowned." Despondent over ill health, Walter Slezak died of a self-inflicted gunshot wound on 21 April 1983 in Flower Hill, New York.

Vincent Leonard Price, Jr. was born 27 May 1911, in St. Louis, Missouri. His father, Vincent Leonard Price, Sr., was president of National Candy Company, and his grandfather, Vincent Clarence Price, invented Dr. Price's Cream Baking Powder, the first cream of tartar baking powder, securing the family's fortune. It comes as no surprise, then, that "Vinnie" was a gourmet and an author – with second wife Mary – of several cookbooks. Price attended St. Louis Country Day School and studied art history and fine art at Yale University. In the 1930s, he became interested in the theatre and was performing professionally by 1935. He made his 1938 screen debut in *Service de Luxe* and landed a part in Otto Preminger's *Laura* in 1944. Price held the distinction of being the longest running incarnation of Simon Templar (the Saint) on radio, reading the character from 1947 until 1951, when Tom Conway assumed the role. He also appeared in Cecil B. DeMille's 1956 star-studded spectacle *The Ten Commandments*. Price appeared as Egghead, the smartest villain in the world (though unable to outwit our Dynamic Duo), in the "An Egg Grows in Gotham,"

"The Yegg Foes in Gotham," "The Ogg and I," "How to Hatch a Dinosaur," and "The Ogg Couple." In *The Official Batman Batbook*, Price says, "I was thrilled to be on the Batman series. I really felt that it was one of the most brilliant TV series ever done." Vincent Price died of lung cancer on 25 October 1993 in Los Angeles, California.

Wladziu Valentino Liberace was born 16 May 1919 in West Allis, Wisconsin. The survivor of a set of twins and wearing a caul at birth, his family believed him destined for greatness. Liberace's father Salvatore, an Italian immigrant who played French horn semi-professionally, instilled a love of music in the boy. By the age of four, young Liberace was picking out tunes by ear on the piano, and after meeting Paderewski backstage at Milwaukee's Pabst Theater at age eight, Liberace fantasized about following in the virtuoso's footsteps. It was Paderewski who would eventually convince the young performer to bill himself by his surname; to his family, Liberace was "Walter," to his friends, he was "Lee." Liberace made his screen debut in 1950's *South Sea Sinner* with Shelley Winters and was wildly popular on variety shows – including his own – and talk shows for the rest of his life. He played twins Chandell (Fingers) and Harry in "The Devil's Fingers" and "The Dead Ringers," the highest-rated installments of the *Batman* series. Liberace died of AIDS on 4 February 1987 in Palm Springs, California.

Otto Ludwig Preminger was born 5 December 1906 in Wiznitz, Austria-Hungary. He was expected to follow his father into law, and he earned a law degree. But the lure of the theatre proved too strong to resist. He proved himself a capable actor and theatre administrator. Suffering from early hair loss, he graduated to directing, eventually making the segue into film with 1931's *Die Grosse Liebe*. His work received favorable notice, and he accepted an invitation to work for 20th Century-Fox, arriving in New York in 1935. The high point of Preminger's American directorial career was 1944's *Laura*, which he also produced. (Preminger's younger brother Ingo was also a film producer, his best-known work being 1970's *M*A*S*H*.) Preminger acted periodically in American films, most notably in 1953's *Stalag 17*, before appearing as Mr. Freeze in the "Green Ice" and "Deep Freeze." He was a terror on the set. "The man insisted on enhancing his reputation as one of the meanest bastards who ever walked a soundstage," Adam West says in *Back to the Batcave*. Preminger had virtually begged William Dozier for a guest spot on the show; he ended up having to pay delinquent Screen Actors Guild dues for the privilege. Otto

Preminger died 23 April 1986 in New York City, suffering from Alzheimer's disease and lung cancer.

Shakespearean actor Maurice Herbert Evans was born 3 June 1901 in Dorchester, England. He made his stage debut in 1926, joining the Old Vic Company in 1934. He made his Broadway debut as Romeo in 1935, opposite Katharine Cornell's Juliet. His *Hamlet* (1938) was the first time that play was produced uncut on the New York stage. During World War II, he headed an Army Entertainment Section in the Pacific, again producing *Hamlet*, this time tailored to the troops. After the war, Evans continued acting and producing on Broadway. In 1953, he began appearing in a series of Shakespeare plays – costarring the likes of Judith Anderson, Richard Burton, and Roddy McDowall – on TV's *Hallmark Hall of Fame*. One of these, the second of two renderings of Macbeth, garnered him the 1961 Emmy for Outstanding Single Performance by an Actor in a Leading Role. Evans played Samantha's urbane father Maurice on the beloved supernatural sitcom *Bewitched* from 1964 to 1971. When Frank Gorshin was unavailable to play Riddler in the "A Penny for Your Riddles" and "They're Worth a Lot More," they were revamped to feature Evans as new villain Puzzler and titled "The Puzzles Are Coming" and "The Duo is Slumming." Maurice Evans died of heart failure resulting from bronchial infection on 12 March 1989 in Rottingdean, England.

Tallulah Brockman Bankhead was born 31 January 1902 in Huntsville, Alabama. Her father, William Brockman Bankhead, was Speaker of the United States House of Representatives from 1936 to 1940; her grandfather and her uncle, John H. Bankhead and John H. Bankhead II, were Alabama senators. Though described as a homely child, Bankhead won a movie magazine beauty contest at age 15. She convinced her father to allow her to move to New York to live with her aunt in order to pursue a career in show business. She quickly won bits on stage and screen but, hoping for greater success, shifted to London in 1923. The move paid off: she became a West End favorite and worked steadily there for eight years. Lured by Paramount to Hollywood in 1931, her private life made bigger news than her acting. Her sexual exploits were legendary: her orgiastic parties lasted days at a time. She soon found herself among the hopefuls competing for the role of Scarlett O'Hara in *Gone with the Wind*, for which her black-and-white screen test was superb. She did not, however, photograph well in Technicolor. Her subsequent portrayal on Broadway of Regina Giddens in Lillian Hellman's *The Little Foxes* garnered her a New York Drama Critics' Circle Award for Best Performance. She won that same award for her portrayal of Sabina in Thornton Wilder's *The Skin of Our Teeth*. She received a New York Film Critics Circle Award for Best Actress for her performance in Alfred Hitchcock's *Lifeboat* (1944). A Tony nomination came from her work in the Mary Coyle Chase play *Midgie Purvis*. Bankhead's last work was her appearances in the "Black Widow Strikes Again" and "Caught in the Spider's Web" on *Batman*. On the set, she snapped at Adam West for using a teleprompter; she was known to have an incredible memory, learning dialog with ease. Tallulah Bankhead died of pneumonia resulting from influenza complicated by emphysema on 12 December 1968 in New York City. Her final words are said to have been "codeine... bourbon."

Ethel Agnes Zimmermann was born 16 January 1908 in New York City. Her father was an amateur keyboard player, and she began singing publicly as a child. Upon graduating high school, she began appearing in nightclubs and soon became a successful vaudevillian. In 1930, she made her Broadway debut, under the name Ethel Merman, in George and Ira Gershwin's *Girl Crazy*. She began film work for Paramount that same year. Her fourth Broadway show was Cole Porter's *Anything Goes* in 1934, and she starred with Bing Crosby in the 1936 film adaptation. Merman's longest-running musical was Irving Berlin's *Annie Get Your Gun*, which played 1147 times from 16 May 1946 to 19 February 1949; she stayed with the production for its duration. She won the 1951 Leading Actress Tony Award for her role in Berlin's *Call Me Madam*; she received nominations for the award in 1957 for *Happy Hunting* and in 1960 for *Gypsy*. She created 13 musical theatre roles in all and introduced such standards as "I Got Rhythm," "Everything's Coming up Roses," and her signature "There's No Business like Show Business." Merman portrayed Lola Lasagne (Lulu Schultz) in "The Sport of Penguins" and "A Horse of Another Color" on *Batman*. "It was *really* exciting to have Ethel Merman on the show. What a career, and what a voice!" Adam West says in *Back to the Batcave*. He was charmed by her soft-spokenness (understandable, considering her belting song style) and by her keen sense of humor. He made a point of spending as much time with her on the set as possible. Ethel Merman died of brain cancer on 15 February 1984 in New York City.

Milton Berlinger was born 12 July 1908 in New York City. At the age of five, he won a talent contest that launched him into a career on the silent screen. His first appearance, uncredited, was in the 1914 chapter play *The Perils of Pauline*. In 1916, he enrolled in Professional Children's School. More uncredited screen appearances followed, including bits in 1917's *Rebecca of*

Sunnybrook Farm, starring Mary Pickford; 1920's *The Mask of Zorro*, starring Douglas Fairbanks; and 1921's *Little Lord Fauntleroy*, starring Pickford. Under the name Milton Berle, he interspersed film work with stage and radio work, and in 1929 Berle became one of the first people ever to appear on TV. In 1948, NBC moved its *Texaco Star Theater* from radio to TV; as one the program's rotating hosts, Berle was among the earliest celebrities to be invited into viewers' homes via the emerging medium, and "Mr. Television" won an Emmy Award for Most Outstanding Kinescope Personality in 1950. On *Batman*, Berle appeared in "Louie the Lilac" and "Louie's Lethal Lilac Time." He is said to have been antagonistic on set. Milton Berle died of colon cancer on 27 March 2002 in Los Angeles, California.

Hubert Prior Vallée (Rudy Vallée) was born 28 July 1901 in Brighton, Vermont. A drummer in his high school band, Vallée went on to play clarinet and saxophone with various New England ensembles. In 1924-25, he performed with Savoy Havana Band at Savoy Hotel in London. Upon his return, he formed Rudy Vallée and the Connecticut Yankees. His sweet voice and boyish looks were wildly popular with flappers, making him a media sensation. As a singer, he was arguably the first of the crooners. Earlier generations of vocalists were required to project in order to be heard by their audiences; with the advent of electric microphones, songs could be delivered in a more intimate style. Vallée's screen debut came in *The Vagabond Lover* (1929). He enlisted during World War II, and Lieutenant Rudy Vallée directed the 11th Naval District United States Coast Guard Band to great success. After the war, he continued work in film, including roles in 1947's *The Bachelor and the Bobby-Soxer*, alongside Cary Grant, Myrna Loy, and Shirley Temple. On Broadway, he originated the role of J.B. Biggley in *How to Succeed in Business without Really Trying* (1961), reprising the character for the 1967 film adaptation. Vallée appeared that same year as Lord Marmaduke Ffogg in "The Londinium Larcenies," "The Foggiest Notion," and "The Bloody Tower" on *Batman*. Adam West remembers Vallée as having "an ego the size of the Batcave... he used to play reel-to-reel tapes of his greatest hits and lip-sync them for the cast and crew. It was a trifle embarrassing." Yvonne Craig says, "I didn't care for those [episodes] because I didn't care for the show's guest villain... that crabby old Rudy Vallée was an absolute curmudgeon... especially when you compare him to a wonderful guest like Vincent Price!" Rudy Vallée died of cancer on 3 July 1986 in Los Angeles, California.

Ida Lupino, scion of a multi-generational performing family, was born 4 February 1918 in London, England. Her father Stanley was an acrobat, actor, comedian, dancer, director, librettist, and singer; her mother, Connie Emerald, was an actor. Lupino was encouraged at an early age by her family to enter show business, and she made her uncredited screen debut in 1931's *The Love Race* (produced by and starring her father, directed by Lupino Lane, her first cousin once removed, and featuring his younger brother Wallace Lupino). Ida Lupino won more significant roles in *Anything Goes* (1936) with Ethel Merman, *The Adventures of Sherlock Holmes* (1939) with Basil Rathbone, and *They Drive by Night* (1940) and *High Sierra* (1941), both with Humphrey Bogart. While on suspension for refusing a role, Lupino developed an interest in directing. She formed an independent film company with second husband, Collier Young. In 1949, Elmer Clifton suffered a mild heart attack while directing the company's *Not Wanted*; Lupino stepped in and finished the project uncredited. With Young, she wrote the 1953 suspense film *The Hitch-Hiker*; directing the piece, she established herself as the first female director of a film noir. She directed dozens of episodes of TV shows, including *The Twilight Zone*'s "The Masks," the only installment of that series to be helmed by a female. Lupino appeared as Dr. Cassandra Spellcraft in "The Entrancing Dr. Cassandra" on *Batman*, alongside her third husband Howard Duff as Cabala. Ida Lupino died of a stroke on 3 August 1995 in Los Angeles, California.

Gábor Sári was born 16 February 1917 in Budapest, Austria-Hungary. The middle daughter of Vilmos and Jolie, she was crowned Miss Hungary of 1936, after which she was invited by tenor Richard Tauber to sing the soubrette in his new operetta *Der singende Traum* at Theater an der Wien. She soon followed her younger sister Eva to America and appeared, under the name Zsa Zsa Gabor, in her first Hollywood picture, *Lovely to Look at*, in 1952. That same year, John Huston directed her, opposite José Ferrer, in *Moulin Rouge*. In 1956, Gabor worked with third ex-husband George Sanders in *Death of a Scoundrel*. (Sanders was later briefly married to Gabor's older sister Magda.) Serious acting opportunities diminished, and by 1958 Gabor was appearing in such camp classics as *Queen of Outer Space*. She was cast in "Minerva, Mayhem and Millionaires" – the series finale of *Batman* – when Mae West was unavailable, and she thoroughly enjoyed the role. According to Adam West, Gabor pursued him after the show's cancellation, presumably with romantic intentions. Resisting her continental charm, West escaped becoming another of her many conquests. As of this writing, Zsa Zsa Gabor resides with ninth husband Frédéric Prinz von Anhalt in Bel Air, California, in a house she bought from Elvis Presley.

For better or for worse, some actors become wedded to certain roles. Similarly, some characters become forever linked to particular performers. The 1960s *Batman* was not the first time many of these characters had been brought to life on film, nor would it be the last. Despite this, none of those who've played these parts has attained an immediate association with his or her character as have the stars of the series. With the possible exceptions of the two recent Jokers – Jack Nicholson in 1989's *Batman* and Heath Ledger in 2008's *The Dark Knight* – the players have been largely forgettable. Magic was afoot during the casting of the *Batman* television series, and the melding of the right actors with the right characters created icons.

POW!: *Batman*'s Visual Punch

by Bill Walko

BIFF! POW! SOCK! There's no doubt the *Batman* TV series left an indelible ZAP! on the public consciousness. Although very much a product of its time, the Pop Art-inspired *Batman* created a visual legacy that still lingers over 40 years later. From its candy-colored cartoon opening to each episode-ending deathtrap, the series provided an undeniably unique creative concoction.

When examining the visual design of the *Batman* TV series, it's especially intriguing to study its main influences. The nascent series drew inspiration from the pop-art trend as well as the original comic-book source material – which then becomes a bit of a head-scratching scenario of who exactly influenced whom.

Consider the origins of the Pop Art movement itself. It first emerged in Great Britain at the end of the 1950s. As a reaction to the serious tone of expressionism, artists began to utilize common popular imagery found in advertising, packaging and comic strips. They employed these elements in designs that expressed new abstract relationships. These artists believed that by fusing elements of popular culture with high culture, they could break down the boundaries between the two. The result: a work of art that could be appreciated by artists and laymen alike.

The trend caught fire in the U.K. and began to emerge on the other side of the pond, particularly in the 1960s. American advertising and media had already adopted a modern art sensibility, leaving artists to discover new means of expression. Pop art offered the perfect creative impetus for the time. Here was an increasingly media-soaked world, populated by artists looking to make a statement. Pop art in America not only used elements of pop culture, but it also said something about consumer commercialism through its design. Tinged with irony, pop artists of the United States produced works that were bolder than their European counterparts.

The most well known American pop artists of the era were Andy Warhol and Roy Lichtenstein. Arguably the most famous figure in pop art, Warhol both celebrated and ridiculed American middle-class values in his work. He used commonplace objects and imagery such as dollar bills, soup cans, soft drink bottles, and newspaper photos. Many of his works featured oversized and minimalist imagery, such as the famous Campbell's Soup can; others employed repetition and color, such as the unforgettable portraits of Marilyn Monroe and Jacqueline Kennedy.

But early in his career, in 1960, Warhol exhibited paintings that celebrated Dick Tracy, Superman, and Batman. Other artists employed comic art in their works as well, but it was the work of pop artist Roy Lichtenstein that became most famous in this regard.

Lichtenstein's paintings would undoubtedly catch the eye of any comic-book fan. His art used elements found in comic books and comic strips, often depicting characters in the throes of an intensely dramatic situation. Largely sampling from the war and romance genres, his paintings made use of modern typography and comic book-inspired printing techniques, such as Ben-Day dots. Lichtenstein's bold and brightly colored works celebrated comic-book panels and enlarged them to spectacular effect.

Like any popular trend, Pop Art soon began to filter into media culture. Ironically, it influenced the very media it was making a statement *about*, as pop-art iconography seeped into advertising, TV, fashion... and even comic books themselves.

There's evidence to suggest that comic creators became influenced by the pop-art trend, whether consciously or subconsciously. Contrary to popular belief, these elements crept onto the comic page before *Batman* even hit the airwaves in 1966. As author Will Brooker notes in his 2000 book *Batman Unmasked*, "The cover of *Batman* #171, for instance [...] has the Riddler in his lime green costume spinning madly against a shocking pink background." This cover, when compared to some of Warhol's seminal works, is undoubtedly inspired by the pop-art movement.

Pop artists also used comic-book sound effects and words themselves as art – enlarged and exaggerated on giant-sized canvases. Brooker also observes, "In keeping with what was seen by audiences, if not artists, as Pop's sense of camp irony, the comic writers threw in more alliteration, more wordplay and more of the clunky dialogue familiar from Lichtenstein's panels." Clearly, the tail had just wagged the dog. Comics were now being influenced by the very pop art they inspired.

Meanwhile, the seeds of Batman's TV debut were being planted at ABC studios in California. Harve Bennet, ABC's director of west coast development, was looking to acquire a cartoon property for early evening programming. The studio tried to negotiate for the rights to Dick Tracy, but the property was deemed too expensive. So Bennet turned his eye to Batman, and after some careful cajoling with ABC executives, the deal was done. Now all *Batman* needed was a producer. That's when William Dozier became involved.

"Batman? Are you out of your mind?" were Dozier's first words after hearing ABC pitch the idea to him, as Bob Garcia reports in the February 1994 *Cinefantasique*. Dozier admitted he had little knowledge of the Caped Crusader. He had never read a Batman comic book, nor was he familiar with the central concept. Still filled with trepidation, Dozier agreed to think about the project. As the story goes, the producer read about a dozen Batman comic books on a flight to New York. His reaction was quite spirited. "So I read all these things," recalled Dozier, "and thought they must be out of their minds. It was all so juvenile. Then a very simple idea struck me and that was to overdo it. I thought it would be funny to adults and yet would be stimulating to kids… the derring-do and that stuff. But you had to appeal on both levels or you didn't have a chance."

The larger-than-life comic books were the first half of Dozier's inspiration for his approach to the series. The second half came from the Pop Art fad – which, by the middle of the 1960s, had gone mainstream. As reported in that same issue of *Cinefantasique*, Batman artist and co-creator Bob Kane praised Dozier's pop-art vision for the series. "It was so original to actually bring the comic script to screen as pop art," the artist noted, "with the actual POW lettering on the screen and the unusual camera angles. The filmmaking was terrific."

The actors prepare to film one of the show's signature Bat-climbs, surely one of its most memorable visuals. Still from William Dozier's archives. Copyright © Greenway Productions, DC Comics, and 20th Century-Fox.

The decision to use Pop Art as inspiration was a brilliant move, one calculated to be failsafe, as illustrated in this John Skow article from the *Saturday Evening Post*, originally published 2 May 1966:

> No one has put it exactly this way, but it seems clear that Dozier, the ABC people, and Dozier's writer, Lorenzo Semple Jr., came to a command

decision last fall: There was absolutely nothing that could make the adult American TV watcher feel silly. The pop art fad, one of whose twitches is an enthusiasm for old comic books, had made *Batman* almost flop-proof. As long as the pop fad lasted[,] there could be no such thing as bad pop art: What in the world could it be? Of course, when the fad fizzled there would be no such thing as good pop art. The trick was to guess how much time was left before the fizzling set in. Dozier and ABC guessed there was time enough; the pop fad would stay alive, or if it didn't, the news of its death would take a long time to reach the sleepless dreamers who watch TV.

So the Pop Art movement, which was influenced in part by comic-book art, had a huge visual influence on the series. And the Batman comic books of the time, which harnessed Pop Art imagery, provided equal inspiration for the show. With overlapping inspirations and influences, it becomes almost impossible to discern what exactly was visually appropriated from where. So tracing the precise origins of the TV *Batman's* vision is almost like staring into one of those maddening "infinity" comic-book covers of the 1960s and 1970s, in which the character is holding the book of him holding the book of him... you get the idea.

Regardless of the exact sources, comic-book art of the 1960s and Pop Art shared many of the same sensibilities. It was a world populated with oversized imagery, bright colors, big words, and bold pronouncements, and all those elements informed Dozier's approach to the TV series.

In 1965, Dozier's vision became a reality. He pitched his idea for the show – as a live-action, Pop Art, camp adventure – to the network. They accepted his unique approach, and Dozier began to assemble his team. He brought in Lorenzo Semple Jr. to pen the pilot episode, which set the tone for virtually everything that followed.

The tale that comprised the first two episodes, "Hi Diddle Riddle" and "Smack in the Middle," was loosely adapted from a story in *Batman* #171 entitled, "Remarkable Ruse of the Riddler." In it, Batman and Robin are sued by the Riddler for his wrongful arrest. As part of the plot, the Dynamic Duo trace hidden clues to a trendy disco called "What a Way to Go-Go," where Batman must perform the Batusi, an unintentionally hilarious dance – for Batman, at least. From the script alone, it was apparent this Batman lived in a surreal world of preposterous excess. Just the idea Dozier had intended.

Indeed, the first five minutes of "Hi Diddle Riddle" were packed with many of the show's trademark visual cues. Commissioner Gordon calls Batman on the blinking, glowing red phone. Once alerted, Bruce Wayne and Dick Grayson race to the phone to learn the Riddler has returned. Ever eager for adventure,

Dick presses the hidden button under the Shakespearean head which activates the sliding bookcase to reveal the Batpoles. The two heroes race toward the poles and slide into the Batcave. The caped crime fighters – now miraculously outfitted – are primed to protect Gotham from evildoers. They race through the Batcave to the Batmobile and ignite its nuclear-powered engine. Within seconds, the Dynamic Duo race through their secret entrance, with only 14 miles between them and their next adventure. And all that transpires before the episode title even appears on screen!

It's amazing how much visual language is conveyed so early in the series – and how much of it remained consistent throughout its three-year run. Much of that credit lies with Semple's writing on the inaugural episode. Semple's script brought all the absurdity of the comic book to life through a colorful and cockeyed lens. It captured the turgid flamboyance of Dozier's vision, but it also began to form the TV Batman's iconography.

Also interesting is the visual nature of the storytelling throughout the series, as established in the very first episode. A viewer could watch an entire show with the sound turned down and still follow everything that transpired. A lot of that is due to Dozier's approach, which was the most literal comic-to-film adaptation to date. Everything was simple, exaggerated, and full of overblown action. Dozier himself contributed many of the ideas for the pilot, including the secret Batpole switch hidden in the Shakespearean bust at Wayne Manor.

Before the opening credits, the sliding bookcase revealed the carefully identified Batpoles, with signs for "Bruce" and "Dick," and written behind the Batpoles, "Access to Batcave via Batpoles." The mobile crime computer in the Batmobile is emblazoned with an identifying sign. While most writers live by the rule, "Show, don't tell," *Batman* evoked a more "show *and* tell" approach. To underline the sledgehammer-subtle storytelling, everything in Batman's arsenal was neatly labeled. Batman's laser gun in his utility belt was accompanied with a carefully labeled pouch. And one of the very first bat-gadgets – the bat gauge – was labeled as well. No doubt the visual labels helped for easy storytelling for young viewers. And for adults, it provided a visual method to relay the inherent *wink-wink* silliness of Batman's gadget-ridden world.

The pilot episode was directed by Robert Butler, who reveled in the audaciousness of Semple and Dozier's impish approach. Butler, as it turned out, was the perfect director to bring Semple's script to life. "Direction is going to be awful important in this thing," Semple observed as he cooked up the first

POW!: *Batman*'s Visual Punch   103

script. "Not so much directing the actors as the camera angles and set-ups: I know that many of the latter should be bizarre, with exaggerated perspectives you get in actual comic book panels."[1] Butler followed Semple's advice and created the show's signature Dutch-angle tilt shots to mimic the comic-book panels. He also pored through Batman comic books, looking to imitate the actual panels through live action.

Also notable in the pilot is how Butler imbued everything with an overblown sense of urgency. As Bruce Wayne gets the initial call from Commissioner Gordon, Dick Grayson is visibly anxious to start their next adventure, twitching and lurching forward. They *run* to the Batpoles. They *race* to the Batmobile. Even as they exit the secret entrance to the Batcave, the film is sped up to give the Batmobile the illusion of atomic speed. And later, in Commissioner Gordon's office, all the characters paced anxiously as they pieced together the clues to the Riddler's diabolical plot.

Then there was Frank Gorshin's perfectly hyper-kinetic portrayal of the Riddler. Maniacally prancing and slithering through his scenes, this live-action Riddler was in deep need of Ritalin. A friend of Dozier, Gorshin was given *carte blanche* with the role, and he took it to extreme lengths, transforming a rather minor Batman villain into a grandiose Prince of Puzzles. Meshing Butler's high-action direction with Gorshin's inspired interpretation of the character, the show had unwittingly established its approach to *Batman*'s live-action Rogues Gallery. From then on, each villain became an exercise in over-the-top scenery chewing. And the actors had a ball with it.

Butler also directed the first of many memorable fight sequences. This set the template for every fight scene in the entire series: the guest villain would order his henchmen to attack the Dynamic Duo and fantastic fisticuffs would ensue – all set to the show's trademark go-go surfer soundtrack. Batman's and Robin's fight moves were lifted from the comic-book source material, with roundhouse punches and chop-socky kicks. Butler choreographed them like dance sequences, with heroes throwing haymakers while villains spun into place to receive each devastating blow. The fight sequences had absolutely no basis in reality and were more akin to musical numbers in a Broadway production. It was a Pop Art spectacle set to music.

The fight sequences presented a problem in themselves, however, as the production started running out of time and money. As producer, Charles B.

---

[1] *Cinefantasique*, February 1994.

FitzSimons devised an ingenious way to speed up production. Instead of directing extra shots for each crushing blow, he decided to cover those areas with an on-screen graphic. "The 'Biffs', 'Bams' and 'Pows' covered the areas where you might have needed an additional shot," recalls the producer.[2] "We had to do that because we couldn't keep going financially." It was also a visceral way to bring the pop-art phenomenon to live-action TV.

The production staff added the sound effect opticals in post-production. As the show went on, this soon caused another problem, since the opticals themselves were expensive. The crew eventually came up with the inventive solution of editing slugs with the sound effects on them. The eight-frame slugs were placed to cover up the contact of a kick or a punch. It was a small change, and one that viewers would not even register, since the effects were only onscreen for a very short time. And little did FitzSimons know his cost-cutting measure had unwittingly created one of the most enduring visuals of the *Batman* TV show.

The pilot combined cartoon and live action in other aspects as well. The scenes would change with a spinning bat logo, or a bat logo would zoom large and then recess into obscurity. It was another way the show meshed the comic-book, Pop Art sensibility with the overblown, live-action tomfoolery.

Then there is the unforgettable punch of the opening credits sequence. Many modern shows have abandoned opening credits in favor of a simple title card and music sting. But opening credits were once an art unto themselves. The best of them, mostly from the 1960s and 1970s, would capture the tone and premise of the program in a unique way. Through a combination of music, lyrics, and images, TV series such as *The Beverly Hillbillies*, *Gilligan's Island*, and *Get Smart* memorably captured the spirit of each show.

Batman's TV opening did the same with its stylized graphic intro but was far from the first series to use animation as an opener. Likely influenced by the Pop Art movement, designer Saul Bass started to revolutionize opening credits in films long before *Batman* premiered. Bass utilized a moving, illustrative approach to opening titles of movies in the 1950s. The 1958 classic, *Anatomy of a Murder,* used eye-popping animation emboldened with a powerful music score by Duke Ellington. Other movies followed suit, and the approach even became a signature way to open James Bond movies for years.

---

[2] Ibid.

A cell from the show's animated opening sequence. Recreation by M. Mrakota Orsman. Copyright © Greenway Productions, DC Comics, and 20ᵗʰ Century-Fox.

Like anything trailblazed in the cinema, animated title sequences soon migrated onto TV. In 1960, *My Three Sons* employed a simple cartoon image of three teenaged male feet as the credits rolled. In 1962, *The Lucy Show* featured lively caricatures of Lucille Ball and Vivian Vance. *Bewitched* famously created a fully animated opening sequence that charmingly captured the fantasy aspects of the suburban sitcom. Likewise, *I Dream of Jeannie* graced us with an animated origin story to the whimsical comedy series, as hapless astronaut Tony Nelson unwittingly unleashed a beautiful, dancing genie. The trend wasn't limited to sitcoms, either, as evidenced by *The Wild, Wild West*, which showcased the fantastical aspects of the Western adventure series with stylized drawings.

So while far from the first series to feature an animated opening, it was perfectly fitting that *Batman* would utilize an eye-popping Pop Art pastiche to introduce each episode; there was perhaps no better marriage of medium and subject. Each and every frame of the lively opening could very well have been pulled from a Roy Lichtenstein exhibit. The Dynamic Duo barrel toward the screen, and it's only seconds before each punch elicits a giant sound effect of

"Sock!", "Pow!", and "Zok!" Among the gaggle of gangsters stood a handful of regular Bat-baddies like Joker, Catwoman, and the Penguin. This was a series willing to embrace the dynamic lunacy of the four-color comic, with villains as audacious as the hero himself. Set to the unforgettable Neal Hefti score, the herky-jerky flat animation worked in its favor, signalling the emphatic stodgy-yet-hip feel of the show itself.

On screen, the *Batman* logo was accompanied by the words: "In Color." And boy, did they mean it! The opener gave a glimpse of the colorful and outrageous world we were about to enter. Originally broadcast in 1966, TV was just making the transition from black and white to color. This was serendipitous for *Batman*, whose Pop Art premise relied on the use of a bright, bold palette. The set designers and Butler established this in the first episodes, using bright greens, pinks, and lavenders throughout. These vibrant hues mirrored the Riddler's color scheme, a chromatic theme continued for each villain during the run of the series. The crew also winked at the show's pop-art inspiration, as evidenced by the set design of the "What a Way to Go-Go" lounge, with Pop Art pieces adorning every wall of the joint. From the very start, it was clear that color would play an important role in the series's sensory experience.

There was another element that was largely inspired by comic books and Pop Art: the show's unique narration. One could argue that it owed much to the movie serials of the 1940s, but it seems equally influenced by the overwrought narration found in comic books. William Dozier and his assistant producer, Charles B. FitzSimons, searched for the perfect voice talent to capture the serious yet wry approach they wanted. Few viewers realize that *Batman* producer Dozier also doubled as the show's narrator! FitzSimons recalled how that came to be:

> We needed a voice that you had to accept as serious narration but also had to make you laugh. It had to have an oily sincerity to it. We desperately auditioned people looking for this quality. I said, "Bill, we really haven't found anybody. I know one person with the right kind of insincerity and phony status in his voice, if we could only get him."
>
> Dozier said, "Who is it? We'll get him." I said, "It's you!" He looked at me, agreed to do a test, and he was sensational. He grudgingly said, "I'll do it for the pilot, but we'll have to find somebody else for the series!" We never did; he did every episode! He was great because he had the humor, the vocal quality[,] and the pompous insincerity needed, God bless him.

He was terrific. Nobody but Dozier could blurt out, "Same Bat-time, same Bat-channel."[3]

As detailed earlier, comics had begun to appropriate elements from the Pop Art phenomenon into their pages. The use of words – particularly in narration – had become an art in and of itself. Pop Art often included the overblown captions and word balloons as part of the art, which encouraged comic-book writers to enliven the language of comics with snappier patter and more creative narrative devices. By the middle of the 1960s, writers like John Broome, Gardner Fox, and Bob Haney used narration boxes for colorful commentary, often engaging the reader into the story by posing questions.

Consider this caption from "The Joker's Comedy Capers!", originally presented in *Detective Comics* #341 in 1965: "Something devilishly familiar about this 'movie producer'? No doubt some of you will already have suspected the presence of that Mad Maestro of Mirth, that Leonardo of the Larcenous Laugh, that Man of a Thousand False Fronts – the Joker!" The script, penned by John Broome, was written at least a year before *Batman* hit the airwaves.

Compare this with the Dozier's voiceover narration in the pilot: "Meanwhile, in an abandoned subway tool room deep under Gotham City, the secret headquarters of the infamous Mole Hill Mob." And later, as the Riddler takes a vice to Robin's skull in the episode's very first cliffhanger ending, "Will Robin escape? Can Batman find him in time? Is this the ghastly end of our Dynamic Duo? Answers... tomorrow night! Same time, same channel!" To accompany Dozier's seriously stiff delivery, the narration is also telegraphed on screen, evoking the feeling of a comic-book narration box. Once again, the show revels in visual storytelling through comic Pop Art sensibilities. This approach would be used to heighten the tension of every cliffhanger ending. TV's *Batman* used a combination of words and pictures to recreate the comic-book reading experience as live-action theatre.

As the series progressed, the narration became more playful and alliterative, hewing even closer to the pop panache of comic writers like Broome and Fox. And the cliffhanger voiceover received one subtle but memorable alteration: each episode would end with Dozier intoning, "Same *Bat*-time, same *Bat*-channel!"

---

[3] Jankiewicz, Pat. "Caped Crusades." *Starlog Presents Batman and Other Comic Heroes*. 1997.

While the pilot established the visual template for everything that followed, the crew prepared for the rest of the season. It was a daunting task because, in many ways, nothing quite like *Batman* had been attempted on TV. The team had to devise a way to deliver the larger-than-life scope of the show – including all its sets, gadgets, and deathtraps – that simply didn't exist in the real world.

The crew followed Dozier's overblown approach, including series producer FitzSimons, who helped Butler and Semple create *Batman's* live-action world for the pilot episode. The producer rifled through *Batman* back issues as his guide to creating costumes, bat-gadgets, the Batmobile, and the infamous Batcave. "The Batcave itself was the most difficult set to build," FitzSimons also recalled, "because it was going to be used so much and had to have so many ingredients in it – the huge nuclear reactor, the computers, and all that stuff. It took up a lot of space."

The Batmobile presented several problems as well. After the network gave the series a go-ahead, the crew had only a few weeks to get *Batman's* famous car ready for the road. Using a modified Ford Futura, the crew created the iconic Batmobile. And although it looked spectacular, its real-life performance was far from super. "It looked great, but performance wise, it was a dog," FitzSimons remembered. "We were lucky it could go over 10 miles an hour. We shot the stuff of it coming out of the Batcave. The gate-lifting cliff entrance was my idea. We had to shoot it with a slowed down camera to get any speed out of the Batmobile."

Like everything in *Batman*, the Batmobile was given a grandiose upgrade through editing and camera trickery. FitzSimons recalled, "[The] Batmobile being run by an atomic pile was not in the first episodes. I said to Dozier, 'You know, the Batmobile should be atomic! We can do it – I can have them build a phony end of the Batmobile and have flames come out and put it in as an insert.' So when Batman presses the button and you see the flames, that was an insert added later." Thus, the show acquired another of its iconic visuals – one equally overblown, though not from the comics.

To film the pilot, Fox employed several art directors, including Jack Martin, Franz Bachelin, and Ed Graves. Bill Self, head of TV production for Fox, then brought in Serge Krizman to function as lead art director for the series.[4] He and

---

[4] Krizman did the bulk of his work in TV during the 1950s and 1960s, notably serving as art director for 17 episodes of *The Fugitive* TV series from 1963-65. Krizman was also a friend of producer William Dozier, which made him a natural fit for the show.

Dozier discussed the approach to the program at great length. Like Dozier, Krizman looked to the original comic books for visual inspiration, and sought to evoke the feeling of those stories on screen.

Everyone on the show looked to the comic books for inspiration. Indeed, many of the signature elements of the show were lifted directly from the Batman comics themselves – a fact many viewers never fully understood. Batman writer and co-creator Bill Finger had already set the template for many of the *Batman* stories told through the course of the series. Batman's methodology, the oversized props and the elaborate deathtraps were just some of the iconic elements Finger weaved into his tales – decades before the first *Batman* TV script was ever written.

Dozier's crew sought to capture that comic-book feeling in every episode. And although the 1966 *Batman* series wasn't the first time a comic-strip character was translated into live action, it was in many ways the most *faithful* adaptation. Consider other attempts at live-action super-heroes up until that point. There were pulp heroes like Dick Tracy, Flash Gordon, and Tarzan, and Batman and Robin had a series of adventures in the 1940s serials. Superman enjoyed a successful TV run in the 1950s with *The Adventures of Superman.* And although those versions borrowed elements from their comic-strip source materials, all of them made concessions to incorporate those characters into the "real world." Some of these constraints were no doubt due to budgets. But the *Batman* TV show was perhaps the first time that someone tried to create a living comic book – with outrageous characters, jaunty camera shots, and bold color schemes. And whereas the previous live-action super-heroes mainly tussled with gangsters and crime-lords, TV's *Batman* squared off against fully-costumed crazies each and every week. It was perhaps the most *comic booky* interpretation of a comic-strip character committed to film at that time.

This was something that Krizman, as lead art director, wanted to capture on a weekly basis. It became quite an endeavor, as *Batman* was an extravagant show to produce. Many of the shows came in over budget, which created an interesting challenge for the show's crew each and every week. Despite the logistical hurdles, Krizman approached the series with a sense of earnest theatricality. He understood that the subject matter was inherently unreal, but he strived for a real-world honesty behind the over-sized props.

To that end, Krizman constantly challenged the crew to bring together this weekly Pop Art production. Krizman also worked closely with Ivan Martin, Fox's lead construction manager, who helped build many of the outrageous set pieces during the course of the show. The talented troupe established the visual look of much of the series, designing the sets, props... and all those elaborate deathtraps.

Each week, Krizman would read a script and see what was needed for sets and props. The crew would create building plans at a quarter inch scale, and the art directors would sketch out the finer details. The plans would then be given to a draftsman, and the construction crew would build it. Krizman recalled one of the first bizarre requests demanded by the script:

> One of the heads of construction happened to ask me what was my next crazy thing. It happened to be the [giant prop] umbrella [...] "We need a thirty-foot umbrella." He said, "Oh, sure." I said, "We do. Make it!" Eventually[,] they just fell in and looked forward to the next crazy thing. It was more fun to do than to make a breakaway door, which I did for years.[5]

True to the Batman comic book, episodes often featured oversized everyday objects that were transformed into instruments of sheer terror. For example, the episode, "Batman's Anniversary," featured a deadly cake trap, an idea inspired by *Batman* #130, "Batman's Deadly Birthday," published in 1960. According to the script, Batman and Robin were slowly sinking in a giant quicksand cake and escaped by using their patented Batrocket boots. Krizman recalled the difficult deathtrap with affection:

> The giant cake was fun. It had four tiers and was 35-feet high. We built most of it with plywood except for the top, which we put foam rubber in so the Dynamic Duo would sink. We had a small elevator installed so they would have something to stand on as they were lowered into the foam. The candles on the bottom were fully lit with electric lights. It was one of the most elaborate deathtraps the show had.

One thing the crew couldn't rely on was heavy use of post-production special effects. Back then, matte shots and trick photography would have been too expensive and time-consuming for a weekly TV series. So the sets and elaborate deathtraps were all achieved entirely with raw camera effects and straight shooting. The size and scope achieved on a weekly basis was a real credit to Krizman's team.

In addition to the intricate sets, each script demanded peculiar props specific to Batman's world. Some were built from whole cloth, while others were raided from Fox's huge prop department. Basically, Krizman used anything he could get his hands on or transform within the show's time and budget constraints. What couldn't be found or altered would be created at the

---

[5] *Cinefantasique*, February 1994.

Behind-the-scenes on the set of the second season's "Penguin is a Girl's Best Friend / Penguin Sets a Trend / Penguin's Disastrous End" (1967). Still from William Dozier's archives. Copyright © Greenway Productions, DC Comics, and 20th Century-Fox.

on-set plaster shop, which could duplicate any object one could imagine, within reason.

The demands of the show were both unique and outlandish. The writers were encouraged to be outrageously absurd, making Krizman's job all the more difficult. Luckily, Krizman worked closely with producer Howie Horwitz, who ensured the art department received scripts well ahead of time. "What was in the scripts originally, that was what stayed," Krizman remembered. "It was heaven for me. Because if you can plot things three or four shows ahead of time, you can plot your revamps. You take one set, and revise it three shows later, with this or that changed. You design it and build it that way. That was entirely to Horwitz's credit." Krizman wisely reused props wherever he could, saving sets and villainous accoutrements. And of course, the various Bat gadgets were tagged, saved, and reused – buying the crew precious time to build the next lovingly ludicrous set demand.

Krizman also made fantastic use of color in *Batman's* world, continuing the bold color themes established by the pilot. As much as possible, *Batman* was a garish, four-color comic made real. Helping to achieve this chromatic overload, the crew used colored lights to accent each villain's signature color. The director of photography would place a gelatin colored lens over the lamp, bathing the set in a particular undertone. The tinted lights were kept away from actor's faces, except for extreme effects. Catwoman's lair was enhanced with a cat-colored amber hue. Riddler's hideout received an emerald-tinted accent, due to his green outfit. And the Penguin's nest was seen through a purple-tinted lens. When the show boasted a "colorful collection of villains," truer words were never spoken. Unlike any previous comic-book adaptation, *Batman* really brought the colorful flair of the comic to screen. "Color played an extremely important part of the look of the show," Krizman noted in *Cinefantastique*. "We had conferences on costumes with designers Patricia Barto and Jan Kemp for a strong and definite coordination of color. Even the effects and gadgets were color coordinated. We were a tightly knit group from the visual standpoint."

In fact, it's said that *Batman* helped sell TV color sets, at a time when most American households still had black and white TVs. Could there be a greater testament to the show's visual impact?

Costume designer Jack Kemp helped Krizman achieve the show's color-saturated style.[6] Kemp endeavored to emulate the absurdly bright palette and personality of the comic book. He closely studied its pages to accurately bring its colorful characters to life. The designer recalled to Bob Garcia in *Cinefantastique*,

> When I received the assignment, I decided to get every copy of the Batman comic books that I could lay my hands on and shut myself away in a room with the phone off the hook and just absorb all the information I could about the characters and their behavior patterns... I spent a lot of time looking at them and in discussions with Charles FitzSimons.

The comic-book Batman had recently gone through his own costume redesign. In the 1960s, DC Comics editor Julius Schwartz had successfully led efforts to update and redesign such heroes as the Atom, Flash, and Green

---

[6] A graduate of the prestigious London Royal Academy of Music and Dramatic Art, Kemp brought his unique touch to film and TV. Kemp was working on the first episodes of *Daniel Boone* when he was tapped to join the *Batman* crew fulltime. With a strong theater background, Kemp injected an ostentatious sensibility into everything he designed for Batman's bright world.

Lantern. With sluggish sales on *Batman* and *Detective Comics*, Schwartz was given the task of updating the Caped Crusader too. The "New Look" Batman debuted in the pages of *Detective Comics* #327 in 1964. Artist Carmine Infantino redesigned the character at Schwartz's behest, making the figure more realistic, shortening Batman's ears, and – most famously – modifying his costume to incorporate a yellow oval behind the bat-insignia.

Infantino's "New Look" Batman and Robin became the template for Kemp's costume designs. Kemp paid very careful attention to every nuance of the printed page, creating almost exact live-action replicas of the four-colored costumes. Kemp knew the outlandish garb had to suit the characters, but also had to be suitable for the actors to wear. He used stretch fabric that would hug the frame, creating that skin-tight look associated with comic-book heroes. For the capes, Kemp sought to emulate the flowing effect often seen in the comics, using specific silk fabrics that gave the capes the proper flow.

Batman's cowl proved a greater challenge. It needed to look like Batman while providing a functional piece through which the actor could see and hear. Ultimately, a clever combination of fabric and hard plastic provided the proper design. The cowl itself had another curious detail: Batman's eyebrows were drawn on the cowl itself, as if to convey a permanent, pensive gaze. That brilliant minor element of design perfectly complemented Adam West's straight-faced delivery and the show's wonderfully absurd dialogue.

Robin's costume was simpler to translate to screen. Kemp strove to match the bright reds and greens of the comic-book Robin. When Burt Ward donned Kemp's Robin mask, he looked like one of Infantino's Robin drawings come to life. There was only one notable derivation from the comic-book Robin: while the four-color Boy Wonder was bare-legged, Burt Ward was outfitted with flesh-skinned tights. Perhaps even in the ludicrous world of TV's *Batman*, a grown man running around in green underwear might have taken things a bit too far!

The villains proved to be the biggest challenge for Kemp and his team, as it became necessary to design new flashy costumes almost every week. Unlike previous live-action super-hero adaptations that often used thugs and gangsters as foils, Batman embraced a cavalcade of colorful criminals. Kemp rose to the challenge, creating costumes that left an indelible impression. Burgess Meredith's portrayal of the Penguin was bolstered by Kemp's design, which used a black cutaway suit over body pads to give the actor a portly appearance, with a vest made of a white fur fabric to resemble penguin feathers. Cesar Romero engendered the persona of a suave, debonair leading man, and Kemp used this to great effect, outfitting the Joker in a sharp tail suit with striped pants – but in bright purples and greens. Combined with Romero's signature laugh, it created the perfect image of a devilish dandy. Likewise, the Riddler's bright green leotard complemented Frank Gorshin's manic performance. And Julie Newmar's curve-hugging cat suit allowed her Catwoman to sensuously slink about while planning her next caper. Kemp's adaptations of the comic villains' costumes proved so influential that that the comic books themselves would later incorporate some of Kemp's designs, such as the Newmar-like Catwoman costume in *Batman* #197 (Nov 1967).

But all those colorful comic-book designs were difficult to replicate on film. As Kemp put it, "The project would require a different approach in regard to costumes and I decided to give the actors a vivid combination of colors and styles that had not heretofore been used in films or TV, and by doing so translate into real life the garish look of the comic book pages." Krizman and Kemp were largely successful in that regard, but those vivid colors didn't come easily – and like many aspects of *Batman*, became a weekly challenge. Kemp worked furiously with co-designer Patricia Barto to meet the show's constant colorful demands. And because of the show's unique use of color, many off-the-rack items were essentially useless. Almost every article of clothing was dyed to meticulously match the eye-popping source material, as Kemp strived to bring that same chromatic intensity to the small screen.

Kemp worked closely with Krizman, matching colors and synching the costumes to complement set construction. The overall result was a well-coordinated visual concoction of costumes, sets, and props. What they created was something beyond an adventure show – it was quite literally a live-action Pop Art exhibit.

As every Bat-aficionado knows, the *Batman* TV program was a massive hit. Soon after it hit the airwaves, "Batmania" swept the nation, as viewers – young and old – all found something to enjoy in the show's camp-tastic style. The series became a marketing bonanza for the studio, as *Batman* inspired all sorts of related merchandise. Feeding the frenzy, many Hollywood stalwarts jockeyed for appearances and cameos on *Batman*, which became the "in" thing to do at the time. As audiences embraced the show's outrageous antics, the crew almost had to top themselves week after week. Over time, the speed and scale of the show began to balloon. As the series progressed, it steadily began to deteriorate. Semple echoed this sentiment in *Cinefantastique*:

It was too expensive to shoot. It got very sleazy. I thought it was produced horribly and very quickly. They didn't know they had a big hit. I think it steadily deteriorated, even the ones I worked on, because it sort of got wilder. They were straining harder. The great thing about the first few episodes is that they were amazingly unforced. They just seemed natural. Then people started with really silly characters.

After ratings declined in the second season, Dozier added Yvonne Craig as Batgirl for the third, in the hopes of reviving the sagging series. Krizman and Kemp succeeded in giving the Dominoed Daredoll an excellent amount of visual appeal. She had her own secret wall where she kept her crime-fighting gear. She rode through Gotham on her customized purple Batgirlcycle. Her color scheme of purple and yellow made her pop visually. And it didn't hurt that curvy Craig perfectly filled out her punchy purple Bat-suit. An accomplished dancer, Craig also gave Batgirl's fighting sequences a graceful kick. To the series's credit, Batgirl was a pro-feminist vision; although she copied Batman in name, she very much lived in her own independent world and played by her own rules. This was supported by Krizman's inventive visual approach to Gotham's lone female crime-fighter.

Despite Batgirl's playful appeal, the third season began to betray *Batman*'s fatigue. There was obviously less money put into the series, as evidenced by the simpler sets and repetitive plots. The novelty had obviously worn thin, and ratings continued to decline. The show was ultimately canceled in January 1968. At that time, Dozier still regarded *Batman* as a "novelty show." He was pleased with its three-year run, but wasn't at all surprised it didn't last too long. He had no idea his little "novelty show" would continue to reverberate years and years after its demise.

On one hand, Dozier's *Batman* could be viewed as a quintessential pop-culture time capsule. The *Batman* TV series was undoubtedly one of those "lightning in a bottle" moments. Consider the exact timing of its genesis. The idea of bringing Batman to TV was formulated just as the Pop Art phenomenon had gone mainstream and shows started broadcasting in color. The counter-culture movement was brewing, giving rise to colorful self-expression, rejection of the norm, outlandish fashions, and experimentation with mind-altering substances. It was the "perfect storm" in which to launch Dozier's vision on an unsuspecting public. The result was an unprecedented jolt of campy, colorful adventure. Certain episodes capture this unbridled visual energy — perfectly reflecting the emerging experimental art culture of the late 1960s.

For example, in "Pop Goes the Joker" and "Flop Goes the Joker," the series even winks at its own Pop Art inspiration. The Clown Prince of Crime actually joins the world of Pop Art in a plot to steal a collection of precious paintings. The episodes are the perfect showcase of the crew's creative use of color and design – while at the same time acknowledging the show's artistic inspiration. The mischievous script even contains some inside jokes for art history aficionados.

In another episode, "Louie the Lilac," evil Louie tries to gain control of Gotham's flower children. This hippy-trippy episode features fantastic use of color, groovy music and counter-culture themes – making it a perfect time capsule to the late 1960s.

Batman also influenced other TV programs at the time, as producers looked to mimic its success. The second season of *Lost in Space* aired in the same timeslot as *Batman*, and it began to adapt a more colorful, campier tone. As a spin-off to the popular *The Man from U.N.C.L.E.*, NBC developed *The Girl from U.N.C.L.E.*, which aired in 1966-1967. Imagined as a more fanciful series, its heroine, April Dancer, began to use more gimmicks and gadgets to escape various deathtraps. In one particularly *Batman*-esque episode, April finds herself trapped in a giant toaster. Clearly, the visual style of *Batman* started to affect other series.

The unexpected mania surrounding the TV series also began to influence *Batman* and *Detective Comics* in the late 1960s. Ironically, editor Julie Schwartz had just removed some of the more colorful aspects of the book in an attempt to depict Batman as a darkened detective. But with the TV show's overwhelming success, the comic-book scripts and art began to reflect the tone of TV's *Batman*, with brighter colors, increased sound effects, and spectacular fight scenes. The costumed villains flooded back into the books, due to the popularity of their live-action counterparts. The Riddler, previously a second-tier villain, emerged as a first-level Bat-baddie, thanks to Frank Gorshin's manic portrayal. And the Joker re-emerged as a giggling gag criminal, much like the Cesar Romero interpretation of the Clown Prince of Crime. Batman also began to rely quite heavily on his arsenal of Bat-gadgets, which became increasingly more implausible with each new tale. The *Batman* TV aesthetic even spilled over into other DC titles like *Teen Titans* and *Justice League* – which prominently featured Batman and Robin, as well as a kooky assortment of gimmick-driven criminals.

As Batmania died down and *Batman's* ratings slid, the show's influence on DC Comics began to wane. The Dark Knight's comic-book tales returned to their roots, with Batman eschewing his absurd gadgets and using his detective skills instead. By the end of the '60s, Batman was on his way back to his original, darker incarnation. The journey was completed in the early '70s, when writer Denny O'Neil and artist Neal Adams charted a bold new course for the Caped Crusader. O'Neil's moody scripts gave us a brooding Batman, while Adams's ultra-realistic pencils provided an intensely *real* crime-fighting vigilante. Serious comic readers were thrilled to have "their Batman" back, utterly rejecting the sillier camp aspects of the TV series.

The mainstream media wasn't as quick to forget the campy Caped Crusader, however. From 1968-1969, Filmation produced a new animated series entitled *The Batman / Superman Hour.* Most of the Batman episodes were two parts and largely mimicked the format and tone of Dozier's *Batman.* The animated series lifted the personalities of the heroes and villains directly from the live-action series, and it retained many of the show's visual quirks, including the zooming-bat screen changes, the red phone, the Batpoles, the outrageous deathtraps, the design of the Batcave, and that of the Batmobile. *Super Friends* also borrowed heavily from the 1966 *Batman* series and featured a serious, scout-leader-style Batman and an overly-exuberant Robin. Throughout its various incarnations, *Super Friends* offered a square pair of Caped Crusaders who relied heavily on their various Bat-gadgets. Clearly, the influence of Dozier's *Batman* was still quite strong in the creative consciousness.

In fact, it never quite left at all. Although canceled in 1968, it hardly disappeared from the airwaves. Episodes continually aired in syndication throughout the 1970s. And while the series had become a pop-culture footnote to adults, it was a rollicking adventure to a fresh new crop of kids every year. The show's continued popularity even helped create a whole Saturday morning sub-genre of live-action, campy comedy adventures. Producers Sid & Marty Kroft launched dozens of kiddie-adventure shows with live actors – including *H.R. Pufnstuf, Sigmund and the Sea Monster, Lidsville,* and *The Bugaloos.* Each show featured wild adventures, oversized props, and colorful characters in surreal surroundings. *Electra Woman and Dyna Girl* was perhaps the most direct offshoot of the *Batman* series: this short-lived action show contained all of *Batman's* the trappings, with the exception of its decidedly female protagonists.

In the 1980s, affection for Dozier's *Batman* began to fade as entertainment became a bit more sophisticated. Even the long-standing *Super Friends* was given a stylized makeover in 1985 and renamed *The Super Powers Team: Galactic Guardians*. Although Adam West continued to provided Batman's voice in the animated series, the character's sillier elements were shunted aside. He relied less on his utility belt and more on his deductive skills. In the comics, Batman evolved into his darkest incarnation yet, as Frank Miller's *Dark Knight* series offered a gritty, urban-warrior version of the character. And in 1989, director Tim Burton drew influence from Miller's Batman in creating his own live-action Batman movie, a dark departure from Dozier's campy version. That incarnation still lingered in the minds of many movie-goers and magazine editors, however, and many articles on Burton's *Batman* would start with a "Biff!" or a "Pow!" somewhere in the headline. Burton's *Batman* was a huge success, and Batmania swept the nation a second time. But this time, the public embraced a dark, gritty Batman. This encouraged Warner Bros. to develop a new animated series with a young Bruce Timm, featuring a more serious Caped Crusader. *Batman: The Animated Series* launched in 1992, stunning viewers with its rich storytelling and lavish dark deco animation style.

It seemed as if the artistic influence of Dozier's *Batman* was dead and buried. Most "serious" comic-book fans were thrilled, as they felt the memories of the 1960s *Batman* prevented anyone from taking their Dark Knight too seriously. But toward the end of the 1990s, the visual influence of Dozier's *Batman* returned. In 1995, Joel Schumacher directed *Batman Forever*, a brighter evolution of Tim Burton's Dark Detective. The set designs were more vibrant, and the villains – Riddler and Two-Face – were more outrageous. Schumacher's affection for the 1960s *Batman* series was even more evident in 1997's *Batman and Robin*. The movie was largely an homage to the campy classic, loaded with bold colors, outlandish set designs, Bat-gadgets, and a steady dose of straight-faced humor.

In 1997, *Batman: The Animated Series* was relaunched as *The New Batman Adventures*. The 1998 episode "Legends of The Dark Knight" featured three different versions of the Batman legend. One story pays homage to the Bill Finger / Dick Sprang era of Batman, while also evoking the '60s *Batman* series. In 2003, producer Glen Murakami developed an animated *Teen Titans* series, drawing from different sources for inspiration when creating Robin. "We combined some different things," Murakami recalled for my website, titanstower.com. "We even gave him some Burt Ward mannerisms by punching his fist into his hand. Stuff like that." And over at DC Comics, writers like Grant Morrison and Mark Waid revived some of the elements of the '60s Batman through a modern storytelling lens. Comic creators and even fans had begun to accept the various incarnations of Batman as valid interpretations of the character. In 2004, Mike Allred even featured a Batusi-dancing Batman in *Solo* #7.

The visual strength and influence of Dozier's *Batman* arguably came full circle with the launch of *Batman: The Brave and the Bold* on Cartoon Network in 2008. This new animated series borrowed heavily from the '60s-era Batman, including some memorable iconography from the TV show. A brighter, friendlier Caped Crusader teamed up with a different hero each episode, often embroiled in oversized deathtraps and ensnared by colorful criminals. The opening credits featured the 90-degree-angle Bat-climb, made famous in the '60s series. Several villains created specifically for the '60s program – including King Tut, Egghead, Mad Hatter, Archer, Bookworm, False Face, Black Widow, Siren, Marsha Queen of Diamonds, Louie the Lilac, Ma Parker, and Shame – all make cameo appearances as prisoners in the episode, "Day of the Dark Knight!" Another episode, "The Color of Revenge!", begins with a flashback that is clearly an homage to the classic live-action series. It makes use of the red phone, the Shakespeare bust, the sliding bookcase, the Batpoles, and the atomic-powered Batmobile. Unknowingly, a whole new generation of children would feel the impact of Dozier's *Batman* – some 40 years later.

It seemed as if everyone discovered that Batman could be many things. In the *Batman: Brave and The Bold* episode entitled "Legends of the Dark Mite!", this point is made quite clear by writer Paul Dini. At the Fifth Dimension Animated Cartoon Convention, a serious-minded fan rails against the series, "I always thought Batman was best suited in the role of gritty urban crime detective. But now you guys have him up against Santas and Easter Bunnies? I'm sorry, but that's not my Batman!" Bat-Mite replies, "Batman's rich history allows him to be interpreted in a multitude of ways. To be sure, this is a lighter incarnation, but it's certainly no less valid and true to the character's roots as the tortured avenger crying out for Mommy and Daddy. And besides, those Easter Bunnies look really scary, right?" Leave it to Bat-Mite to put everything into humorous perspective!

Undoubtedly, the visual impact and iconography of the '60s *Batman* TV series still lingers to this day. It was an innovative adventure series told as a bravura pop-art spectacle. Unlike any comic-strip adaptation of its time, it was a literal, living, breathing, live-action comic book. Its visual language, bold palette, and inventive imagery continues to deliver a POW! into the hearts and minds of its audience.

"Known Super-Criminals Still at Large": Villainy in *Batman*

by Chuck Dixon

For a long time, it was referred to as "the Show" among the comic-book *cognoscenti*. Now it's "the Adam West show," to differentiate it from the many cartoon incarnations and movies that have featured the Dark Knight.

The 1966 TV show wasn't popular with the more diehard fans of Batman comics. While the rest of the nation was captured by Batmania, devoted readers of the Caped Crusader's monthly adventures in *Batman* and *Detective Comics* were in deep mourning. I was a kid at the time and recall punching a school friend when he proudly showed off his new Batman T-shirt. He thought I'd dig the shirt, since I had the largest Batman comic collection in class. But instead, I saw red. I knocked him into the coat closet. And I was never the class troublemaker or any kind of bully. I wasn't the kind of kid to resort to slugging someone unless you said something about my mom... or Batman.

The Dark Knight, Tarzan, and Spider-Man formed the holy trinity of my childhood heroes. I was dedicated to them in their purest forms. Hell, I quit buying Spidey when Ditko left. I was hardcore, man.

So I took it all very personally that Wednesday night in January when the series premiere broke my heart. This wasn't *my* Batman! Hell, my parents were *laughing* at the show. Laughing at *Batman*! Batman and Robin running around in the daytime! Bruce and Dick acting like scolded kindergartners in front of Aunt Harriet. And who *was* this Aunt Harriet anyway? And Batman was dancing! *Dancing*, I tell you! I was outraged. I was wounded. My hero was besmirched, maligned, desecrated, and made a mockery by those morons who make TV shows. How could creators of the same ilk who polluted the airways with *Gilligan's Island* and *I've Got a Secret* possibly do Batman justice? The Dark Knight was no two-dimensional shill for breakfast cereal or deodorant. They'd ruined the Caped Crusader, and they ruined him for eternity.

To compound my miseries, the series spawned acres of merchandising both authorized and not. Bat-pencils, Bat-gum, Bat-candy, Bat-waterguns, Bat-yo-yos, and anything else a bat symbol could be pasted on crowded the shelves of newsstands, fives-and-dimes and department stores. It all seemed to spring up overnight, and there was no escaping it. Even the Top 40 radio stations were packing Batman-inspired songs onto their playlists. Long-forgotten R&B groups recorded deservedly-forgotten 45s about Batman and Robin, and the single of Nelson Riddle's arrangement of the TV show theme was on the chart and the airwaves for months.

My poor pal Doug paid the price for all this just because he wanted to show me the Batman shirt his mom bought him at Kresge's. He got knocked on his ass among the galoshes in the coat closet of Mrs. Buckley's sixth-grade classroom because he'd stoked the incandescence of my fanboy rage.

Looking back now, as a more mature, reflective fanboy, I realize that the show *saved* Batman.

As stupid a medium as TV was (and remains), it was considered a more legitimate form of entertainment than comic books. Comics were still suffering from the cultural malaise brought upon them by Wertham's book, *Seduction of the Innocent*, more than a decade before. Comics had been made toothless and "wholesome," but they were still trash to the wider public. While my 11-year-old self was appalled at the atrocities being committed against my hero by TV, others were wondering why ABC had sunk so low as to adapt a funnybook for primetime viewing.

And things on the comic-book end were already pretty bleak by '66. DC Comics had run the franchise into the ground years before, with silly stories of aliens and space travel that took Batman and Robin away from the kind of gang-busting detective stories they'd starred in for decades. Foreshadowing to the shock stunts later in vogue in comics, Robin even died on an alien world only to be brought back by a *deus ex machina* too stupid to relate. The comics had gone off the rails, and DC Comics looked like they had no direction for Gotham's denizens.

Forced back into the more familiar, iconic formula by the TV show, the comic books really didn't improve much (Batman's best comic-book years wouldn't begin until the early '70s). But they did bring the emphasis back onto the Dynamic Duo as crime-fighters. Mysteries returned, along with villains who offered Batman and Robin more of an earthbound challenge than bee-men visiting from outer space. Batman returned to his roots.

And most importantly, the villains were back.

As I got older and watched it in endless syndicated reruns, I made my peace with the show. Though I still took joy in seeing Bruce Lee kick Burt Ward's ass, I began to appreciate the finer elements of the four-color adventures that the show got right and even (gasp!) improved upon. It would be my first lesson in altering aspects of an entertainment property to suit the needs of different media.

My nephews (whose first exposure to Batman was the TV show) watched the show in the same earnest way that I read the comics at their age. They were six and eight years old and didn't see that the show was played for laughs. They were digging the fights and traps and crazy crimes. From their reaction, I learned that you can write on two or more levels and appeal to a broader audience. There was the camp and satire for the older viewers, but the writers paid just as much attention to character development, plotting, and action. They provided a framework on which to hang the comedy aspects. Remove the humor, and you still had a solid story.

Years later, an impossible fantasy came true when I was invited to join the team of writers scripting Batman for DC Comics. Those endless hours of daydreaming and staring out the classroom window, imagining Batman and Robin poised atop the monkeybars in the playground, *weren't* wasted. Thousands of drawings of the Batmobile, made at the kitchen table, turned out to be research. The Batsignal my dad made for me out of an old slide projector was preparation for my longest run in comics. I may not understand how to balance a chemical equation, but I knew the Batcave like the back of my hand.

But as any writer knows, there are pitfalls in every dream assignment. Sometimes, it's better to come at a project cold, without nostalgia or opinions formed from childhood associations. You can love a character too much. You can hold them too sacred.

So I get this job, and I'm expected to produce. I'm running in the majors now. I have a Robin limited series to write, and everyone has certain sales expectations for it. I have comic-book legends like Denny O'Neil and Archie Goodwin overseeing my work. Everyone else on the team has been writing these characters for years. I blow this, and it's back to second-tier super-heroes and smaller publishers – and a shortened career in funnybooks.

As I was thinking and plotting and blue-skying my first plotlines, I kept thinking of the Show. Not the comics. It was the Adam West show that kept pushing itself forward. How could that be? How could that travesty of a pastiche trump the decades of comics I'd read ever since I could read? Could it be that those thousands and thousands of pages of Batman comic books I read as a kid were secondary to that stupid TV show? Was Lorenzo Semple more of an influence on me than Bill Finger? Did I finally get my Numero Uno dream assignment, only to find that I'm *not* the Bat-fan I thought I was?

I couldn't tell anyone about this. Those three seasons of tongue-in-cheek mockery still stung in the comics biz. And I was working for Denny O'Neil, the man revered for rescuing Batman from the "Biff! Pow! Wham!" legacy left by the TV series. This was a guy dedicated to erasing the Batusi from the zeitgeist. If he thought for a moment I was marching to the Neal Hefti theme, I'd be hounded out of the profession for eternity. Denny was always a wonderful and generous editor to me, but there's a line you do not cross.

Oh, I managed to slip some sly nods to the Show into my scripts. No one noticed an obtuse reference to the "bat-turn" I wedged into one scene, or that I named a major span over Gotham Harbor the "Westward Bridge." But I did get caught when I went a step too far on one story. More on that later.

As I outlined and plotted and dialogued more scripts, I examined what the Show had done to shape my own take on Batman's universe.

It wasn't the gimmicks, because beyond the Batmobile, the ones on the Show were all silly. Shark repellent? Come on! I wore a home-made utility belt when I was a kid, and I had more practical stuff than that in it.

It wasn't the detective work, because this Batman and Robin were flummoxed by mysteries that a child could see through.

It wasn't Gotham City, because this sun-washed burg had nothing to do with the shadowy noir-scape I'd come to love. It looked no different than the town the Beverly Hillbillies lived in. Where were the crime-haunted docks? The dark alleys? Even the Batcave looked too brightly lit and… cheery.

So what was I channeling here?

The villains.

What I was doing in my initial efforts is what the writers on the TV series had to do. They had to find what would work for their purposes. They knew going in that this would not be an earnest or serious portrayal of the Dark Knight. They'd already decided on a parody approach. But they understood that a great comic-book hero (no matter how campy) is defined by his foes, and so they went back and took a long hard look at Batman's rogues gallery.

Oh, and what a gallery it is. From classic criminal masterminds like the Joker to frankly ridiculous goofballs like Firefly, Gotham City had its share of costumed miscreants. Most of these were inspired, in the early runs of *Detective Comics* and *Batman*, by the super-criminals from the Dick Tracy comic strips. Chester Gould's lantern-jawed cop faced down an endless parade of hideously-deformed gangsters, killers, and thieves. Flat-Top, BB Eyes, Mumbles, and the Mole were all monsters in human form who would always meet justice in the most gruesome and deadly form when they chose to go up against Tracy. These bad guys were presented in the broadest strokes and without shades of grey. Each was unique and fully developed, with themes and language of their own.

Bob Kane, Bill Finger, Jerry Robinson, and the other Batman contributors were heavily influenced by the look and the success of the Gould strip. The look of Batman evolved over time to resemble the heavily-outlined caricatures of *Dick Tracy* and its multi-plane approach to panel composition. The Dark Knight even developed a jawline to rival Tracy's signature profile.

And the traps, the glorious traps. A trademark of *Dick Tracy* was the ingenious traps that the cop would find himself in again and again. Tracy and his allies were often left to drown, asphyxiate, burn alive, or be crushed by tremendous weights on a fairly regular basis. These cliffhanger traps and the characters' eventual escapes could play over weeks of the strip, as Gould cranked the suspense higher and higher. Kane, Finger, and the rest would place Batman and Robin into traps much like those Tracy fell prey to. As a kid, that was my favorite aspect of Batman stories: his indefatigable resourcefulness. Unlike other comic characters, who used brute strength to thwart their foes, Batman used his mind to save himself in most cases.

Batman's villains weren't as vicious and sadistic as Tracy's. They were madder for madness's sake, real psychos without much of a gameplan beyond making a big show out of crime and embarrassing the police and their costumed nemesis. Gotham's villains didn't just anticipate the Dynamic Duo's interference, they *longed* for it. They needed to demonstrate their superiority. Super-crazy egomaniacs, the whole bunch of them. Dick Tracy's Chicago gangland enemies were more focused on successful lawbreaking than their attention-hungry Gotham counterparts. This plays into a major difference between the two creations.

Gould's storylines would most often focus on the criminal. Each new baddie was presented in his own personal gangster epic, in which Tracy was always the force of law and order. In many stories, we would see Tracy one step behind the crook for the bulk of the story, but the focus was solidly on the current rotten apple.

In Batman's stories, the Dark Knight is always the focus. That's why his enemies have to be needy mental cases, I suppose. Their unhealthy obsession with Batman is expected to match the reader's fascination with the hero. It's easy to say (and has often been posited to the point where it is a conceit of the franchise) that without Batman there would be no Batman villains. They practically spring up overnight once he begins his nightly crusade against crime.

As an aside, it's no coincidence that, before picking Batman as the subject for an early primetime action show, ABC was trying to obtain the rights for a Dick Tracy TV show. When those plans fell through, the network began casting around for a similar property, and there was really only *one* that came close.

Once they got down to work, the show's writers and producers plucked the best from the decades of comic material they had to choose from. Most comic fans are either ignorant of the fact or loath to admit it, but the TV show made classics of several baddies who were long-forgotten in the comics pages.

First and foremost of these would be the Riddler.

The conundrum-themed Riddler was featured in the first two-parter to air on ABC when the series premiered as a mid-season replacement in January 1966. "Hi Diddle Riddle" and "Smack in the Middle" were not the first installments filmed, but the network wisely chose them to make the best first impression on the TV audience.

I'm not the first Bat-scholar to say that Frank Gorshin, a gifted comic actor and impressionist, set the tone for the entire series. Cast members and production people have evinced this opinion as well. Gorshin threw everything at the role of the mad, green-clad puzzler. He based that falsetto giggle on Richard Widmark's portrayal of the psychopathic killer Tommy Udo in *Kiss of Death* (1947). Gorshin practically defined the phrase "over the top" as he pranced, preened, shuffled, and leapt about the set, practically daring the rest

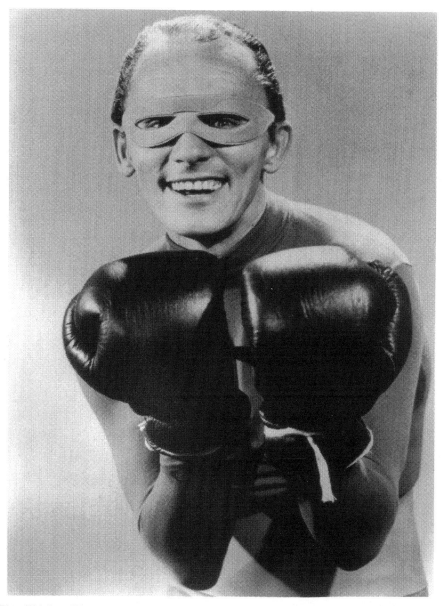

The Riddler (Frank Gorshin) challenges Batman to a boxing match in the third season's "Ring Around the Riddler" (1967). Publicity still. Copyright © Greenway Productions, DC Comics, and 20ᵗʰ Century-Fox.

of the cast and crew to keep up with him. His Riddler would rise to heights of giddy hysteria, only to fall, seconds later, into brooding menace or compulsive introspection. By bringing his performance to a level of ham never seen before, Gorshin provided the bar for those who came after him to reach for.

And the writing was a match for Gorshin's mad characterization. Prior to the TV show, the Riddler had only appeared three times in two decades. To comic-book fans, he was a minor villain. In fact, as dedicated a Bat-fan as I was, I'd never heard of him until the TV show. Even the Batman annuals I treasured as a kid never reprinted any Riddler stories. The TV writers were looking for bad guys with high-concept hooks. They found one in Eddie Nigma, an obsessed egomaniac whose theme was leaving clues in the form of riddles that offered the Dynamic Duo a shot at catching him.

I'm a big fan of John Astin, but he was given big shoes to fill when Gorshin had to bow out of one of the stories in the second season. It's tough to walk into a role *owned* by another actor like that.

Now, nothing against writers like Bill Finger (whose shoulders I stand on whenever I write Batman) or Gardner Fox, but those initial Riddler stories suffer from a lack of coherence. Sure, they're colorful and action-packed, but there's no building upon the idea of a riddle-themed criminal; he's just another misfit with a mask and gimmick. The crimes are contrived, the riddles make little sense, and the payoffs are lame. In the defense of anyone writing for DC Comics in the '40s and '50s, the company line to creators was "anyone over the age of ten still reading comic books is an idiot."

And apparently they didn't have a high regard for the intelligence of ten-year-olds either. Any writer who showed the least concern for story structure (or solid plotting or even challenging mysteries) risked ridicule or even firing. The DC editorial staff was focused on a bait-and-switch philosophy to sell their super-hero comics. The covers would feature outlandish scenarios, in which the comic book's lead character was shrunk to the size of an insect or transformed into a gorilla or mysteriously invisible to the public. The stories inside rarely lived up to these high-concept covers and, even when they tried, offered unsatisfactory resolutions.

Given these low expectations and ego-crushing restrictions from editors, it's a wonder these stories are as good as they *are*. Rereading these stories as an adult, I realized how much I had projected on them as a child. The events in the comics and the way I remembered them were wildly at odds. My recollections of the stories were far better than they actually were.

With little to play with other than a colorful costume and an easy-to-grasp theme, the writers of the TV series concentrated on Riddler's *modus operandi*. The original comic-book stories were, to be charitable, disorganized. Why was the Riddler doing what he did and was there a method to his madness? The idea of a criminal who leaves clues to his crimes wasn't a new one. The Victorian serial killer Jack the Ripper left riddles and tantalizing poems to taunt the police. Sherlock Holmes, Professor Thorndyke, and Hercule Poiroit all solved their share of puzzles to find their way to the killer. Pulp detective fiction was full of criminals who couldn't resist the urge to tease their pursuers. Stories like these are engaging because they invite the reader to join the hero in deducing the identity of the evildoer.

But Batman and Robin simply solving children's riddles and using the answers to stay one step behind the villain until the climax was lifeless as a story. Again, it was a battle of egos rather than wits. There was little at stake in the stories, other than bragging rights for whoever stumped who. The Riddler might prevent Batman and Robin from interrupting his crime *du jour* but had to know he was playing against the odds the longer the game went on. What worked as an eight- or 10-page comic-book story in 1949 would be sheer tedium over two nights of TV. So the TV writers added a new wrinkle to the Riddler's gimmick: dual-purpose clues.

The riddles delivered to Commissioner Gordon to be forwarded to Batman would serve at first to mislead our heroes. The answers to the queries would often be obvious to Batman and especially easy for Robin, who was adept at coming up with responses. Once the viewer got into the rhythm of it, he could even try to beat the Dynamic Duo to the answer. But that darned Robin was so quick!

Some of the better examples of the Riddler's puzzlers:
Q: When is the time of a clock like the whistle of a train?
A: When it's two to two.
Q: Which president wears the largest hat?
A: The one with the biggest head.
Q: Why is an orange like a bell?
A: Because they both must be peeled [pealed].

Corny? Sure. But these riddles were designed to mislead. The first answers invariably led Batman and Robin away from the Riddler's true intentions and often into a deadly trap. The real clues were hidden in the double meanings of the riddles' answers or a hidden significance or pattern. The Riddler counted on "those costumed dolts" to act on their initial responses to his questions. This fed his ego because he was able to demonstrate, time and again, his intellectual superiority to the World's Greatest Detective. Temporarily, anyway.

And watching Adam West strain his brain for an answer was great theater. So was the moment of satisfaction he allowed himself when he put his and Robin's solutions together to arrive at their (often incorrect) conclusions. In the endgame, West's Batman was always the better brain, but he resisted self-congratulation. The Riddler was in this for the ego-stroke, but the Dark Knight's reward was knowing that Gothamites were safe once more from the predations of yet another sick monkey.

The TV writers revised and established the template for what makes a classic Riddler story – and that template is a mother, let me tell you. I think the Riddler is my favorite of all of Batman's villains but, holy brainlock, is he a tough one to write.

At the height of Batmania, DC Comics re-introduced the Riddler to the comic pages after a decades-long absence. But he only appeared a few times and was largely and inexplicably replaced by the Cluemaster, a much weaker character who copied Nigma's *modus* but expanded his repertoire to other puzzles beyond complex riddles. The Cluemaster was a pale imitation who wasn't provided a clear motivation or even a secret identity. (I would provide him with the street name of "Arthur Brown" when I revived him in the '90s.)

I think that's why most writers avoid the character of the Riddler and, when they can't, often write stories wherein he gives up his riddle obsession or which *examine* his methods rather than showing them in practice. In a recent comics storyline, Eddie Nigma had reformed and worked as a private investigator *solving* crimes rather than inventing them. Way to avoid heavy lifting.

Even screenwriters (who are paid lots more than us lowly comic scribes) throw in the towel when it comes to Eddie Nigma. In *Batman Forever*, the Riddler leaves only one riddle for Batman and Robin to solve – and the answer is his own name, which was revealed to the heroes earlier in the film anyway. Aside to Jim Carrey: if you're going to go over the top, do what Frank Gorshin did and take the audience *with* you.

For my money, the best Batman and Riddler movie is *Die Hard with a Vengeance*. Think about it. What an awesome Riddler Jeremy Irons makes: vain, sneering, cruel, and coldly intellectual. His conundrums are clever, and John McClane and Zeus must figure them out in order to save their own lives and the lives of others. But in the end, the Irons character was only using these riddles to lead McClane and the police *away* from the true crime (stealing the gold reserves from the basement of the federal depository). Pure Eddie Nigma.

Much as I love the character, I only wrote two Riddler stories in my 11-year tenure on Batman-related comics. I featured him in the background in lots of stories, but I set my standards for stories featuring him so high that I intimidated myself. In one outing, I simply retold his origin and revisited some of the crimes of his earliest stories, in an effort to make sense of them. *My Riddler* was obsessed with gamesmanship and creating a deadly gauntlet for Batman to run through, for which Nigma set the rules. I followed the pattern set in place by Lorenzo Semple, right down to the double-entendre clues that would send our heroes off chasing hares (and possible extinction) while the Riddler got down to business. This required combing through countless riddle books and, eventually, having to create dozens of riddles of my own to fit the serial heists I wanted the Riddler to commit.

My second Riddler adventure was a long arc in *Detective Comics* in which the riddles were themed to baseball scoring. It took me two years to write. My hat is off to the TV scripters who wrote at least four Riddler two-parters in the first half season of the show. But each is by a *different* writer, and one is essentially an old Joker plot with few actual Riddler tropes – all of which only proves my point that the Riddler is a tough gig.

Speaking of the Clown Prince of Crime, the Joker is considered Batman's arch-nemesis and was played on TV with manic glee by Cesar Romero. This was wildly against type for the actor, as Romero was most often associated with playing suave Latin types or straight dramatic male leads. The pancake make-up and green wig liberated him to play *big*. But he didn't go for spastic or manic, as Gorshin had done. Romero's Joker is a vain ringmaster with huge gestures and the painfully-correct elocution of an American theater actor. In effect, he is a ham portraying a ham. His sense of self-worth ranges from loud pronouncements of his own brilliance when things are going swimmingly to nauseating self-pity when Batman finally thwarts his schemes. He is always buoyed by his sycophantic thugs and clueless moll, as were the other Batman baddies. But Romero's Joker genuinely seems to *need* this cheering section. He's a clown; he has to have applause and laughter to motivate him.

Cesar Romero was a great choice for the role. He was tall and could carry off the ludicrous zoot-suit clown tux that is the Joker's signature togs. He moved with all the phony grace and contrived elegance of a quiz show model. And his laugh was filled with gusto rather than madness. His Joker didn't care if the world laughed with him.

Writer Chuck Dixon unscrambles the origin of Prince of Puzzlers in *Detective Comics Annual* #8 (1995). Art by Kieron Dwyer. Copyright © DC Comics.

The Joker seemed to present the least challenge to the TV writers. They had lots of material to choose from, as the Joker had appeared more frequently in the comics than any of Batman's other rogues. The clown or comedian theme of the character was far less constricting than the Riddler's tightly-defined schtick. All the Joker needs to be is sadistic and funny in equal measure. And let's face it, clowns are scary, right?

And Romero *was* funny. The jokes themselves were stale and shopworn by design. The idea was that only the Joker honestly finds his tired vaudeville tomfoolery amusing. Everyone else titters politely or simply appears frightened when he's tearing up the floorboards or cadging laughs with ancient one-liners and excruciating puns. When Romero got sincere laughs was when the Joker was in defeat. At his most miserable and woe-is-me, Romero's Joker is hysterical. His plaintive cries of "justice is blind!" beg for real laughter. The most fitting revenge for this bad guy is when we are finally laughing *at* him, when we never laughed *with* him.

Writing the Joker for comics is a greater challenge because he's had so many memorable stories. From David Vern Reed's definitive "The Joker's Aces" in *World's Finest* #59 (July 1959) to Alan Moore's *Batman: The Killing Joke* (July 1988), there are so many strong Joker stories that to write a weak one is a risk to a comic scripter's legacy. The main rule to the Joker is that there are no rules. He is wide open to the interpretation of the individual writer. He can be played as a fun-loving criminal mastermind, a kind of Professor Moriarty with a seltzer bottle. You can dial him all the way over to Hannibal Lector in greasepaint, or anywhere in between. From complex crime caper to apocalyptic mass murder scenario, it's all good. It only has to *read* good.

When coming up with Joker outings, I always took special care that they be solid crime stories that showed the Clown Prince off to his best advantage. And I always made certain that his jokes actually read *funny*, rather than the place-holder jokes he would so often be supplied with. Without a performer like Cesar Romero (or Mark Hamill's snarky / scary voice portrayals in the cartoons) to pull the role off, the idea of a Joker spouting streams of old groaners just doesn't work. He's a tiresome hack at that point, rather than the charismatic showman he needs to be. And to me, that's what he is; a performance artist who works in blood and misery. A comedian to whom "slaying the audience" takes on a double meaning.

Because the restrictions to the medium at the time along with the conceit that the show was aimed at kiddies, the TV show took the higher road with the

Joker and emphasized the grandiose narcissism of the character. And while he obviously fully intended to commit mass murder, our heroes always thwarted him with only seconds to spare. The TV Batman was not permitted to fail. The current comic-book Batman fails repeatedly, in order to raise the stakes for the reader and to demonstrate that, though he is a near-perfect specimen of the self-made man, he is not infallible.

In the end, that's the Joker's job, right? He exists to show that, given the slightest opening, the merest moment of weakness on Batman's part, the right villain at the wrong time could be the Dark Knight's undoing. We all know that, should this eternal saga ever have an unhappy conclusion, it'll be the Joker who enjoys the last laugh. I mean, could any lesser villain make that claim?

On the subject of lesser villains, we move on to Oswald Cobblepot. Of all of the show's recurring badguys, he got the best makeover of all. The Penguin was, frankly, an inexplicable character who got a new lease on life from his TV appearances. I mean, the *Penguin*? Seriously? Who's afraid of penguins? A little guy who dressed like some antiquated fashion victim and sports an arsenal of trick umbrellas? *This* is a formidable foe for the Dark Knight?

But Burgess Meredith makes the Fowl Fiend work – and how. Meredith's Penguin is a dirty little bird who fancies himself a player. While all the bad guys had their trophy girlfriends, lounging around and pouting like so much scenery, the Penguin was the only one to whom they were a necessity. He liked the chicks and, as long as the filthy loot kept rolling in, they liked him back. My impression was that the Penguin, like a garage band drummer, was *in it* for the babes. Let's be honest: what chance did the guy have on his looks?

Meredith attacked the role with total conviction. He made his mark with that silly waddling walk and the series of bird noises he used for emphasis. His squawking when alarmed, the cooing when he was making time with a moll, and that quacking chortle of approval became part of his repertoire to great effect. Meredith even carried off the monocle and cigarette holder – the whole *boulevardier*-gone-wrong look.

This was a character who never held any appeal to me. I don't care for reinventing icons just to suit myself and so, for a long time, I stayed away from Oswald Cobblepot and his ornithological ploys and deadly bumbershoots. If any character was an instant throwback to the '60s TV show, it was this guy. Major comic-book talents have tried to find the finer points in the old buzzard and come up against a wall.

Then, in one of the many crossovers I participated in, we needed someone to fill the role of a fixer, the kind of underworld enabler often played by Sidney Greenstreet in old movies. For you youngsters, I mean someone like the Merovingian from the *Matrix* sequels. We needed the kind of crime figure who sat in the middle of the underworld web in some sort of quasi-legal business establishment.

Who better than the Penguin? This would be a re-purposing rather than a reboot. As the charismatic owner of the Iceberg Lounge, the Penguin was a perfect fit. There, he could command power from the center of a citywide network of crooks but appear legitimate. He could play the *bon vivant* and raconteur with a chilled martini in his hand and a babe on his arm. Now we could play up his intellect and cunning, rendering his less-than-intimidating physique irrelevant. The Penguin alone could do his evil from a corner booth, taking on a whole new persona of malevolence, and still be true to the core creation.

Other villains borrowed from the comics fared poorly. Mr. Freeze was never a big-name crook in the comics. In fact, his name was Mr. Zero in the appearance closest to the show's incarnation. It didn't help that he was played by three different actors and never associated with a single, signature player like the other villains were. George Sanders played him indifferently in the first season, followed by Eli Wallach portraying him as too lively for a guy with ice-water for blood. Otto Preminger gave Freeze a truly creepy feel, but there seemed to be a disconnect between his performance and the rest of the cast. His signature shouts of "Vild! Vild!" didn't help matters. The fact that the character was house-bound for the most part didn't help matters much either.

It's a pity, because Freeze is a tremendous character with and loads of potential buried in his frigid depths. Not to mention a great visual hook, with his bluish pallor and the refrigeration suit. Freeze never really evolved as a character until Paul Dini and the other writers at Warner Animation provided him with a richer backstory and more pathos-driven motivations. I played off their reimagining of Freeze in a number of appearances. In fact, I have the dubious distinction of having killed Freeze *and* brought him back to life in the comic pages.

The Mad Hatter, played with a kind of fussy panache by David Wayne, was too one-note a character even in the comics. How far can you go with a chapeau-themed lawbreaker? I've written the character only twice in my career and only then as a small part of a larger storyline. The current Mad

Hatter draws his visual style directly from the Mad Hatter of *Alice in Wonderland*. The original incarnation was a larger man with a wild mustache and flaming red hair. I always thought he looked like the comedian Rip Taylor. What a piece of casting *that* would have been.

Other villains were created from the ground up by the show's staff. King Tut is the most successful and memorable of these, with Victor Buono cast as a rotund faux-pharaoh who fancies himself the potentate of Gotham's underworld. He's effete and boorish, and Buono played him with relish. But without the cachet of a comic-book legacy he fails to rise above merely interesting. I know more than one writer proposed adding him to Batman's print continuity, and he finally has become comic-book canon in a recent arc in *Batman Confidential*.

Egghead is one of the show's weaker creations. This intellectual powerhouse, with his inexplicable obsession with eggs of all kinds, was played with wasted enthusiasm by Vincent Price. Of all the actors hamming it up on the series, Price had the greatest reputation as a Hollywood ham. His style of working with too-correct enunciation, those athletic eyebrows, and theatrical posturing were a perfect fit for the series. He was, perhaps, the Elvis Presley of ham, the Michael Jordan of pretentious scenery chewing. Price was famed for his shameless mugging and overbearing puffery. I say this as a huge fan of the guy's work. He was fearless and unapologetic and, like William Shatner today, was willing to gleefully mock his own image. That he was cast in a role that required him to make endless, awful puns involving eggs ("Eggs-cuse me," "It's time I eggs-ecute you," "That was eggs-cruciating") was a missed opportunity. It would have been a much better use of his talents were he cast in the role of a ham actor, as he was in *Theater of Blood* or his marvelous turn in the Robert Mitchum vehicle *His Kind of Woman* (a movie that any fan of ham must see for Price's hijacking of the entire third act of the film). Price as a sinister Shakespeare-quoting hysteric would have been a classic.

A more promising character, to my mind, was the Bookworm. Roddy McDowell played the larcenous know-it-all with his usual charm and wit. McDowell was a gifted actor and a seemingly effortless scene-stealer. He brought a mannered body language to the character, with plenty of theatrical gestures and flourish, but always kept in mind that his character eschewed physical violence for mental gymnastics. The Bookworm's gimmick was a workable one (a braniac who's a walking storehouse of knowledge), and his costume was clever: a tailored Barnaby Street suit made of leather bindings and that awesome fedora with its built-in reading light. Unfortunately, he only appeared in one two-parter. Especially in the light of Vincent Price's Egghead and Cliff Robertson's Shame ("You're a sham and a shame, Shame") each getting two outings. Bookworm, to me, is the perfect Batman foil. His madness was more internalized and didn't really interfere with his criminal endeavors. And as the intellectual equal (and possible superior) of Batman, he could provide real challenges for the Dynamic Duo. The added bonus of literature-themed crimes should have assured him a permanent place in the line-up. I know I would have dug putting him through his paces in comic stories.

Other attempts at recruiting new talent for the Gotham crime scene are mostly forgettable. I'm sure Van Johnson and Art Carney regretted answering the phone when the Minstrel and the Archer were cast, respectively. These were simply awful characters with thin motivations and bankrupt themes.

There's a final evildoer worth mentioning. In fact, I saved the best for last. One character's portrayal on the show explores an area of the Batman mythos that is often disregarded. And by introducing this character in the way that they did, the show's creators demonstrated that maybe they understood this franchise better than the comic-book talents who came before *and* after them.

I'm talking about Catwoman.

Julie Newmar as Catwoman has that one ingredient that so often goes missing in Batman's world: sex.

See, Batman has no recurring love interest either in the show or in the comics, and his significant others in the movies have a life span that would seem unfairly brief to a fruit fly. There's no Lois Lane to his Superman. No Tess Trueheart to his Dick Tracy. No Leia to his Han. Oh, they trot out Vicki Vale every decade or so, but she never takes. And Bruce Wayne is *supposed* to be a millionaire playboy. But he always leaves his dates at the door without even a peck on the cheek. And should either alter ego take an interest in a member of the opposite sex, that lady is in for an awful fate. Batman and Bruce's paramours have a regrettable track record of nasty accidents, suicides, homicides, and in one memorable instance, having her mind reduced to that of a child. Girls, beware of any kind of commitment from this guy.

The reason that Batman has never had a lasting, recurring paramour is simply that creators were always looking at the Lois Lane paradigm for him. But Bruce Wayne has never served the same purpose in his franchise that Clark Kent does for Superman's. Kent's sole reason for existence is so that the last son of Krypton can interact with the world of normal humans. Bruce Wayne (even though he is a real person) is a fictional construct designed to limit or excuse Batman from the world of everyday society. As a reporter, Kent allows Superman to participate in the world of men in a hands-on way. As a bubble-headed billionaire, Wayne offers Batman a convenient "out" to explain his many absences.

Where it is feasible and desirable for Clark Kent to have a love interest like Lois Lane or Lana Lang, the same kind of relationship is unworkable for the aloof and unknowable Bruce Wayne. Besides, Batman works nights.

But this lack of a romantic partner is a special problem for a guy who lives alone with his elderly butler and teen-age ward. People talk. In the '50s, some pseudo-intellect even wrote a bestseller about it. As every gander needs his goose, so Batman needs his Catwoman. As series producer William Dozier wrote in a production note to Lorenzo Semple, Jr, "Let's remember we must work dames into these scripts, both for Batman and Robin, wherever feasible."

Dick Grayson was established as having girlfriends and being able to charm, however ineptly, the occasional bad girl back to the path of righteousness. But both Bruce and Batman seemed to be confirmed bachelors. In the '60s, that was a codeword for gay.

The need for someone to show that the Dark Knight did indeed like the ladies was amply filled by Julie Newmar's Catwoman. She was tall and leggy and had a figure, to quote Raymond Chandler, "to make a bishop kick out a stained-glass window." The long auburn hair and the slightest exotic slant to her eyes added to her irresistible allure. Newmar's voice was also unmistakable and invaluable to her portrayal. She could move from little girlish pout to husky seductress in seconds.

The TV version also differed greatly from the comic-book Catwoman. In the comics, Catwoman wore a demure costume that was far from daring and even had a skirt that reached below her knees! There was little cleavage visible, and even her arms were fully covered. The show provided the femme fatale with a far hotter skin-tight bodysuit. She sometimes wore a matching cat's-eye domino mask and sometimes went without. The ensemble was completed with clawed gloves, those ever-present kitty ears, and a broad, hip-hugging gold belt.

The writers imbued her with mercurial mood swings that only added to the seductive draw. What is it about an attractive woman who also happens to be crazy? She was dangerous *and* hot. A lethal combination. This feline fury could take you places you've never been before.

And the feline persona didn't begin and end with the costume. Newmar's Catwoman had a cat's personality. She was self-centered and indifferent to all but her own immediate needs. Catwoman only showed affection when she thought it would get her somewhere, and she demanded that affection be returned at her convenience. As with a cat, others existed only to serve Selina Kyle, and their needs and desires were secondary (or irrelevant) to her own.

How could Batman find some squeaky reporterette the least bit intriguing when you had *this* chick prowling the Gotham rooftops by night? They were made for each other, despite the fact that they stood on opposite sides of the law; the pair obviously had the warm mushies for each other. No matter how much he denied it, you could see Batman's longing whenever they were together. The scenes between Newmar and West are the only times we see that Batman might just have a human failing. It is only in these instances that he is clearly tempted to violate his own rigid code of behavior. You get the sense that if Bruce and Selina were allowed five minutes alone without interruption from the Boy Wonder, they might point the Batmobile toward Reno and never come back. The only thing that brings Batman back from the brink of seduction is the reminder that Catwoman is an amoral lunatic. There's no future for these crazy kids.

But Catwoman understands Batman in a way no other woman could. She doesn't question his motivations, his need to act out his naive dreams of battling crime as a reaction to a childhood trauma, or even his crazy costume. She shares the need for the buzz he gets from being a daredevil. Sure, he insists that everyone buckle up in the Batmobile, but how can a guy like this deny he digs living on the edge? It's this edge where Catwoman and Batman meet. It's where they both feel most *alive*.

In what is for me the series's most brilliant scene ("Scat, Darn Catwoman" from the second season), Catwoman swears that she could reform only with Batman's help. She goes so far as to suggest that she and Batman team up to fight crime together. The Dark Knight wavers, but when Batman asks what they'll do about Robin, Catwoman replies instantly, "We'll kill him."

The producers and writers broke through into a creative goldmine buried within the Batman legacy. Batman and Catwoman were made for each other but can never be together. This is classic stuff. Star-crossed lovers. Love denied. Eternal unrequited longing. They'll have their dalliances, their infatuations. But for each, there's only one who truly knows their heart.

This is killer stuff and it's rarely touched upon outside of a few comic stories and the second Tim Burton film. To my mind, they've always been destined for each other. I've put that notion center stage only a few times. In one, Catwoman has a fantasy about her wedding day with Batman, only to wind up beating him to death with her whip when he tries to leave their honeymoon bed to answer the Batsignal. Other times, I only hinted at it, both characters too driven by their separate demons to ever admit to how they feel about each other. It seems like this is the creative third rail of the Batman series and, as I put more distance on the years in which Batman was my day job, I regret that I wasn't allowed to explore this aspect more.

Perhaps one day, the cycle will come back around and Catwoman will take her rightful place as Batman's object of desire.

And just for the sake of completeness, Lee Meriwether's stand-in for Newmar in the Batman movie was no replacement for the original, and I found Eartha Kitt to be more frightening than anything else in her two storylines. Given the taboos on interracial relationships on TV back then, I have to wonder at that casting. But regardless of any other issue, Kitt played the role as more of a predatory female. She went too far with the kinkier side of Catwoman.

There's also a cellblock (mental ward?) full of villains that might have been perfect for the small screen but were not considered. Some are obvious. A character like Clayface would have been problematic and remained so until the later developments in CGI. Certainly, he would have been beyond the budget to a TV show in that era.

But why create the one-note Siren (played with her usual sly suggestiveness by Joan Collins) instead of introducing Poison Ivy to the series? Ivy has a fascinating premise that could easily be played up or down to suit the purposes of a story, and her costume is striking and would have translated well in real life. And like Catwoman, she holds the promise of sex. In fact, with her herbal potions, its *guilt-free* sex she's offering. But Ivy came along at the same time the show was airing, and the TV team seemed to be looking only at Batman's legacy characters.

It's easy to understand why Two-Face didn't make the jump from the funnybooks to TV. The make-up was probably considered too frightening for the early, 7:30 prime-time slot. It would also require whoever played Harvey Dent to spend many extra hours in a chair getting make-up put on his face. Those bifurcated suits would have been pricey and could only ever be used for that role. And half-assing Two-Face (pardon the pun) would have been an injustice. Certainly, the show's writers regretted this, since Two-Face's duality theme provides fertile ground for dialogue, gimmicks, gags, and other assorted business. Two-Face is a generous character for creators, and I've always found that he's one bad guy who writes himself.

Scarecrow is another recurring Bat-baddy who would have fit the show's style to perfection. His gimmick of inducing fear in his victims would have added to the frantic delirium already present in the series. And I can't be alone in imagining what Adam West might have done with the scene-chewing possibilities of a Batman paralyzed by terror. Perhaps there was a concern that he would be confused with Disney's *The Scarecrow of Romney Marsh* that would still have been fresh in viewers' minds. Or maybe the costuming was too close to *The Wizard of Oz*'s scarecrow – the classic MGM film was still shown annually on CBS at the time. Maybe no actor wanted to be hidden in the full-face sackcloth mask.

Killer Moth, despite his ridiculous name, would have been a worthy addition to the TV cast of evildoers. Although there was a short Batgirl promo film made for ABC affiliates that featured Killer Moth as the villain, it was never aired and was used primarily to trumpet the addition of Batgirl to the show's third-season cast. In his original incarnation, Killer Moth set himself up as a criminal version of Batman. He was meant to be the polar opposite of both the Dark Knight and Bruce Wayne. Cameron van Cleer was a millionaire playboy who would be the protector, rather than the scourge, of Gotham's underworld. He had his signature car (the Mothmobile), a hidden lair, and an impressive assortment of gadgets to thwart the forces of law and order. All of this was done for mercenary motivations, rather than from the goodness (or badness) of the Moth's heart. Killer Moth would use his talents and arsenal to help your criminal enterprise succeed... for a portion of your loot. A little competition for the Dynamic Duo might have made for some fun episodes. Perhaps he would have been introduced to the revolving roster of rotters, had the show continued beyond three seasons.

Hugo Strange is another early Batman foe but very much a cipher of the mad scientist character with little to recommend him. Yet another iconic villain, Gorilla Boss, would have exceeded the ludicrous factor even for a show with as dangerously a high degree of silliness as *Batman*. Calendar Man, the aforementioned Firefly, Crazy-Quilt, Kite Man, Signalman, and Tiger Shark were all shallow gimmick characters who either didn't rate a second appearance on their own or would have proven problematic to present.

The influence that the show and its portrayal of Gotham's criminal element had on me as a writer are most evident in an arc of *Detective Comics* that Graham Nolan and I collaborated on. In issues #687 and 688, Graham and I set out to tell what we saw as a classic Batman story in the mold of Bill Finger and, yes, Lorenzo Semple Jr. The story presents a new villain named Cap'n Fear (a name borrowed from an earlier DC Comics character who was the lead in a short-lived back-up feature in *Adventure Comics*, 20 years earlier). Fear was a pirate-themed badguy who talked in antiquated "yo-ho-ho" nautical phrases. His henchmen were also buccaneer types, though demonstrably less enthusiastic than their boss. In an employer / employee relationship straight out of the TV show, the moll and underlings would kiss up to their scenery-devouring skipper and try to ape his lingo. But in whispered asides to one another, they mocked Cap'n Fear. This swaggering, hyper-dramatic costumed creep played for the cheap seats with the same breathless bravura as the hams on the TV show. He was writ broad and with tongue firmly in cheek. At the same time, he was menacing and driven, and his grandiose posturing evoked as much unease as laughter.

In a direct homage to the TV version, we ended the first part of the two-parter with Batman ensnared and left to die in an "inescapable" trap. All that was missing from the conclusion was the famous "Same bat-time, same bat-channel" reference. In our story, the Dark Knight was left chained to a free-drifting marker buoy being carried further and further out to sea in shark-infested waters. He makes his escape in the second chapter and, with the aid of Robin, defeats his freebooting foes in a fight scene on the high seas.

Graham and I were pretty happy with ourselves. We not only tipped our hats to the creators of the Golden Age Batman stories we loved and admired, but we also slipped in some oh-so-subtle references to the Show.

Maybe we weren't so subtle, after all. After publication of that two-part arc our editors told us that those issues were, by far, their least favorite of all the work we'd handed in on DC Comics's flagship title. Graham and I were scolded never to do anything like them again. Their most bitter recrimination? The story was too much like – GASP! POW! – the Adam West TV show.

I personally felt like I'd been knocked on my ass into Mrs. Buckley's coat closet next to my old pal Doug.

But like all of Batman's recidivistic rogues, I'd do it again in a Gotham City minute!

May I Have this Batdance?

by Michael S. Miller

It leaps forward with an unhinged, whirling-cyclone string introduction and segues to a Duane-Eddy-on-speed guitar assault. Brass accentuates the kinetic rhythm in tuneless bursts. A "Ticket to Ride" drumroll kicks into a chanting chorus, and the production builds to a "na-na-na-na-na-na-na-na-na" climax. It lasts barely 50 seconds, but it has defined a character for more than 40 years.

As arranged by Nelson Riddle for the show's opening, Neal Hefti's "Batman Theme" benefited from its brief length, planting that propulsive bass line in the brain and exiting before the repetition wears thin. It evokes spy music, surf music and 12-bar blues in an alternatively menacing and goofy mix. The simple animated montage of the smiling Batman and Robin pummeling a legion of foes perfectly meshed with the theme's modest desires, aligning every "Sock!", "Pow!", "Zok!", "Whap!", "Biff!", and "Oooof!" with a blast of brass.

There have been thousands of pieces of instrumental music written for TV shows, but only a handful perfectly complement and encapsulate their source material. Some establish an organic connection the first time the music's notes are heard over a program's title card. The mystical, languid seduction of Angelo Baldementi's *Twin Peaks* is such a work; so is Mike Post's melancholy, determined piano theme for *Hill Street Blues*. Some theme music achieves cultural permanence through years of repeated exposure until it is inconceivable to imagine any other music in its place, and yet remains vital and exciting. Danny Elfman's rollicking, jovial theme for *The Simpsons* comes to mind, as do Lalo Schifrin's urgent title theme for *Mission Impossible* and Mark Snow's haunting theme for *The X-Files*.

Rarest of all are the themes that encompass both qualifiers: instant classic status *and* timeless relevance. Neal Hefti's title theme for the ABC series *Batman* stands astride both touchstones, sending echoes through more than 40 years of popular culture. What other theme music unites the Who, Snoop Dogg, Jan & Dean, the Flaming Lips and Eminem, and echoes in scores of records, from Cyndi Lauper's "She Bop" and R.E.M.'s "Winged Mammal Theme" to Weezer's "Hash Pipe?" What other theme music can evoke knowing, appreciative laughter on *The Simpsons* and *Family Guy* with a 10-second snippet?

The recording of "Batman Theme" won Neal Hefti a 1966 Grammy for Best Instrumental Theme, placed versions by two artists in the *Billboard* Top 40 (Neal Hefti reached No. 35 and The Marketts placed No. 17), inspired complete albums of original music and the creations of one-shot groups (The Sensational Batboys and Bruce and the Robin Rockers) and was named the fifth-best TV theme by rock critic Dave Marsh's *Book of Rock Lists*.

Serious Legacy

In its heyday, music legends as disparate as Mel Torme, Frank Zappa, Link Wray, Sun Ra and Peggy Lee would toy with the *Batman* theme, and musicians continue to be fascinated with it; Iggy Pop, The Jam and the Smithereens have all recorded it, and Prince, who would have his own 1989 dance with Bat-music, has said Neal Hefti's theme was the first piece of music he learned to play on the piano.

That is a heavy, serious legacy for such a modest composition, but equitable to the effort Neal Hefti said it took to create it.

"I tore up a lot of paper," Neal Hefti told Jon Burlingame, who wrote the 1996 book on TV show music, *TV's Biggest Hits*. "It did not come easy to me. I just sweated over that thing, more so than any other single piece of music I ever wrote. I was never satisfied with it."

"*Batman* was not a comedy," Hefti, who died in 2008 at age 85, told Jon Burlingame. "This was about unreal people. Batman and Robin were both very, very serious. The bad guys would be chasing them, and they would come to a stop at a red light, you know. They wouldn't break the law even to save their own lives. So there was a grimness and a self-righteousness about all this."

Jon Burlingame reports that it took Hefti "the better part of a month" to write the music. Burlingame said, "I was almost going to call them and say, I can't do it. But I never walk out on projects, so I sort of forced myself to finish." Hefti's "musical solution to a combined dramatic and comedic problem," Jon Burlingame writes, "was perfect: bass guitar, low brass and percussion to create a driving rhythm, while an eight-voice chorus sings 'Batman!' in harmony with the trumpets. It was part serious, part silly: just like the series."

The night the series premiered on ABC, 12 January 1966, Hal Lifson was five years old. Lifson, author of *1966! A Personal View of the Greatest Year in Pop Culture History*, said in a 3 September 2009 interview for this book that promos for the show had run for months and caught his attention. "I watched that first night," Lifson said.

> There had been nothing like *Batman*. There were old *Adventures of Superman* reruns with George Reeves, *Zorro* in reruns, the *Lone Ranger*, but no modern super-hero like Batman. It took pop art and TV to a new level; it reinvented the sitcom format as it had no laugh track like a straight family sitcom. It was existential, and existed with no apology or explanation. There was no back story for Commissioner Gordon or Chief O'Hara, no explanation for their loyalty to Batman.

Lifson credits the show's theme song for much of its pop-culture impact. "It was brilliant music, the 'Batman Theme.' What made that song was the drum beat, that go-go flavor with the chorus of women and horns mixed," Lifson said.

> It set the mood of triumph and fun. It was magical when you heard it. It was like blowing a bugle and you knew Batman would come rushing out of the Batcave. I would use the Ventures' version as the soundtrack when I played Batman with my buddies. It was great background music for capturing arch-villains and staging mock Bat-fights, which included jumping off my bed into the melee.

Lifson owned the original Neal Hefti album, *Batman Theme*, and its sequel, *Hefti in Gotham City*, which Lifson describes as a "masterpiece":

> The first album sold so well, even though it did not contain the Nelson Riddle version heard on the show, that Neal Hefti released a follow-up, *Hefti in Gotham City*, which was just a brilliant idea. It is more common today for movies or shows to have "music inspired by" soundtracks, but this was way ahead of its time. Neal Hefti wrote about the experience of living in Gotham City, expressing it through great songs and arrangements.[1]

---

[1] The iTunes service currently offers "Batman Theme and 19 Hefti Bat Songs," which combines the two albums into one package.

"That music was so cool, it inspired a lot of other cool things," Lifson said. "The Marketts, Al Hirt, Duane Eddy and many other groups recorded the theme. Jan and Dean recorded an entire album about Batman."

Lifson said a CD companion to his book, *1966! The Coolest Year in Music History!* was the first CD to contain the original Nelson Riddle TV arrangement.

In an interview for this book, rock critic Dave Marsh said, "How did the music fit with its time? Good lord, [anyone who asks that] has never heard the Who's version, all thrash and rattle and thunder, or *Jan and Dean Meet Batman*, which is one of the greatest audio comedy records ever made. Neal Hefti created a great riff, particularly a great bass line, at a time when you could humble Archimedes with the ease with which a great riff and / or bass line could move the world."

The .38 and the Gong

Helping the "Batman Theme" thunder roll was Rock and Roll Hall of Fame drummer Hal Blaine, who played on tracks with Elvis Presley, Simon & Garfunkel, the Carpenters, the Beach Boys and on more than 30 No. 1 records. Blaine sat behind the kit for Neal Hefti on his original *Batman Theme* album.

In a 14 September 2009 interview for this book, Blaine said he played drums on a number of different versions of the song, but not the Nelson Riddle-shortened TV version. "I did do the album for RCA with Neal Hefti and The Marketts version. I don't think that I did the Ventures version, but I might have," Blaine said. "I thought that I had done the TV show but my research shows I did not, unless there is a glitch there. I thought that I did because I did so much at 20th Century-Fox with Billy May and Nelson Riddle at Capitol."

Blaine said he had not seen the show before the music was recorded. "I had not seen *Batman* because I was working very late sessions through all of the Batman craze," Blaine said. "Everyone else did, though!"

Where does the "Batman Theme" fit into the legacy of the man who drummed on Frank Sinatra's "Strangers in the Night," Simon and Garfunkel's "Mrs. Robinson" and "Bridge Over Troubled Water," the Beach Boys' "Help me, Rhonda" and "Good Vibrations" and the Mamas and the Papas' "Monday Monday"?

"Batman was a stellar classic," Blaine said. "As far as fitting into my legacy, it was one of the great sort of novelty albums that I had the pleasure of doing during my fortunate career. The one thing that stands out in my mind was the huge orchestra at RCA Victor studios in Hollywood."

Blaine said he added a unique element to the Neal Hefti track. "I was on my drums and my good buddy Emil Richards was on all of the percussion instruments and toys, as we refer to them," Blane said.

> At one point I thought that some gun shots would be great as part of one of the tracks we were recording. Neil Hefti said, "Emil, got a gun?" Emil went into his trunk and came up with a starter pistol. It just gave off a small pop. It was just too soft. Finally[,] I told Neil that I had a real .38, loaded with blanks – I was licensed to carry a concealed weapon, which is a long story. Emil brought out his large gong and I shot blank wads at the right times; it came out perfectly. Everyone was delighted. It just added a realism to the song. That's sort of how I made my name in the recording business, coming up with sounds for songs. It always seemed to work for the producers. Fortunately, for me too!

The song endured one minor controversy. In his 1994 book *Back to the Batcave*, Adam West claimed the "Batman!" chants in the Nelson Riddle TV version of the theme were made by brass alone, with no chorus – he claimed the lo-fidelity recording gave the impression of voices – but this account was reportedly discounted by Neal Hefti and Nelson Riddle.

The Batusi

Of course, *Batman* also inspired its own dance, the Batusi. The Batusi Fever Web site offers these helpful instructions:

> First, take your index finger and middle finger and make a peace sign. Then turn your hands with the fingers still in place so the front of your hand is facing your face. Now draw the positioned fingers on the right hand across your eyes, with the eyes in between the positioned fingers. This should be done with the left hand and at the same time as the right hand is doing it. Now shake your ass a bit. Seriously. Do some weird things with your arms while you are shaking your ass. Only shake your ass for 5 seconds or the effect will be lost. Rub your hands downwards across your body till you reach mid-hips. Then grab both sides of your cape and twirl around for 5 seconds.

The Batusi has made myriad appearances over the years, most notably as performed by John Travolta in *Pulp Fiction* and by an animated Adam West on an episode of *The Simpsons*. It has been incorporated into dances on *Everybody Loves Raymond*, *Xena Warrior Princess*, and *Dancing with the Stars*, and was named runner-up for "Greatest TV Dance Craze" at the 2006 TV Land Awards. It lost to "The Fonzie," a dance from *Happy Days*.

Batman dances the batusi in ""Hi Diddle Riddle" (1966). Publicity still. Copyright © Greenway Productions, DC Comics, and 20ᵗʰ Century-Fox.

The 1966 Explosion of Batman Music

In the wake of the TV show's success, music provided a major element of Batmania, as both albums and singles proliferated. Almost all came from 1966, the peak of Batmania. These include the most obvious entries, Neal Hefti's *Batman Theme and 19 Hefti Bat Songs* and Nelson Riddle's *Batman Original TV Soundtrack* by Nelson Riddle, along with copious entries by bands unrelelated to the show.

Many of these other albums prominently covered Hefti's theme. The Marketts even got a whole album out of this idea: 1966's *The Batman Theme Played by the Marketts*. Their version of the theme even charted higher than Hefti's own. Jan and Dean, the group composed of the Beach Boys backbenchers, released *Jan and Dean Meet Batman* (1966), which included riffs on Hefti's theme.

No less than the Who recorded the Batman theme for its 1966 EP "Ready Steady Who." The Who's version, a mere 1:34 in length, is currently available on *A Quick One (Happy Jack)*. It avoids camp or humor and is played with punk and garage band energy, with Pete Townsend and Roger Daltrey belting out

Even the Hootenanny Hotshots want to sing about the Dynamic Duo. From the lead story in *Batman* #164 (June 1964), at the beginning of the "New Look" era. Written by France Herron with art by Sheldon Moldoff (credited as Bob Kane) and Joe Giella. Copyright © DC Comics.

"Batman!" after "Batman!" as if believing enough intensity would summon the Dark Knight in a cloud of smoke. A rumbling, thick take on the Neal Hefti classic.

Among the many other versions of the theme recorded in 1966 was the Ventures' "Batman Theme" (2:16), which 1966 buff Hal Lifson lists as his favorite. This version strips the recording to its essentials: bass guitar, surf drums and a relatively subdued female chorus chanting "Batman!" The middle of the recording features two guitar solos, one heavy with spy movie accent, one twangy and loose. It's a rare version without brass, but like the Who's take, the energy of the music makes up for the lack of horns.

Also of note, Link Wray's 1966, predictably lo-fi version (2:08) is interrupted throughout by impersonations of Batman and Robin, which distract from a

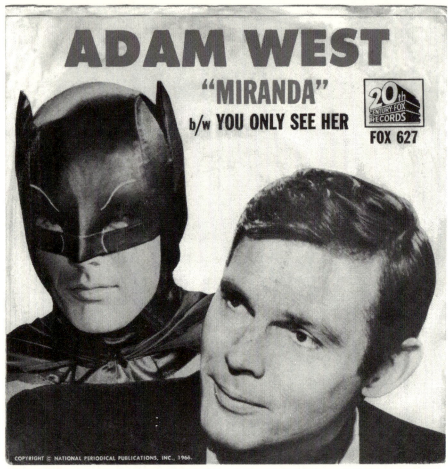

Adam West, caped crusader *and* crooner. "Miranda" single record sleeve (1966).

clever and gradually faster tempo take. No chorus chants "Batman!", but a lead guitar perfectly captures the sound.

Beyond this, 1966 also saw at least 43 other singles and six additional albums, all inspired by Hefti's theme. A full accounting of music inspired by the show more generally is open to debate and may never be made.

Some musical responses to Batmania, while incorporating Hefti's theme, were considerably more experimental. Dan & Dale, a combination of centers of Sun Ra's Arkestra and Al Kooper's Blues Project, offered the experimental, largely instrumental 1966 album *Batman and Robin – The Sensational Guitars of Dan & Dale*. Another album in this vein, although much less successful, was 1966's *Batman Theme* by the Dynamic Batmen, which incorporated electrical noise.

Adam West even got into the act himself. In 1966, he released a single, "Miranda," the lyrics of which have West, apparently as Batman, debating whether to reveal his identity to the title heroine wearing a mask.[2]

In the spirit of these recordings, producer (and Rock and Roll Hall of Famer) Frank Zappa took Burt Ward into the recording studio in June 1966 to record "Boy Wonder, I Love You," a reading of Ward's fan mail set to music Zappa wrote – after two minutes of "I love you, please come live me" recitation, Ward pauses and reads, "I hope you know this is a girl writing." A bootleg recording of that studio session, "The Boy Wonder Sessions," captures a number of stop-and-start moments, including a hideously out-of-tune Ward warbling Nat "King" Cole's "Orange-Coloured Sky." Reportedly, Zappa's widow refuses to allow these recordings to be officially released. Good for her.

Several of the above-mentioned albums remain available on CD.[3] Parental Warning: exposing your three-year-old son to any version of the "Batman Theme" will result in repeated and endless chants of "na-na-na-na-na-na-na-na-na-Batman!"

The Batgirl Theme and Later Works

After Batgirl was added to the show for the third season, she got her own theme, composed by Billy May and Willy Mack. It features a filtered-down version of Hefti's lesser themes, borrowing the chorus and brass from the main track. It appeared only twice, debuting in the episode "The Wail of the Siren." Mercifully, it appeared only once more, in a noticeably slower version in "Louie the Lilac."

Its lyrics speak for themselves:

Batgirrrl, Batgirl! Batgirrrl, Batgirl!
Where do you come from, where do you go?
What is your scene, baby? We just gotta know.
Batgirrrl, Batgirl! Batgirrrl, Batgirl!
Are you a chick who fell in from *outer space*?
Or are you real with a tender warm embrace?
Yaaa, whose baby are you? Batgirrrl, Batgirl!
Yaaa, whose baby are you? Batgirl!

---

[2] It is currently available on *Batmania: Songs Inspired by the Batman TV Series*.
[3] Please see my appendix for a track-by-track recounting.

One internet site describes the song as "the worst TV theme ever."[4] One can only imagine the difficulty in singing such a song with a straight face: "Are you a chick who fell from outer space?" actually sings better through a cheesy grin.

But the Batgirl theme does show what a remarkable achievement Hefti's original theme was. One false lyrical step away from the repeated "Batman!" chant, and we could have ended up with a theme more dreck than hip.

And even decades later, the Batman theme continues to inspire. Take, for example, R.E.M.'s "Winged Mammal Theme," a B-side on some singles from their 1992 album *Automatic for the People*, recorded when the group was the most popular band in the U.S. Although the music is much changed, the only lyric is still "Batman!"

Conclusion

When Neal Hefti died on 11 October 2008, every wire service obituary and tribute contained the word "Batman" in the first sentence. Hefti is buried at Forest Lawn Memorial Park (Hollywood Hills), which overlooks North Hollywood and Burbank in the San Fernando Valley — the same cemetery as Batman creator Bob Kane.

To the very end, Hefti's "Batman Theme" inspired praise and yet more curiously defensive prose. In his obituary, *The New York Times* wrote, "Hefti's most famous tune is among his least musically interesting, even if it was somehow brilliantly apt." Even Hefti's son, Paul, echoed this sentiment: "He had to find something that worked with the lowest common denominator, so it would appeal to kids, yet wouldn't sound stupid. What he came up with was a 12-bar blues with a guitar hook and one word."

Despite this impulse to apologize for the theme, it continues to inspire legions of Batman fans and to encapsulate a moment in time for many who experienced the TV phenomenon. Even today, the theme remains instantly recognizable; it has survived in pop culture's memory bank longer than most of its day's biggest songs. It can sum up the middle of the 1960s as well as any quote or image. It is simple but memorable, lightweight but insistent, brief but immortal. It echoes and drives with the insistence of a right hook from Batman himself. Within seconds, it evokes and summarizes every climbed wall, every

---

[4] The cleanest version of the song is posted at yvonnecraig.com. YouTube has a video version with the shapely but clad-like-a-nun Craig sitting on her Batcycle as a wind machine blows through her hair and a screen behind her shows "Gotham City" being passed at a safe and moderate speed.

Joker laugh, Riddler giggle and Penguin quack, every "Pow!" and "Biff!" and "Bam!" If you're a fan, it symbolizes the best of the TV show; if not, the worst.

The Best-Dressed Women in Gotham City

by Jennifer K. Stuller

The dance craze the Batusi is replaced by the Catusi. The Siren hypnotizes the male of the species, while girls remain impervious to her captive call. The Joker follows Catwoman's lead. Batgirl saves the day.

In Gotham City, women rule the school – or more accurately the cave, the hideout, the prison yard, and even the public library. That is, of course, when they're not otherwise busy nurturing their inborn desire to outsmart men – or so Batman claims.

Through the self-conscious use of humor and irony – components of the camp aesthetic that defined *Batman* – the series walked the line between presenting progressive women, who challenged social perceptions of gender, and reinforcing normative notions of femininity. Through three seasons, we are alternately shown women who are powerful figures, even leaders – stereotyped bad girls who just want to be loved – and independent, intelligent role models who reflected the modern girl.

As Batman put it, "What's a nice girl like you doing in a situation like this?"

Popular culture can give us insight into social mores in a given time or place. In effect, it serves as a historical record of attitudes and ideals.

Representations of women in American 1960s media were only beginning to evolve out of the repressive, heteronormative depictions of women that dominated post-War popular culture. Samantha Stephens of *Bewitched* (1964-

1972) and Jeannie of *I Dream of Jeannie* (1965-1970) may have had supernatural powers that enabled them to perform magical feats, but they were also both housewives whose transgressions (usually an exertion of their powers) generally led to trouble and the necessity to contain that power – if only to please their men. Their antics were all too reminiscent of Lucy Ricardo, that feisty wife whose zanily subversive behavior led her to frequently have to 'splain her actions to her husband Ricky on *I Love Lucy* (1951-1960).

1950s stereotypes about middle-class suburban life outgrew their usefulness as baby boomers became teenagers and young adults. In the '60s, boomers were the catalysts for an evolution of American culture that included an exciting young president in JFK, as well as the momentum of several social-justice campaigns, including civil and gay rights, as well as the youth and women's movements. The second wave of feminism was already in motion by 1963, what with the landmark publications of Helen Gurley Brown's *Sex and the Single Girl*, Betty Friedan's *The Feminine Mystique*, and Gloria Steinem's exposé on working conditions in Playboy Clubs. Additional indicators of social change included the Equal Pay Act of 1963, the Civil Rights Act of 1964, and the establishment of the Equal Employment Opportunity Commission.

Pop culture would again need to reflect the changing social landscape in order to remain relevant. Comics, film, and TV all attempted to evolve in ways more suitable to the times, while simultaneously trying not to offend those consumers who might not be happy with social changes – a conundrum navigated with varying degrees of success.

1966, the year *Batman* first aired, was a landmark one for TV roles for women. *Honey West*, one of the first TV dramas to feature a female lead in an action-adventure role, starred Anne Francis in the title role. Capable, brave, and wicked smart, Honey was the head of her own detective agency and skilled in martial arts. Her handbag carried not just the requisite gun, but also gadgets such as a lipstick microphone, radio transmitters disguised as martini olives, teargas earrings, and an exploding compact. (We would soon see similar examples of feminine subterfuge used by Catwoman and Batgirl.) And in an all-too-rare reversal of gender roles, she had a male sidekick who deferred to her authority. Unfortunately, the show only lasted through the 1965-1966 season.

British export *The Avengers* arrived in the United States in 1966 and wowed audiences with Diana Rigg's Mrs. Emma Peel (though the series had been enjoyed across the pond since 1961 and had already featured another kick-ass femme in Honor Blackman's Cathy Gale).

Actress Nichelle Nichols co-created her own landmark TV character, Lt. Nyota Uhura, with Gene Roddenberry for his *Star Trek* (1966-1969), and she was the first black woman on TV in a non-stereotyped role. Racist and sexist prejudice from network executives diminished her screen time, but not her presence's promise of the future.

But until the introduction of Batgirl in the third season, women on *Batman* generally filled one of two roles: the mother-figure or the villainess / femme fatale. (Or as in the case of Shelly Winters's Ma Parker, the villainess mother.)

She's a Woman, Robin

Dick Grayson's Aunt Harriet Cooper, who had been introduced to the comics in an effort to combat Frederic Wertham's assertions that the Dynamic Duo were in a homosexual relationship, was played on the show by veteran actress Madge Blake. The TV incarnation may have been ditzier than her comic counterpart, but in both versions, her female presence served to complete the family dynamic. You know, just your everyday nuclear family – aunt, butler, millionaire playboy, and his youthful ward.

She also provided comic relief by keeping the men of the house on their toes to protect Bruce and Dick's secret. Harriet never approached her nephew or his mentor directly about their suspicious activity, but she did venture to occasionally ask Alfred about such matters as the beeping that came sometimes from Bruce's study or why she wasn't allowed in there. (Alfred provides a crafty, if lame, excuse about how "every man likes to have a sanctuary from the opposite sex," and explains that, while "those less fortunate" – a.k.a. poor people – go to the barber shop for this purpose, Bruce, being a man of means, retires to his study. Harriet seems to buy it.)

The role of the femme fatale, villainess, or temptress, was present from the very first episode, with a go-go dancing moll named Molly, played by Jill St. John. In "Hi Diddle Riddle," Batman and Robin find their way to the What a Way to Go Go club, after solving two of the Riddler's puzzles that gave them an address. As Robin is underage and can't enter, he waits in the car while Bats checks out the scene. Batman heads to the bar and orders a large, fresh orange juice, bopping to the music and eyeing the luscious Molly all the while.

> **Molly:** Looking for a friend? Maybe you could help me? I've got a problem. Why is a quarrel like a bargain?
>
> **Batman:** Well, well. What master taught you the riddle?

Molly: The answer is, it takes two to make it. Like beautiful music. Like a dance. Shall we?

Batman: What's your name?

Molly: Molly.

Batman: You interest me, strange lady. I accept your invitation.

Together, they dance the Batusi, but Batman's orange juice has been drugged. While he's recovering, the Riddler and his gang kidnap Robin, make a mask of his face, and send a disguised Molly back to the Batcave in his stead. But Bats was hip to her plan. When Molly discovers he's disabled her weapon, she climbs on top of the Batmobile's nuclear power source. Naturally, her wicked ways are her undoing, and though Batman tries to save her, she slips and falls to her doom.

Batman: "Poor, deluded girl. If only she'd have let me save her. What a terrible way to go-go."

When all is said and done and the Riddler's scheme stopped, Bruce and Dick reflect in the sitting room at Stately Wayne Manor...

Bruce: I have only one regret in the whole affair; one thing that makes me heart-sick. [In case we can't guess, a ghost-like headshot of Molly appears for added effect.]

Dick: Molly? You kinda liked her, didn't you?

Bruce: If only I could have helped her somehow – weaned her from that tragic alliance with the underworld...

Batman has a passion for justice but also compassion for humanity. While shady ladies on the series were alternately called such inventive and gender-laden insults as "tricky little she-devil," "feline devil," "hateful hussy," "titian-haired wench," and... you get the picture, there's no doubt that Bats is drawn to the villainess. Whether this speaks to something darkly innate within himself or is a symptom of his arrogant belief that *he* can save *her* depends on the interpretation of Batman.

There were many guest villainesses throughout the series, including Joan Collins as the Siren, Anne Baxter as Zelda the Great, Carolyn Jones as Marsha, Queen of Diamonds, Ethel Merman as Lola Lasagna, Tallulah Bankhead as Black Widow, Ida Lupino as Dr. Cassandra, and Zsa Zsa Gabor as Minerva. But of course, the most famous guest villainess of all – and the one our hero tried hardest to rehabilitate – was Catwoman.

A Woman's Greatest Weapon

"The only true Catwoman is Julie Newmar, Lee Meriwether, or Eartha Kitt," Adam West said playfully in a cameo on TV's *The Simpsons*. Indeed, three different women donned the cat-eyes and kitty-ears to play the Catwoman to his Batman: Julie Newmar in the first two seasons, Lee Meriwether in the feature film, and Eartha Kitt in the third season. Each actress brought something feisty and fur-ocious to the character, but the most recognized for the role would be Newmar, whose Amazonian figure, dancer's stretches, and giggles peppered with tantalizing "meows" defined the live-action character.

Catwoman has been around almost as long as Batman, having debuted as "The Cat" in *Batman* #1 in the spring of 1940. In his autobiography, Bob Kane, who co-created the feline fatale with Bill Finger, writes, "We knew we needed a female nemesis to give the strip sex appeal. So Bill and I decided to create a somewhat friendly foe who committed crimes but was also a romantic interest in Batman's rather sterile life." Though the cat-burgling Catwoman has been many things to the Batman over the years – femme fatale, nemesis, lover – she was never intended to be entirely evil or cruel, as were other villains in the Bat-mythos. Kane felt she could appeal to both female and male readers: girls through identification and boys because they'd "appreciate a sensual-woman [sic] to look at."

Unlike Wonder Woman, who was introduced the following year, Catwoman wasn't exactly intended as a feminist role model. In fact, the blatantly chauvinistic Kane noted in his 1989 book *Batman & Me* that the character expressed what he saw as typically female behavior:

> I felt that women were feline and men were like dogs. While dogs are faithful and friendly, cats are cool, detached, and unreliable. I feel much warmer with dogs around me – cats are hard to understand, they are erratic, as women are.

Uhhhhhhhh huh.

Catwoman also served to reinforce the bond between Batman and his young ward, Robin, the Boy Wonder. Kane writes that men always feel more comfortable in the company of other men, and he claims that women need to be kept at arm's length because, as he wrote, "we don't want anyone to take over our souls, and women have a habit of doing that." (One can only *hope* Kane had a barber shop or study to protect him from too much contact with those soul-sucking X chromosomes.)

Catwoman (Julie Newmar) teaches a young admirer the "Catusi," on the set of "Hot off the Griddle / The Cat and the Fiddle" (1966). Still from William Dozier's archives. Copyright © Greenway Productions, DC Comics, and 20ᵗʰ Century-Fox.

Although a source of sexual desire and frustration, as well as a threat to the relationship between a man and his Boy Wonder, comics herstorian Trina Robbins, notes that Catwoman frequently saved Batman's life – sometimes at the risk of her own. In her book, *The Great Women Superheroes*, she observes that Catwoman was a character "very much in the tradition of Milton Caniff's

Dragon Lady, or the shady ladies of Will Eisner's comic strip, *The Spirit*, who harbor soft spots in their hearts for the hero and are never really bad."

This soft spot for the Caped Crusader was evident in Newmar's incarnation – though not at first. As Adam West notes in his 1994 autobiography, *Back to the Batcave*, "Julie felt that Catwoman should be pure evil, teasing Batman rather than actually falling in love with him."   Indeed, in her first few performances as the Catwoman, Newmar conveyed the character as maniacal, devious, and dangerous. From "The Purr-fect Crime" through "Batman Displays His Knowledge," she softens somewhat, going from man-eating tigress to naughty kitten.

Newmar, tall and graceful, her self-designed black metallic Lurex catsuit gratefully clinging to her every curve, paraded around like she owned the place. Not surprising then that when Catwoman was on the prowl it became *her* show – as evidenced by the end-of-episode reminder-to-tune-in-tomorrow's change from "same Bat time, same Bat channel" to "same *Cat* time, same *Cat* channel."

She devises deadly schemes – most involving cats, or at least the word or prefix "cat." Her tools are an array of cat-tastic cat-paraphernalia, including a cat o' nine tails and a cataphrenic.   But she doesn't do any actual fighting herself. You get the impression that it's not that she can't; rather, she's simply above it – and she has plenty of minions willing to do it for her. After several attempts to kill Batman and Robin, her romantic interest is piqued when, even after all she's done, Batman saves her life at the end of the second-season episode, "The Cat and the Fiddle."

> **Catwoman:** Batman, you saved my life!
> **Batman:** It was the least I could do.
> **Catwoman:** Batman, are you spoken for? Married? Engaged? Going steady?
> **Batman:** Hm. Em. My crime-fighting leaves me little time for social engagements.
> **Catwoman:** Boy, have I got a girl for you!
> *Batman blushes.*

From this point on, she makes it clear (if it wasn't already) that she's the "girl" in reference, and she does everything in her power just to hear Batman say the words, "Catwoman, you're under arrest."

One scheme, in "The Cat's Meow / The Bat's Kow Tow," involves stealing the voices of a popular British musical duo and then demanding ransom from the British Counsel for their safe return. By the end of the episode, Catwoman has Batman staring down the barrel of a laser gun – which we know his Bat-gadgets could easily deflect. Yet entranced by her beauty and bemused by her moxie, he allows the scene to play out, happy to have a moment alone with her:

Batman: What are you waiting for?

Catwoman: *(sultry and girlish)* Can't you see how I feel about you, Batman? How *I want you*... by my side?

Batman: It won't work, Catwoman. If you're going to kill me, you might as well get it over with.

Catwoman: I can't kill the only man that I've...

She doesn't need to finish her sentence. She lowers her weapon and tells him how to foil her diabolical plan and restore the stolen voices. He praises her ingenuity and calls her "genius." Bats is impressed – this one's got beauty and brains. But alas, she *is* under arrest.

Catwoman: *(with sweetness and trepidation)* Batman? When I get out of jail, will you take me on a date?

Batman: We'll have plenty of time to think about that, Catwoman. Several years, I'm afraid.

Catwoman: If I were to kiss you... would you think I was a *bad girl*?

Batman: *(clearly turned on)* No... of course not... Catwoman.

Just as they are about to lock lips, Robin interrupts their romantic moment. Seeing them arm in arm leads to a disgusted, "Holy Mush!"

It seems the biggest barrier to Batman's heart (other than their being on opposite sides of the law) is that damn Robin. Catwoman, who believes that "teenagers should be seen and not heard," comes up with the idea to take on a protégé to seduce – and thus distract – the Boy Wonder. In "That Darn Catwoman," she recruits Pussycat, played by singer Lesley Gore, out of the Milkshake a Go-Go for the mission. Gore, famous for her 1964 Girl Power anthem, "You Don't Own Me," is dressed head-to-toe in pink. The color emphasizes her girlishness and blossoming sexuality, just as much as Catwoman's skintight black catsuit is suggestive of a more seasoned seductress.

Catwoman: There he is, Pussycat. Do your duty.

Pussycat: He's kinda cute. Say, why'd you get me involved in this anyway, Catwoman?

Catwoman: *(playing with Pussycat's ears)* Well, Batman has his protégé, and you're mine.

Pussycat: But I'm just a rock 'n' roll singer! I'm not a crook!

Catwoman: Oh, forget it! You're 20 years old. You're over the hill. Now you just do as I tell you and scratch your way into his heart.

Pussycat manages to drug Robin with a "cataphrenic" that causes him to act like Clark Kent on Red Kryptonite — all id. He knocks out Chief O'Hara after the policeman calls Pussycat a "little banshee."

Later, Batman finds the gang hiding out at Catlair West. It's clear from the signs saying "Secret Entrance to Catlair West" and "Catwoman's in here" (the latter with an arrow, no less) that Catwoman wants him to find her. She wants to be chased. And chase her he does, straight to a rooftop. When she realizes there's no escape, she contemplates jumping into the river 100 feet below. Batman tells her there's no chance of survival.

> **Catwoman:** Anything's better than facing prison again.
>
> **Batman:** I'll do everything I can to rehabilitate you.
>
> **Catwoman:** Marry me.
>
> **Batman:** *(much too quickly)* Everything except that. A wife, no matter how beauteous or affectionate, would severely impair my crime-fighting.
>
> **Catwoman:** But I could help you in your work. As a former criminal, I'd be invaluable. I can reform! Honestly, I can!
>
> **Batman:** What about Robin?
>
> **Catwoman:** Robin!?!? *(rolls her eyes)* Oh, I've got it! We'll kill him!
>
> **Batman:** I see you're not really ready to assume a life in society.
>
> **Catwoman:** I guess you're right, Batman. Can't teach an old cat new tricks.

As Catwoman gives up one of her nine lives by jumping into the West River, Batman sheds a tear. And speaking of tears…

In "Catwoman Goes to College," Bruce Wayne helps Catwoman get out of prison and serves as her parole officer. (Since the series isn't big on continuity, we just have to accept that at some point between "Scat Darn Catwoman" and now, the Princess of Plunder has resurfaced and been arrested.) Catwoman announces that she owes her life of crime to the fact that she's a drop-out and that she's returning to Gotham City University.

As is to be expected, Catwoman is incapable of staying on the right side of the law. Atop yet another rooftop, we find her commanding her henchmen to attack the Dynamic Duo. They, of course, subdue the gang and corner her with a reprimand:

> **Batman:** You had your chance, Catwoman, but you blew it.
>
> **Robin:** You're a blot on the name of Gotham City University. When the students find out what kind of a person you really are, *they'll hate you forever*.
>
> **Catwoman:** *(beginning to cry)* Nobody loves me.

Batman: *(stiffening)* There... there... Catwoman. It'll be alright.

Catwoman: *(sniffling)* Can I use my cat-kerchief? I'm ruining my eyeshadow.

Batman: *(awkwardly)* Of course.

The Dynamic Duo are at a total loss for what to do with a crying woman and watch uncomfortably as Catwoman dries her tears. Naturally, she's staged this distraction to provide an opportunity to remove a concealed spray, armed with a drug that knocks them unconscious. "Fools!" she says. "Don't they know that tears are a woman's most effective weapon?"

In Newmar's final Catwoman adventure, "Batman Displays His Knowledge," she steals Batagonian Cat's Eye Opals with the intention of selling them on the black market. But since they are so rare, no one will buy them because they could easily be identified as hot merchandise. Catwoman then discovers the opals are fakes planted by Batman and sends him a hand-delivered message at Police Headquarters: "I'm willing to give myself up. But only to you, Batman."

She invites him to meet her at a model home at midnight and tells him to come alone. When he arrives, Catwoman struts down the stairs to greet him.

Batman: You're very beautiful, Catwoman.

Catwoman: Yes. You're quite right. I am.

Batman: Your propinquity could make a man forget himself.

Catwoman suggests they throw caution to the wind, since they're both adult human beings interested in the same thing: happiness. Batman, who has a gorgeous, brilliant, sensuous woman standing in front of him and offering to be his life partner, responds by asking her, "What about Robin?"

Moron.

Oh well, Catwoman was attempting to poison him anyway. Her henchmen jump out from their hiding places. Robin has also tagged along in secret to protect Batman from the Cat's charms. "You were taken in by her," he says. Ever the late-bloomer he adds, "But I'm too young for that sort of thing."

A fight ensues, and Catwoman tries to escape in her getaway car but can't find her keys. Batman shows up with a velvety smooth "Going my way?"

Catwoman: I wish I were, Batman. But we're fated to travel in different directions. You on the straight and narrow and me on the crooked and wide.

Batman: Catwoman, it would be so easy for you to tread the path of righteousness.

Catwoman: I'm afraid not, Batman. *(sighs)* I need what every woman needs: the love of a good man.

The villainess's potential power is contained by her affection for the hero – after all, she's usually a supporting player in *his* story. Her threat is minimized by the possibility of rehabilitation, usually through "the love of a good man," though occasionally she's subject to a self-sacrificial or even accidental death (as with Molly the moll). Newmar's Catwoman kept her feisty charm from beginning to end, but her plans end up merely being ploys to get her man's attention, rather than a criminal's desire to do any real damage.

In the third and final season, chanteuse Eartha Kitt played Catwoman. Kitt was one of the first, if not *the* first, black women to play a comic-book character on screen. With her fluency in French, Kitt's accent turned Catwoman's soft, playful meows into cat-in-heat, deep-throated, "r"-rolling purrs. Her sing-song pronunciations made every line a melodious threat that returned ferocity to the character. And she was just as sexy as her predecessors, though in a 2006 interview with *Psychology Today*, Kitt claimed she "didn't try to be sexy or anything." On NPR's *All Things Considered* in 2008, she said she didn't have to think about the role. "That's the way I am. I just went ahead and did myself." Rrrrrrrrooowwwwrrrrrr.

With Kitt in the claws, Catwoman's role as the Princess of Plunder once again took precedence over romance with Batman. She appreciated his musculature but neither desired him nor craved his desire for her – though this may have been an attempt by producers to avoid the taboos of the era. Additionally, it seemed that this Countess of Criminality seemed much more concerned with a different Costumed Crime-Fighter – one whom she must have supposed posed a much bigger threat to her devious designs.

Femininity Gave Us a Break This Time!

After the second season, with *Batman*'s initial success dwindling, the show's producers wanted to introduce a new regular female character in hope of rekindling interest. The comics had seen previous incarnations of Bat-females: Batwoman was introduced in 1956 and Bat-Girl followed in 1961. Both were removed from the comics when Julius Schwartz took over the series in 1964. Batgirl 2.0 came about only as a solution to the TV series's ratings problem. As Carmine Infantino recalls in *The Batcave Companion*:

> Billy Dozier asked for some female characters, and I had to come up with three or four characters there, and he picked two... I think I called Poison Ivy "the Crimson Rose" or something like that. Dozier loved the character Poison Ivy. He was going to use her on the TV show but didn't. I don't know what the hell happened with that... And he picked the Batgirl. In

fact, this Batgirl character had no ears on her at the time I first drew her. I remember Dozier then said, "Put ears on her. Make her Batgirl."

The new Batgirl – a different entity from the previously titled character – was introduced in the comics several months before her first TV appearance.

Comic-book representations of women in the 1950s and '60s had been just as bad as those of TV. In the '40s, Wonder Woman had been an advocate for women's independence, and in a reversal of gender norms, she rescued her male love interest, Steve Trevor – a man she rejected in favor of duty. But in the '50s, Wonder Woman's covers showed her in more appropriately feminine roles. One image depicted her as a romance editor. Another showed her being carried across a stream by Steve – as if it'd be abhorrent to get her dainty, *Amazon* feet wet. "Wonder Women of History," a feature that had appeared regularly in her comics, was replaced with another that documented wedding customs across the globe.

Lois Lane, once a saucy, snarky reporter who fought to be treated equally in the workplace (instead of being relegated to "women's news") had received her own comic book in 1958. But as the title made clear, she was *Superman's Girl Friend, Lois Lane*. Generally, Lois's stories involved attempts to trick Superman into marrying her and fights with other women over his affections. In two of her issues from the mid-1960s (#70 & 71), Lois is hypnotized by Catwoman into thinking she is the Princess of Plunder – so that Lois will take the fall for the villainess's crimes. When Lois recovers her memory and finds that Superman has been turned into a Super-Cat, she tells Catwoman, "You'll need a cat's nine lives before I'm through with you!" They bare their claws at each other, and the teaser for the continuation of the tale reads: "Coming up – the cat fight of the century!"

In 1966, the same year that the National Organization for Women was founded, DC Comics' *Brave and the Bold* #63 printed a story called "Revolt of the Super-Chicks," in which Supergirl and Wonder Woman shirk their responsibilities as crime-fighters and run off to Paris to model high fashion and make out with French men. Even though the "chicks" do return to crime-fighting, the not-so-subtle message is that, given the opportunity, women will quickly abandon independence and heroics in favor of stereotyped female desires such as romance and shopping.

In "The Million Dollar Debut of Batgirl" (*Detective Comics* #359, Jan 1967), we meet the unassuming Barbara Gordon, daughter of Police Commissioner Gordon, sewing the finishing touches on her "Batgirl" costume for that evening's Policemen's Masquerade Ball. Barbara, a professional librarian who's tired of being seen as a "Plain Jane" and a "colorless female brain," hopes people will see her as a "far more imposing girl" in her Bat-garb. (In a bit of post-adolescent rebellion, she also hopes to give her stuffy Daddy a shock.)

Sadly, Babs, who has a Ph.D. from Gotham State University and a brown belt in judo, thinks this night will supersede those accomplishments to become the highlight of her life. Serendipitously for her, she stumbles upon an incident that proves to be an awakening.

In her costume (not yet a disguise for her identity) and on the way to the ball, Barbara Gordon encounters Killer Moth and his henchmen attacking Bruce Wayne's car. Without thinking twice, she springs to his aid. "Make a run for it, Mr. Wayne – before you get hurt! *Batgirl* will handle these human moths!" Barb proceeds to kick ass – throwing puns left and punches right: "Her eyes sparkle! Her breath comes faster! Her heart thumps with alarming speed! Babs Gordon is having the time of her life – fully alive to this new excitement and danger – and loving it!"

The following day, Barbara is lost in thoughts of the previous night's fantastic events. She decides to repair the tears in her costume and starts training in the basement storeroom of the library where she works in order to keep herself in fighting shape. When dropping off a book one evening at Wayne Estate, Babs hears gunshots. Peering in the window, she sees Killer Moth hovering over what appears to be Bruce Wayne's dead body. She quickly changes into her new alter ego, Batgirl, and attempts to bring down the villains. Though well-intentioned, she soon discovers that Batman and Robin had staged the event to capture Killer Moth and that her interference had cost them this.

As Batman and Robin run after him, Batgirl insists on accompanying them. "No, *Batgirl*!" says Batman. "This is a case for *Batman* and *Robin*! I'm sorry – but you must understand that we can't worry ourselves about a girl…"

"*Hah!*" thinks Batgirl. "If they think they can cut me off from where the action is, they're mistaken!" She ends up saving the Dynamic Duo, but instead of thanking her or encouraging her pursuit of crime-fighting, Batman informs her that he "*could* have escaped – and was about to when you appeared – by firing my laser torch."

And here we all thought it was Superman who could be a real dick.

But then, in the very next panel, Batman tells Commissioner Gordon that he'd welcome Batgirl's aid any time, adding that, from what he's seen of her work, "She doesn't have to take a back seat to anybody!" In the final panel,

Gordon sings Batgirl's praises to his daughter Barbara, adding, "*Harrumph!* Too bad *you* couldn't be a little more *like* her, Babs!"

As Michael Eury and Michael Kronenberg rightly observe in *The Batcave Companion*,

> It's unlikely that Schwartz and Fox, winking at the audience as they tacked on an 'If Dad only knew!' coda, were aware of how insulting Gordon's remark was to Barbara, particularly since this is the first time the two characters were seen together as father and daughter.

Obviously, over at DC, there was some confusion over female identity, desire, and power. This complete lack of understanding of femininity rears its ugly head again and again in Batgirl's appearances with the Dynamic Duo. On the one hand, she's brave, skilled, and independent. She's shown as innovative and a thorough researcher with a photographic memory. She has an education, a career, and a desire to better the world.

On the other hand, there's "Batgirl's Costume Cut-Ups" from *Detective Comics* #371 (Jan. 1968). The introduction alone should warn us to the sexism ahead: "When is a woman a woman? Every moment of the day – and night! Even *Batgirl* during her most hectic moments – when she is battling criminals – is always conscious of her appearance!"

While Julie Newmar's Catwoman manipulated the trappings of femininity to her advantage, the comic-book Batgirl was continually thwarted by her feminine vanity. Throughout this story, a superficial idea of what constitutes femininity serves as a detriment to Batgirl's crime-fighting efforts. While fighting criminals, she stops to adjust her headpiece so that it's centered, and the crooks get away. Upset that her vanity betrayed her, she sets out to prove that she can overcome her feminine instincts by sheer concentration. As she reasons, "It wasn't personal vanity that made me adjust my headgear – it was an instinctive female reaction!" Yet as the story continues, these "instincts" continue to handicap Batgirl. She screams like a girl and alerts criminals to her presence. She wipes mud off her face and allows more crooks to escape. She resolves that she *will* be "a *crook*-catcher first – and a *glance*-catcher second."

On her next night out on patrol, she rushes to Batman and Robin's aid, then suddenly slides to a halt and lifts her leg to examine it.

Robin: *Batgirl*, get over here! *Help us!* We've got a problem!

Batgirl: I have a bigger one – *a run in my tights!*

Crime-fighting girls are so silly. But her frivolity pays off! As she studies the tear in her leggings, the criminals Batman and Robin are fighting are distracted

A tear in her tights puts the Dominoed Dare-Doll in danger of becoming a stereotype, in "Batgirl's Costume Cut-Ups!" from *Detective Comics* #371 (Jan 1968). Art by Carmine Infantino and Murphy Anderson. Copyright © DC Comics.

by her "gams" (yes, the word "gams" *was* used – and *not* ironically). The Dynamic Duo take advantage of the diversion and smash their assailants appropriately. Robin exclaims, *"Batgirl's* femininity gave us a break this time!"* Batman later praises her, "You see, *Batgirl?* That was one time where you turned a feminine trait to your advantage – and the disadvantage of the criminals!"

Holy sexism, Batman!

To top it off, it seems Babs purposely tore her tights to give her an excuse for showing off her legs and distracting the crooks, in order to prove that, while her feminine weakness had often betrayed her in the past, it had its strong points too. Compared to the TV Catwoman, Catwoman is aware of her feminine power from the get-go – and embraces it. Babs considers it a weakness when it concerns her "instinctual vanity" but an asset when it's an intentional use of her sexuality. It almost seems hard to believe that, as the editors of *The Batcave Companion* claim, Batgirl was the strongest female character to have emerged at that time "from the desk of old-school editor Julie Schwartz." (But this is also coming from an era when Wonder Woman gave up her Amazon gifts and opened a clothing boutique.)

Though both the comic-book and TV versions of Batgirl were presented as physically and intellectually capable, the TV incarnation was less burdened with stereotypes. In fact, on the TV show, the *men* more often came off as one-dimensional, and their preconceived ideas about women were played as a joke.

You are No Longer Alone, Caped Crusaders!

In 1967, a short presentation reel was filmed for advertisers to generate interest in the show. It featured Yvonne Craig, a former ballet dancer, in the cowl, cape, and titian wig. Barbara is working at the library when the villainous Killer Moth and his henchmen attack patrons Bruce Wayne and Dick Grayson. The henchmen grab Barbara and lock her in a room. The young woman calmly turns around and relocks the door from the inside, walks into a secret closet, and soon remerges in a purple suit, ready for action.

"Holy Transformation!" exclaims the narrator. "Batgirl, modeled after her idol, Batman. Ready for this crucial moment and off to make her first foray in her own beautiful and beguiling way through her secret exit."

Barbara, now disguised, climbs onto the fire escape to stage her dramatic entrance. Kicking in the window, she shatters glass to make a "smashing entrance." Arms akimbo, she announces, "I'm Batgirl! You are no longer alone,

Caped Crusaders!" – then proceeds to kick moth ass with a bevy of "Boff!"s, "Zlopp!"s, and "Zlonk!"s.

According to Adam West in *Back to the Batcave*, ABC had originally considered having a Batgirl spin-off series, "which would have run before ours, with Robin and me helping to wrap up a case begun on her show. But visions of NBC's failed *Girl from U.N.C.L.E.* two years earlier danced in their heads, and they gave her to us instead."

Changes were made to Batgirl between the aforementioned short and the resulting TV version. In the short's script, "Batgirl was quite a flirtatious character – very loose, witty, and much less straight-laced. But," West writes, "changes were made based on feedback we got from potential sponsors (women were not quite liberated, yet), and Batgirl ended up more stolid than Yvonne wanted."

Still, with the exception of the (cancelled) Honey West, (the underused) Lt. Nyota Uhura, and (the imported) Mrs. Emma Peel, there wasn't a female character on TV at the time like Batgirl, who was first seen by the public in the third-season premiere, "Enter Batgirl, Exit Penguin." Barbara Gordon had a Ph.D. and her own mid-town apartment in a big city. She was even successful enough to not need to share her flat with a roommate. She wasn't married – and unlike some of her TV contemporaries, her actions were not contained by any man. She's a modern girl, with access to modern technology that must have made her entry to crime-fighting seem natural.

Babs has a secret room with her Batgirl garb, gear, and all sorts of Batgirl-gadgets, including an electronic compact, antidote pills, and an anti-eavesdrop plug. She has a library prowler alarm system by her bedside and keeps a Batgirl bike in a secret freight elevator (Craig rode the bike herself). When she arrives on the scene, you get the impression that she's been preparing for this for quite some time.

Batgirl is an ass-kicker who impresses even Robin, who upon seeing her in action exclaims "Holy Agility!" In fact, the petite redhead is such a powerhouse that Catwoman moves from arching Batman to engaging Batgirl as her nemesis.

In "The Catwoman's Dressed to Kill," Eartha Kitt's Catwoman is crashing an awards luncheon, at le Maison du Chat, for the Ten Best Dressed Women of Gotham. An extra category has just been created, called the "Batty," for the Best-Dressed Crime-Fightress in Gotham City. The first recipient is Batgirl. Commissioner Gordon and Chief O'Hara accept on behalf of her. Gordon declares that "this award goes to prove there *is* room for style – even in crime fighting," just as Catwoman arrives with her henchmen.

> **Catwoman:** You ladies with your fancy hairdos, what do you know about beauty? After you suffer the effects of my hair-raising bomb, you will never be able to raise your heads in public again. Then we'll see who's the fairest of them all!
>
> **Lady:** No! Not our hair! Anything but that!

When the story of the day's events is relayed to Barbara Gordon, she says, "Ruined their hair forever! Catwoman *really* knows a woman's weak spot." Barb suggests that the way to catch Catwoman would be to use Batgirl as bait – an idea Batman immediately rejects. "I wouldn't dream of endangering that fair lady's head. No," he says, "better leave the crime fighting to the men."

Batman, of course, doesn't realize that he's talking to Batgirl in her alter ego – but would it make a difference if he did? Just as women on the show teeter back and forth between female empowerment and female stereotype, men walk a fine line between chivalry and chauvinism.

Catwoman's plan is to steal the Golden Fleece. She explains it's "the single most valuable piece of clothing in creation. It's a million dollars worth of 24-carat gold cloth, all woven into one gorgeous garment." But she doesn't want it for herself; rather, she's exploiting other women's desires. The gown belongs to Queen Bess of Belgravia and is considered a national treasure. Catwoman intends to sell it back to Belgravia at an inflated price.

Soonafter, Catwoman crashes a fashion show intending to steal the one-of-a-kind garments to add to her personal collection. But the Dynamic Duo arrives as well.

> **Catwoman:** Let no one say that Catwoman is not the best-dressed woman in the world.
>
> **Batman:** There are no fashion shows where you're going, Catwoman.
>
> **Robin:** How can a feline villainess like you also be a fashion model!?
>
> **Batman:** Uh-uh. Credit where credit is due, Robin. She may be evil, but she is attractive. You'll know more about that in a couple of years.

Catwoman distracts the men while her henchmen capture them in a net. Catwoman laments the presence of Batgirl, who quickly arrives on the scene. Batgirl rescues the Caped Crusaders, as Catwoman makes her escape. Batman, upset that Batgirl found out about the event, informs her that "We can fight our own battles!" (A "thank you" might have been nice.)

Batgirl is kidnapped by Catwoman and placed on a giant seam cutter. (Batman arranges to have a disguised Alfred save her.) Catwoman steals the gown, and when Batman and Robin arrive to foil her plan, she is simply amused. But when Batgirl shows up, she hisses at her, making it clear that capturing Batgirl would have been a bigger prize. It may not be much, but it's a far cry from the comics, in which Catwoman tries to destroy Batgirl because she fears she's a rival to Batman's affections.

While ideas about gender and power were certainly muddled on *Batman*, it could be argued that the series was self-conscious enough to perhaps subvert gender stereotypes by playing into them.

For example, Batman repeatedly tells Batgirl that he can fight his own battles, but she continues to show up and save them. Occasionally, he'll express some gratitude, as in "The Sport of Penguins." Afterward, she jokes that she knew their whereabouts because she has the one thing Batman couldn't have in his utility belt – a woman's intuition.

It's a joke because her femininity had nothing to do with it – a fact she'd tried to make clear before, in "Ring Around the Riddler." When the Riddler leaves behind a blinking metal box in Gotham Square Garden, Batgirl brings it promptly to police headquarters for examination. Batman tells her, "It's lucky you were in the vicinity of Gotham Square Garden." "Yes," she replies. "'Luck' is an important weapon to a woman crime fighter, Batman." She looks for a reaction, but the comment flies right over his head. Batgirl didn't need luck or intuition, because she had smarts and training. She was no one's girlfriend, and unlike Robin, no one's sidekick either.

As Yvonne Craig told *Femme Fatales* magazine (in the December 1998 edition), "I meet young women who say Batgirl was their role model. They say it's because it was the first time they ever felt girls could do the same things guys could do, and sometimes better. I think that's lovely."

Batgirl would remain an emblem of female empowerment after the series was cancelled. In the early 1970s, Craig reprised her role as the Dominoed Dare Doll in a Public Service Announcement for the U.S. Department of Labor. In the short, Batman and Robin are tied up in a warehouse with a time bomb about to explode when Batgirl arrives. Batman calls out, "Quick, Batgirl! Untie us before it's too late." She calmly, yet firmly, replies, "It's already too late. I've worked for you a long time and I'm paid less than Robin. Same job, same employer means equal pay for men *and* women."

Robin: Holy Discontent!
Batman: No time for jokes, Batgirl.
Batgirl: It's no joke. It's the Federal Equal Pay Law.

    Robin: Holy Act of Congress!

Holy Act, indeed! The Equal Pay Act had been passed over a decade before. In a short version of the PSA, Batgirl closes by saying, "If you're not getting equal pay, contact the Wage and Hour Division, U.S. Department of Labor." And instead of untying them, *she* defuses the bomb.

The Best-Dressed Women in Gotham City

    Catwoman also was (and like Batgirl remains) a symbol of female power. Suzanne Colon, author of *Catwoman: The Life and Times of a Feline Fatale*, has noted that "this was one of the first female characters we saw on TV that really spoke to empowerment. Not only empowerment; a proto-feminism that was very sexy and pretty and female, and yet very take-charge." She adds, "This woman had her own gang of men who wore little cat ears and striped shirts to please her. Knowing that she was the boss."

    Catwoman and Batgirl were proto-feminists at best, but they were far more independent and empowering than many of their contemporaries – as well as their comic-book counterparts. Not only were they two of the most progressive representations of women on TV in the late 1960s, but they were also the best-dressed women in Gotham City.

"Holy Contributing to the Delinquency of a Minor!": Youth Culture in *Batman*

by Michael D. Hamersky

Night falls across Gotham City. Children wait with bated breath for the next episode of *Batman*. But is it actually a wicked Establishment trap to trick the young into listening to the platitudes of their parents?! Will the young fall victim to the patronizing schemes of the show's creators? Or will they escape in time? Tune in to this chapter to find out...

Robin, the teenage half of the Dynamite Duo, represented America's youth. How he was portrayed, how he was treated, and how his character was elevated from comic-book sidekick to TV co-star clearly demonstrated the desire of the *Batman* producers to capture the youth audience.

Prior to this ABC TV show, there really hadn't been many super-heroes on primetime TV. Of course, there was *The Adventures of Superman*, but that had first been televised years earlier, from 1952 to 1958. The youth of the 1960s saw it only in reruns.

Batman was the only primetime show other than *Peyton Place* to be broadcast twice in one week. It aired at 7:30 p.m. (Eastern) Wednesdays and Thursdays, early enough for even the youngest viewers. But *Batman* had to appeal on at least two levels. For young viewers, it played as an actual live-action comic book. "Zap!", "Pow!", "Bam!" and other socko words were splashed across our TV screens as the fighting broke out between Batman and Robin and the villains with their henchmen.

But to attract and hold the interest of the adults in the household, which was key in those days when most homes had only one TV, villains and their sidekicks were portrayed by popular guest actors easily recognizable to the adults in the audience. Movie, stage, and TV stars like Ethel Merman, Steve Allen, and Gypsy Rose Lee each had guest roles or cameo appearances in the series. Even a young Joan Collins, playing the very adult role of the Siren, vamped her way through a couple of episodes, long before her *Dynasty* days.

To further interest the older viewers, the writers played up the so-called "camp" aspect, using humor that zinged over the heads of the younger audience. I was a little too young to totally understand the show's "cheekiness." While interested in the villains and the molls, I almost completely missed the tongue-in-cheek satire that I appreciate today when re-watching the series.

The *Batman* TV show could be enjoyed by the entire family. By 1966, the generation gap was growing between the baby boomers and their parents. Control of the only TV set in the house was just one area that could cause friction in households of that era. What better way to ensure a solid viewership than by trying to please both generations in the same household?

While trying to keep the peace for the sake of ratings, *Batman* was clearly aimed at younger viewers. That said, the show made a valiant yet misguided attempt to portray youth and the counter-culture of the '60s in several different areas.

Holy Keystone Cops!

In the *Detective Comics* version of Batman, Bruce Wayne's parents were killed by a violent criminal, thus providing the motivation for his emergence as a crime-fighting super-hero as an adult. Amazingly, the TV show never touched on Batman's origin beyond the pilot episode and rare references to the Wayne family. This was probably because Bruce Wayne's parents were killed in cold blood in front of Bruce when he was only a small boy – not exactly the kind of scene parents would want their youngsters to see on TV in 1966. Remember that Batman was created back in 1939, during an era of gangsters and molls, which fit perfectly in the hard-hitting stories that were published in those days.

Unlike the grim and gritty portrayal of Batman that became dominant in his 1970s comics, most of the TV episodes were filmed during daylight hours. Thus, this series was quite unlike the dark and sinister Gotham City of the later comic books where psychotics roamed, terrorizing the citizenry.

Whereas the Batman in the early comic books was a vigilante, in the TV series he is a "duly deputized officer of the law." Batman really took this to heart, as seen in this civics lesson he gives the young Robin in 1966's "Hot Off the Griddle":

> **Batman:** *(seeing Robin is not going to feed the parking meter where they've parked the Batmobile)* Better put five cents in the meter.
> **Robin:** No policeman's going to give the Batmobile a ticket.
> **Batman:** This money goes to building better roads. We all must do our part.
> **Robin:** Holy taxation, Batman! You're right again!

At the end of "Rats Like Cheese," Robin asks why the police took so long in getting to where the action was. Chief O'Hara replies that they "took a wrong turn on Route 49," which seemed to satisfy Robin, strangely enough. This wasn't the only time the coppers were late to the scene. At the end of "Batman Stands Pat," Chief O'Hara tells Batman, "We had a devil of a time finding this place!" Just how large and confusing of a city was Gotham that the *Chief of Police* couldn't find where he was supposed to go?

As a kid, I didn't understand why the police were shown to be so ineffective, but I now understand it was a nod and a wink to the youthful rebellion of the time. Whereas the police had been shown as effective and fair enforcers of the law in early TV shows such as *Dragnet*, by 1966 the police were more widely called "cops" or even "pigs" and other such names of derogatory nature. The writers of *Batman* didn't go as far as name-calling, but they showed that the police force wasn't as effective as the public had been led to believe in earlier TV shows. And in doing so may have appealed to the youngsters of the time.

Holy I'm Totally Hip!

Both Robin, the Boy Wonder, and Dick Grayson, young ward of Bruce Wayne, expressed the exuberance common to youth culture of the time. Burt Ward always expressed surprise or wonderment at what was happening to him. His enthusiastic delivery added the exclamation marks common to comics dialogue. He was 21 when he began playing a high-school-age Boy Wonder.

But his exuberance and neophyte status in show business helped lend him an air of "golly-gee-willikers" that helped us believe he was younger than his true age.

Robin used a total of 352 "Holy...!" expressions throughout *Batman*'s 120 episodes – and one more ("Holy Sardine!") in the theatrical film (a shark was circling him and Batman). The very first, in the show's first episode, was "Holy Barracuda!" These expressions were typically tied to the circumstances. In "Fine Feathered Finks," Robin exclaims "Holy Popcorn!" in response to a movie star possibily being in trouble. During the same episode, when stuck to the wall with Batman by a Penguin magnet, Robin exclaims, "Holy Flypaper, what a fix!" In "Instant Freeze," when the Batmobile won't start because of Mr. Freeze icing the car, Robin says, "Holy Snowballs!" – and exclaims "Holy Iceberg!", when referring to Mr. Freeze. These expressions could easily cross from funny to painful. Take "Holy Ravioli!" when Robin hears an Italian opera playing in "The Joker is Wild."

There's little sign that any kids adopted "Holy...!" as part of their everyday speech. The youth did use (and overuse) slang, especially "fab" words to signify liking something. Those words would later be adopted by TV and comics. Unfortunately, by the time adult writers picked up on these words and put them into publications, the words had often already become stale. Holy behind the times!

Watching the show's producers and writers try to co-opt the day's "hip" slang could grate on the ears. Sometimes, seeing older people trying to be "hip" in the show was somewhat funny at times for the younger viewers. Aunt Harriet dancing the "Catusi" at stately Wayne Manor was funny to see, but watching the dancers at Catwoman's Pink Sandbox in "Hot Off the Griddle" with Batman trying to fit in with the crowd was even funnier.

Viewing those quite older actors sporting "mod" gear in the series pointed out exactly how hard the producers were trying to win the loyalty of the older viewers while simultaneously appealing to the young viewers. Cabala, played by Howard Duff, kept throwing in "groovy, groovy" so annoyingly often in "The Entrancing Dr. Cassandra." The same episode uses slang such as "Cool it, love, we don't want to blow the scene." With those phrases coming from obviously much older people – well, let's just say this didn't come across so well to the youth of the time.

Although he would try to be "cool" in several episodes of the show, Dick Grayson was obviously also brought up to be polite. Try as he might, he was

A youthful Robin (Burt Ward) stands as an example for young men everywhere. Publicity still (1966). Copyright © Greenway Productions, DC Comics, and 20th Century-Fox.

not truly rebellious.   His politeness often came through after his youthful enthusiasm briefly took over.   For example, in "Rats Like Cheese," Princess Sandra asks Dick how he was feeling; he quips, "Better – like real cool, ma'am. I mean, your Highness."

Robin's language often attempted to be "hip," as in "Hi Diddle Riddle," when Robin tells the Riddler, "You flipped your lid!" In the same episode, Robin phrases even attempts to be modest as "Aw gee, it was nothing, Batman!" However, phrases such as "Golly, Batman!", in "A Riddle a Day Keeps the Riddler Away," came across as a tad old by that time. It didn't let up by "The Thirteenth Hat," where Dick uses "Gosh!" in an exclamation. Make up your mind, Robin!

Regretfully, normally staid Batman gets into the "hip" act – or tries to – when he says of the Riddler's moll, Molly, falling into the Batcave's nuclear pile: "What a terrible way to go-go!" But since that was in the pilot episode, we can forgive him. More unforgivable (but somewhat funny) is when Batman wants Robin to be the one to act as intermediary with the young hippie-looking people in "Louie the Lilac":

> **Batman:** Go back outside and calm the flower children.
> **Robin:** They'll mob me!
> **Batman:** Groovy.

In that episode, Batman seems to sense that Robin was torn between being a square and a "mod." He later tells his sidekick, "You're far from mod, Robin. And many hippies are older than you are."

Even more out of touch with the youth of the time, Batman used words for Robin that you would typically hear older English gentleman say about each other: "old chum," "old man," and "old friend." These were used so often in the early episodes that they quickly wore thin.

Holy United Nations!

In many episodes, Bruce Wayne seemed highly concerned about teaching Robin about international relations.   This often came up when foreign dignitaries visited Gotham City – which seemed to occur frequently. Typically, the reason Batman wanted to solve the crime at hand was to preserve our international relations with some made-up country.

Writer Stanley Ralph Ross was ahead of his time when he wrote this exchange in the third season's "Catwoman's Dressed to Kill":

> **Batman:** *(gravely)* Nobody wants war.

Robin: *(brashly)* Gee, Batman. Belgravia's such a small country. We'd beat them in a few hours.

Batman: Yes, and then we'd have to support them for years.

As guardian to Dick Grayson, Bruce took every opportunity to make sure Dick studied so he would be adequately prepared to further our country's international relations. Witness this exchange when Dick complains about learning a foreign language at the beginning of an episode:

Dick: Aw, heck! What's the use of learning French anyway?

Bruce: Dick, I'm surprised at you! Language is the key to world peace. If we all spoke each other's tongues, perhaps the scourge of war would be ended forever.

Dick: Gosh, Bruce, yes. I'll get these darn verbs if they kill me!

In another scene, Bruce takes the opportunity to teach Dick a lesson in geography *and* international relations:

Dick: I thought Lima was the capital of Ecuador.

Bruce: As you can see, I was right. It's the capital of Peru.

Aunt Harriet: Oh, I just love this game of capitals. It's just so educational!

Bruce: Not only that; if we don't know all about our friends to the south, how can we carry out our good neighbor policy?

Our world wasn't the only place Batman wanted to have good relations with. He even wanted good *interplanetary* relations, as seen in "The Joker's Flying Saucer." As Batman says, "It is the duty of every good citizen of Gotham City to report meeting a man from Mars in a public park."

Holy Homework!

Most kinds complain about homework. But in his downtime from fighting crime as Robin, Dick always had his head in a book – with Bruce Wayne close by supervising his studies. Robin's home life was all work and no play. It's as if the show's patronizing producers wanted to teach kids the value of studying, despite its actual low priority among youths.

Although *Batman* was clearly aimed at young people, the show creators didn't know much about appealing to youth. 1960s counter-culture told the young not to trust anyone over 30. Naturally, this put the youth at odds with teachers and parents. But not Dick Grayson.

Apparently, school was very important to Dick; he was always learning, even in his role as Robin. When Batman figures out an answer to a question using geometry, in "Batman Sets the Pace," Robin says, "I'll never neglect my math again!" In "While Gotham City Burns," Batman saves Robin, who's tied to the clapper of the Wayne Memorial Clock Tower timepiece. Batman then explains how he did so: like electrical charges repel each other, so the clapper and the bell were made to repel each other, saving Robin. Another lesson learned by our school-loving young hero.

In the opening of "Hot Off the Griddle," Bruce is helping Dick with more science, offering advice: "Don't look directly into the lens. It will cause damage to the retina of the eyes." Obviously, this was Batman's own patronizing version of "You'll shoot your eye out, kid."

Speaking of clichéd adult advice, there's always grammar. In "The Cat and the Fiddle," Batman tells Robin, "Good grammar is essential, Robin!"

Studying a foreign language was also part of Dick's itinerary. However, instead of learning to speak Spanish or French, in "Fine Finny Fiends," Bruce asks Dick to "put your Latin verbs away." With no real complaint from him, he definitely was not a rebel when it came to schooling.

Batman also echoed the establishment view that successful people finished school – and that people who didn't wouldn't make it very far in life. Many of the show's villains had backgrounds that highlighted a lack of schooling. For example, in "When the Rat's Away, the Mice will Play," when the Riddler's moll Mousey was revealed as a "bad girl," it was said to be because she was a high-school dropout.[1]

Bruce is so serious about school as the key to success or reform that, in "Catwoman Goes to College," we discover that he is also on the prison parole board.[2] Catwoman is granted a parole, approved by Bruce Wayne. The reason she is granted a parole? Turns out she was a college dropout and wanted to go back to Gotham City University.

Batman's role as teacher also extended to lecturing Robin more generally on American civics. In "The Unkindest Tut of All," Batman says, "Robin, the Constitution provides that a man is innocent until proven guilty. And the Constitution is the cornerstone of our great nation. We must abide by it."

---

[1] She wasn't given the chance to redeem herself at the "Wayne Foundation for Delinquent Girls," which we learn about in the following week's "Batman Stands Pat." Or reformed by the "Bruce Wayne Rehabilitation Fund," like Blaze was at the end of "Holy Rat Race." Some bad girls are more deserving of sympathy than others, apparently.

[2] In "Fine Finny Fiends," we're told that Bruce Wayne's great-grandfather founded Yale University's "Skull & Bones," a so-called "secret society." So education runs in his family.

In "True or False-Face," Dick is seen reading the "Book of Nature" for his studies. Bruce and Dick were even having a discussion about it before Alfred came in to the room:

> **Dick:** Gosh, botany is tough. I'll never learn to recognize all these trees!
>
> **Bruce:** Come, come, Dick. Pine, elm, hickory, chestnut, maple. Part of our heritage is the lure of living things, the storybook of nature.
>
> **Dick:** That's true, Bruce. I'll learn to read that book of nature yet!

Bruce's also lectures about botany in "Louie the Lilac," when the Dynamic Duo is caught by Louie the Lilac's plants. "Man-eating lilacs have no teeth, Robin," Batman teaches. "It's a process of ingestion through their tentacles." Well, holy homework, Batman — thanks for the education. Talk about your single-minded educators.

Holy After School Special!

The moralizing of the infamous *After School Special* series of TV movies had a forerunner in *Batman*. Hardly an episode went by that Batman didn't teach Robin, the symbol of America's youth, an important civic or moral lesson.

In the third-season opener, "Enter Batgirl, Exit Penguin," we see Dick Grayson coming out of the Department of Motor Vehicles with Bruce Wayne. Dick has just passed his driving test on his birthday, so Bruce proceeds to tell Dick that Robin is now legally allowed to drive the Batmobile. This was kind of funny, considering we had seen Robin driving the Batmobile a few times before; in fact, he first did so in the very first episode. So much for Batman's law-abiding nature.

As an added bonus for passing the driving test, Bruce has a new car waiting outside the DMV as a birthday gift for Dick. Yet even at that moment, Bruce can't help himself from moralizing. As they step into the car, He says to Dick, "Remember, this is not the Batmobile, Robin. Highway safety is everyone's responsibility!" This sounds like Batman is excusing the Batmobile's wreckless driving.

Batman's moral instruction often carried a tone of talking down to Robin. When Robin is going to cross the street in "Fine Finny Fiends," he doesn't stop before attempting to cross. Batman yells out, "Always look both ways!"

This sometimes reached absurd heights. In "Ring Around the Riddler," Dick exclaims how good the camel grass juice is. Bruce warns, "Beware of strong stimulants, Robin." Drugs were part of the counter-culture scene during the sixties, but this was never directly addressed in the TV series.

In another patronizing example, in "Walk the Straight and Narrow," Commissioner Gordon admonishes Robin to "tell Batman to eat all his vegetables!" That was certainly odd to hear, coming from the Commissioner of Police of a major metropolis to a "duly-deputized officer of the law."

The importance of good personal hygiene also came up. In "The Riddler's False Notion," Batman uses a Batrope to save Robin, and the Boy Wonder clamps onto the Batrope with his teeth. His comment afterwards? "Holy Molars! Am I glad I take care of my teeth!"

Holy Hippies!

Part of 1960s counter-culture was student rebellions and demonstrations at colleges. While not a constant element on *Batman*, the student movement did appear on several occasions.

The writers made reference to this phenomenon in "The Curse of Tut," when explaining the origin of the villainous King Tut. Apparently, Tut was a college professor before being struck on the head during a student riot. It was then that he lost his memory and woke up believing he was the famous boy king of ancient Egypt.

Another reference to the then-current student rebellions on campus is when Catwoman, in "Catwoman Goes to College," led a "sit-in." Too bad, then, the show's narrator says, in part two of the story, when cluing in viewers on what had happened previously: "Hold on to your beanies! They may not get out of this!" As if students wore beanies at this time period.

The student rebellions and flower children aspect wasn't fully explored until the third season's "Louie the Lilac." Louie attempts to exploit the "flower children" of Gotham City by capturing the organizer of their planned "Flower-In" demonstration, Princess Primrose, and bend her to his will. Louie's scheme is to first control the youthful hippy Princess, then the flower children, then Gotham City, and finally the world (in tried-and-true arch-criminal fashion).

Barbara Gordon, daughter of Commissioner Gordon, knew "Princess Primrose" when the young hippy was just a girl named Thelma Jane. Barbara couldn't figure out why Thelma Jane / Princess had "flipped a petal or two" and was listening to Louie the Lilac.[3]

---

[3] One wonders, in this episode, about the age difference between Barbara Gordon and Bruce Wayne. If Barbara knew Thelma Jane from her school days, then there would be an even wider age discrepancy between Barbara and Bruce – yet the

Louie corners the flower market in Gotham, leaving the flower children with no flowers for their "Flower-In" event. He then gives the purchased flowers away free to the kids as a way to control their minds, a clever way to take over the youth movement.

The episode also has a funny scene in which Batman and Robin discover a flower decal on the Batmobile. Truly, this was the era of Flower Power, and the story's two episodes did much to place Batman and Robin in the era of the student rebellion.

The writers couldn't leave the flower children alone for long. In "Catwoman's Dressed to Kill," Alfred dresses as the world's oldest hippie to save Batgirl. It's interesting that Alfred could loosen up but the show's "teenage" co-star, Robin, couldn't.

At the time, hippies were still more of an amusement than anything else for older folks. This was before Woodstock, where the flower-child youth culture was "exposed" as a "Free Love and Stop the War" movement. And before Altamont, where actual violence erupted. This was still the "Summer of Love" period, where good-natured ribbing went on in mainstream culture. And *Batman* was no exception.

Holy Teenage Hormones!

In the middle 1960s, America's youth was also involved in the sexual revolution. An awakening to sexual possibilities was discussed more freely than ever before. Sex symbols could be found in multiple media outlets, including TV.

Could Robin, the Boy Wonder, also be considered a sex symbol of his time? Not in the comics. But on TV, that very possibility was pointed out in "The Joker is Wild," in which a group of girls on the corner at the Comedians Hall of Fame cry out, "There he is! It's Robin, the Boy Wonder!" So by that early episode, Robin was being pushed as an "idol" for the pre-teen and teenage girls.

Yet this is the same Boy Wonder who, as Dick Grayson, would be fed milk and cookies by Alfred in same story's the concluding episode, "Batman is Riled." Even Aunt Harriet got into the babying act a few times, bringing him milk and cookies as a snack in "Zelda the Great."

---

show's writers would attempt to throw them together as a possible couple several times in the third season.

For someone being molded into a sex symbol, Dick was really a novice in dating too. In the third-season episode "Catwoman's Dressed to Kill," Dick prepares for his school prom.

Dick: Sorry, I'm not interested in dance lessons.

Bruce: Wait a minute, Dick. The junior prom is coming up, isn't it?

Dick: Yes, but...

Bruce: Well, we don't want you to be a wallflower, do we? Dancing is an integral part of every young man's education.

Dick: Gosh, Bruce, you're right.

So although Dick wasn't already a sex symbol *per se*, he was certainly being groomed as one – by Bruce, no less.

The first episodes truly centering on Dick Grayson / Robin were "The Joker Goes to School" and "He Meets his Match, the Grisly Ghoul," which occured at the same high school Dick attended. (Of course, his high school would have an old-fashioned name, Woodrow Roosevelt High.) The school's basketball team found themselves playing against a more "mod"-sounding high school named "Disko Tech" in an upcoming game. Dick's high school had been Gotham City champions for five years in a row, and the two-episode story was about the Woodrow Roosevelt High players being coerced by the Joker into throwing the game.

We see Dick lifting weights in the gymnasium – an opportunity to give the female teens and tweens some eye candy. He's also shown to be a student leader (though it's hard to imagine where he finds the time) with more than a casual interest in another student leader, Susie, who is also the head cheerleader.

Batman asks Dick to be an "undercover agent" to infiltrate the Joker's kid gang, the "Bad Pennies." The Pennies are high-school dropouts – what else? Try as he might, Dick seems to be a fish out of water when playing a delinquent, and he's found out when he can't smoke without coughing. To be fair, he does do a good job in greeting Susie as "Sue baby." Way to impress a girl, young master Grayson.

Here too, Batman seems to have a patronizing tone with the young. He uses a megaphone to tell students to return to class, saying, "Boys and girls, go back to your studies! Believe me, nothing in life is free!" Batman is definitely representative of the older generation – it's surprising that Robin doesn't rebel for real after three seasons of the Caped Crusader's condescension.

When it comes to teenage hormones, the most telling scene in the series occurs when Robin is looking at Batgirl, who had been Bat-gassed to sleep to keep her from learning the location of the Batcave:

Robin: You know something, Batman?

Batman: What's that, Robin?

Robin: She looks very pretty when she's asleep.

Batman: I thought you might eventually notice that. That single statement indicates to me the first oncoming thrust of manhood, old chum.

Interesting word choice, Batman.

Holy Headlights!

1960s youth counter-culture also included women expressing their individuality. But until the advent of Batgirl, most of the show's young women were the villains' molls — apparently attracted to the "bad boy" type. Because the villains and their henchmen usually looked much older, the molls even more overtly stood out as young people.

The first young female shown on the show was "hip chick" Molly, who was working for the Riddler in the first episode. She ended up the first casualty in the battle against crime in Gotham — not the usual fate for a villain's moll in the series. After Molly, no more deaths would occur in the series — perhaps so as not to scare the kiddies.

In the third episode, "Fine Feathered Finks," Miss Dawn Robbins was posing for *Funboy Magazine*, a clear euphemism to another famous magazine at the time. This early in the series, young, good-looking women were either criminals or models. Not exactly that type of forward-thinking role models that young women were looking for in the 1960s.

Batman would typically "sympathize" in some way with the villain's moll, usually saying patronizing things such as "poor deluded child" (said about the Joker's first moll, Queenie) or "some hapless female trapped in a life of crime" (in "The Curse of Tut").

Batman also used the molls as examples for teenaged Robin, as in "The Bookworm Turns," when Robin was referring to Lydia Limpet:

Dick: Gosh, Batman, those look like honest eyes.

Batman: Never trust the old chestnut, "Crooks have beady little eyes." It's false.

Batman warns Robin, "When you get a little older, you'll see how easy it is to become lured by the female of the species." This combines both Robin's hormones with the Caped Crusader's somewhat misogynist attitude.

Social values concerning young females were also brought up during the series run, voiced by the Boy Wonder, significantly. In "Hot Off the Griddle," Robin commented on the Penguin's new moll:

> **Robin:** Venus seemed like a nice girl in that costume.
>
> **Batman:** I suspect she is a nice girl down deep, but she's fallen in with bad companions. And who knows what her home life was like?

For all his apparent misogyny, Batman did correct Robin when the youngster innocently noted, "I guess you can never trust a woman." Batman quickly stated, "You've made a hasty generalization, Robin. It's a bad habit to get into."

After Barbara Gordon, a.k.a. Batgirl, was introduced in the third season, the Penguin stated that when Barbara became his bride, she would learn the wife's first virtue: obedience. Then again, the Penguin is portrayed (by actor Burgess Meredith) as an older man in the series.

But at least Batgirl represented the younger woman as strong and independent – unlike the molls and models on the show before her.

Holy Conclusion, Batman!

Batman made a valiant but misguided attempt to portray 1960s youth and counter-culture. It felt like a caricature of what was actually happening during the time period. Watching the show is more than just an exercise in time travel back to the mid-1960s. It is a window into how the youth of the period were thought of by their elders.

While the show elevated the role of Robin from comic-book sidekick to co-star, the writers had Batman talking down to Robin and the youth he represented in nearly every episode. Whether lounging at Wayne Manor or struggling to escape a villainous trap, Batman always seemed to have plenty of time to moralize to Robin about the evils of crime, the importance of studying, or the responsibilities of citizens.

Even though the show wanted to appeal to the youth audience, it didn't want to embrace or glorify the counter-cultural interests and practices of young people at that time. The most "far-out" characters, flower children and "hipsters," were either victims or villains – never law-abiding citizens or heroes.

Instead, the heroes were decidedly "square" and the show's message clearly "establishment."

Viewing the episodes now, *Batman* seems almost like some adult propaganda show. On the surface, the characters reflect the youth and counter-culture of the day, but the dialogue and moralizing reflect the opinions and beliefs of the older generation.

Gotham City R&D:
Gadgetry in *Batman*

by Michael Johnson

In 1966, the Batman TV show arrived on the scene during a major technological renaissance. The Cold War was in full swing, unleashing a world of spies and espionage upon us. The Space Age had dawned, making new technology a necessity. *Batman* competed with other television shows like *Star Trek* and with movies like the James Bond series. In order to maintain the "sci-fi action" edge, the writers needed gadgets.

And gadgets there were: the Caped Crusader had hundreds of different devices to help him keep Gotham safe. He had the coolest car, and his belt carried dozens of items that could get him and his sidekick out of any jam. A motorcycle, boat and helicopter rounded out his collection. Storage was no problem for Batman because of the Batcave, which held an arsenal of crime fighting equipment that would make the CIA jealous. The amount of gadgets paraded before viewers of the 1966 TV show is staggering not only in their number but in their complexity and, often times, their seeming impossibility. It'd be an understatement to say that technology, or *science-fiction* technology, was a major component of *Batman*.

There's also no argument that these gadgets were a big part of the show's success. To feed 1966's Batmania, Ideal Toys offered the "Batman Utility Belt" to eager children and beleaguered parents. For many collectors of Bat-paraphernalia, it's something of a Holy Grail. The set offered a bright yellow belt, from which dangled enough plastic opium to send any materialist kid into nirvana: a Bat-Rocket Grenade, a Bat-Rope, a Bat-a-Rang, a Batsignal Flash, Bat-Cuffs, a Batman Message Sender, a Bat-Gun Launcher, a Dummy Transmitter, and a Bat-Storage Pouch for other sundry items. Was there any other toy of the time that so epitomized the sheer love of gadgetry? *Batman* was a TV series about *stuff*, baby, and companies like Ideal were more than happy to reproduce it for the masses.

But while some *Star Trek* gadgets are now in your house, car, or pocket right now, were the gadgets used on the Batman TV show equally predictive? The sheer volume of Batman's gadgets argues in his favor, but *Batman* didn't take place in outer space or the future. Rather, it took place in a fictional city, in an unnamed time period that more or less resembled the 1960s. Batman fought eccentric criminals, not aliens. His show wasn't science fiction. So how does his tech stack up against that of the 1960s and of today? To answer this question, we'll have to get our hands on some of his gadgets.

Above all, the Batcave was the site of Batman's detective work, aided by analytical machines that seemed years ahead of their time. In the aughts, the popular TV show *CSI* and its many spinoffs present the impression that any tiny piece of evidence can be analyzed to incriminate a suspect. In the sixties, *Batman* gave the same impression. The Batcave's machines illustrate the scientific concept of forensics, offering information on any piece of evidence. At the time, most detective shows didn't even focus on forensics; rather, the main character visually saw the evidence and used it to solve the crime.

Batman's collection of criminal forensic tools also extended to the gadgets on his utility belt and the Batmobile, but the Batcave housed the most advanced tool: the Batcomputer. Tech-savvy people look at the sixties as a time of great technological advancement; it doesn't get much more technological than going to the moon. In the early '60s, the computer was still unknown to most people, but with the dawn of the rocket age, its application possibilities became endless. But was the Batcomputer and its advanced functions truly ahead of its time?

The Batcomputer had a variety of audio forensic devices, such as the Anticrime Voice Analyzer and the Bat-Sound Analyzer. Audio forensics employs the use of audio recordings to determine things such as the location of the crime, its approximate time, and its perpetrators. In several cases, Batman used voice recognition to identify the evildoer, as with the Joker in "He Meets his Match, the Grisly Ghoul." Voiceprint analysis became a reality in the late

1960s and went on to become a valuable tool in the ensuing decades; the *Batman* TV show used the concept but not the exact technology. Batman may have gotten the jump on the widespread use of audio forensics, though only by a couple of years.

One frequently used piece of equipment on the show was the Hyperspectrographic Analyzer – one can see it in both "The Ring of Wax" and "Batman Sets the Pace." Its purpose was to analyze key pieces of evidence gathered at the scene of the crime and to determine its origin. The device worked simply: Batman placed a piece of evidence on a flashing screen, which would then give him information on the object. The Analyzer was able to take small traces of materials, such as dust, metal, or cloth, and give Batman the information he needed. But the Hyper-Spectrographic Analyzer was only one of many such "analyzers" in the Batcave, such as the Precious Metal Bat-Analyzer, the Batroscope, and the Brain-wave Bat-Analyzer. Such devices obviously didn't exist in the '60s, although they do illustrate the idea of using machines to aid criminal investigation. Although a variety of machines can give results like some of Batman's analyzers, they don't duplicate all of their functions. Nor are they so simple to use, yielding results in plain English rather than abstract data. One day, such a device may well be possible, as well as the consolidation of such analysis into a single machine. Unfortunately, this technology might put a crime-fighter like Batman out of a job.

The modern computer has many of the same features that the Batcomputer had. It certainly provided a multitude of functions beyond just analyzing evidence. One of its basic functions, now commonplace, is to simply maintain detailed information on a variety of criminals. This made it easier for Batman to narrow his search of villains. Today, most law enforcement agencies have access to various such computerized databases, some of which keeps tabs on the whereabouts, status, and profiles of certain types of criminals. While the idea of such a database of information has antecedents, Batman's impressive collection of data on the Batcomputer was considerably ahead of its time, rivaled only by computers decades later. With the Internet, we often take information for granted; Batman certainly had the jump on this.

The Batcave also housed its own atomic power plant that supplied power for the computers and the Batmobile. Commercial atomic power first saw light in the 1950s, and this technology grew in the '60s. Today, much of the world gets its energy from nuclear power plants. But the Batcave's atomic power is unrecognizable as a real atomic power source. A nuclear reactor is, in the simplest terms, like an old steam-powered train engine, with the obvious difference that it heats the water differently. Once the uranium core heats the water, the resulting steam is pressurized to move turbines that create the electricity, and this is why nuclear power plants emit vapor clouds from their tops. The Batcave's atomic pile apparently didn't produce any steam, or at least none that could be seen rising over stately Wayne Manor – thank goodness. Another difference comes in terms of size: nuclear power plants can be seen for miles. This makes Bruce Wayne's private nuclear reactor, which could easily fit in a cave under his home, quite unique. Also, the complications of dealing with a radioactive power source would require much more work than Batman and Robin could handle on their own, even with Alfred's help. Even today, this requires a multitude of highly-trained technicians.

The Batcave may have pushed several technological boundaries that had yet to be breached in the 1960s, but let's see how Batman's utility belt stacks up. Today, when we leave the house, we have to grab our keys, cell phone, music player, wallet, sunglasses, etc. The utility belt was a handy accessory that contained everything that he needed to leave the Batcave with on short notice. When the Dynamic Duo found themselves in an elaborate deathtrap, something was always on hand that could get them out.

One important device in the utility belt was the Remote Control Batcomputer Oscillator. In "Caught in the Spider's Den," the Caped Crusader was able to use this device to remotely communicate with the Batcomputer and retrieve information. This is a great example of forward thinking on Batman's part. The smart phone is a relatively new technology, giving one access to the same information that one has on one's home computer. With some programs, one can even access programs on one's home computer and make changes to information stored there. The Caped Crusader was using mobile technology decades before such portable devices, let alone such advanced ones, hit the market.

Among its other wonders, Batman's utility belt contained infrared eye goggles. This handy device, which resembled sunglasses from the 1980s, allowed Batman and Robin to see clearly at night. Utilizing a variety of spectra, infrared technology can make the darkest environment appear well-lit. It first saw application in World War II, but these early infrared vision devices were so large they had to be mounted on the back of trucks. During the 1950s and '60s, night-vision technology advanced, so that by the late '60s, portable night-vision devices existed but were primarily used by the military. Civilian usage of night-vision technology wouldn't begin until the 1980s and wouldn't become commonplace until the late '90s. Night vision has since become vital and commonplace in law enforcement and the military. Yet Batman's infrared goggles were considerably smaller than even today's designs. So while this equipment was not a new invention by the show, it still illustrated the future of this technology.

Another nifty gadget Batman's belt was the Batlaser. This device, about the size of a small pistol, could fire a thin, green laser beam. Batman used his Batlaser in a variety of situations, such as cutting down a net and to removing metal bars from a window, as in "Hi Diddle Riddle." In the '60s, the laser was in its early stages of practical application, but many science-fiction stories used the laser as a form of weapon; typically, a futuristic device in the shape of a gun would fire a beam of light, harming or disabling a foe. Just like early computers that were large enough to fill a room, early lasers were very large machines. Today, anyone can carry a laser in his or her pocket, though such lasers are only powerful enough to serve as pointers (or annoyances), not metal-cutting devices. Batman's laser was miniaturized long before its time, but lasers of its strength are still unavailable to the public.

On his belt, Batman also carried a Mini Charge capable of an electrical charge of 5000 volts. In "Caught in the Spider's Den," it sent this electricity through Batman and Robin to free them from a giant spider web in which Black Widow had ensnared them, and the only drawback was a minor shock, from which the duo instantly recovered. In the 1960s, such portable technology didn't exist. In the 1990s, however, law enforcement agencies began employing just stuch a device: the stun gun. About the size of a pistol, the stun gun can carry a charge much higher than 5000 volts. Used as an alternative to lethal force, it disrupts a person's nervous system, with accompanying brief but intense pain. Batman and Robin's survival of the shock is thus realistic, although the resulting discomfort would be more severe. While Batman's use of a personal electric charge is different from its application today, it illustrates another concept not fully realized at the time of the series that has become commonplace.

Despite these forward-looking devices, most gadgets in the utility belt were really just common items with the "bat" prefix added to them. For example, the Bat-rope, Bat-tweezers, and Bat-knife are just a few examples of this. Rather than a collection of advanced items, many of these common items duplicate functions of any Swiss Army knife.

Of course, Batman's most famous technology is probably the Batmobile. Other vehicles would play an important part in the series's history, and the Batcopter and Batcycle were featured on several occasions. But the Batmobile stood head and shoulders above the rest in its frequent and successful use. This reflects the car's supreme role in American culture and in the industrial age. And Batman's first choice in transportation is filled with his trademark bat-gadgets.

The simplest such gadget was the car's Safety Batbelts. While seat belts have been around since the first automobiles, the 1930s saw the beginnings of safety belt awareness, and the '50s saw the earliest forms of this device's legislation and regulation. In the '60s, most U.S. vehicles included standard seatbelts, but that didn't mean you had to wear them. For example, Ohio didn't enact a seatbelt law until the mid-1980s. Yet in the '60s, Batman and Robin could be seen on TV putting on their Batbelts before leaving the Batcave. The Dynamic Duo wasn't ahead of the times by having Safety Batbelts, but they were ahead of the times by actually using them consistently. (Incidentally, the Dynamic Duo didn't use seat belts in their first episode. It wasn't until some right-minded civic groups of the time complained to the show's producers that the omission set a poor example that Batman began to buckle up.)

Many of the Batmobile's features later became standard. For example, it could be remotely started. But perhaps its most impressive such feature was the Batphone on its dash. When Batman was on the road and needed to get in touch with Commissioner Gordon, all he had to do was pick up the mobile Batphone. The mobile phone was just budding technology in the 1960s; it made its public debut in the '70s and remained a costly luxury throughout the '80s. Cellular phones thrived in the '90s in part because people wanted them in their cars, to call in case of accident. Today, most of us probably have a mobile device close at hand at any given time.

The Bat-scope, a television monitor built into the Batmobile's dash, could pick up Gotham City broadcasts. Such video systems have also become commonplace, especially in mini-vans; today, one almost cannot drive along a highway at night without seeing the familiar glow of a TV monitor.

The Batmobile also had several anti-theft devices. Security devices have become standard on most vehicles. True, these are limited to sirens, horns, automatic shut-off devices, and LoJack tracking systems, while the Batmobile was more flamboyant. As seen in "Hi Diddle Riddle" and "Batman Stands Pat," it shot fireworks and rockets up from the car.

The Boy Wonder (Burt Ward) takes the wheel as Batman (Adam West) readies the Batmobile's Emergency Bat-Turn Lever. Publicity still (1966). Copyright © Greenway Productions, DC Comics, and 20ᵗʰ Century-Fox.

The Batmobile also had a unique feature, seen in "Better Luck Next Time," that allowed its tires to repair themselves if damaged or flattened. Today, so-called "run-flat tires," available on some higher-end vehicles, have reinforced rubber sidewalls that hold the tires' shape after a puncture; the tire must still be replaced, but you should be able to make it to the nearest tire shop. Another analogue is the self-inflating tire system (SIT), which keeps a tire at optimal pressure, using tubes inside the tire and the vehicle's own weight to fill the tire with air; once filled, a valve shuts off the intake of air until the tire falls below optimal pressure. This technology, a product of Coda Development, is still in the prototype-and-development phase, although it did win the Tire Technology of the Year award in 2009. While neither of these technologies duplicates the self-repairing functions of the Batmobile's tires, those tires still illustrated a general direction that tire technology would eventually take.

The Batmobile also had the ability to navigate roads without a driver, either through remote control or by preset coordinates relayed through the Batmobile's remote control unit. The Batcycle also had an auto-drive feature, as featured in "Come Back, Shame." While such cars have been theorized since the 1950s, the 1990s brought the first cars that could navigate without a driver. Today, yearly competitions between engineering schools promote the development of a fully autonomous vehicle. While such tech isn't yet perfected, it's close to being so. Here again, the Batmobile proves predictive.

The Batmobile also had a Bat-glove compartment, which housed the Antimechanical Bat Ray. In the third-season episode, "The Foggiest Notion," this device was used to cut power to the Tower Bridge in Londinium before Robin was crushed by the bridge's winch. A similar device, called the Bat Ray Projector, was able to fire a pulse at a fleeing suspect's vehicle to shut it off, as seen in "Smack in the Middle." Such technology resembles the effect of an EMP (Electro Magnetic Pulse), which renders nearby electronic devices useless. The idea of an EMP, first theorized as a side-effect of a nuclear explosion in the upper atmosphere, predates the show by about 20 years. Some have theorized about a small, precision EMP, but such a device has yet to be achieved.

The Dynamic Duo's familiar checklist before leaving the Batcave began with "Atomic batteries to power!" (As Marty McFly put it in *Back to the Future*, "Are you telling me this sucker's nuclear?") Yes, the car's atomic batteries were charged by the nuclear power core at the center of the Batcave. In the 1950s, futurists imagined atomic-powered cars and robots for every home, and Ford Motor Company even unveiled a concept called the Nucleon, which was to be powered by a small atomic reactor. Of course, the Nucleon didn't get much further than that, and we've since given up hope of home-based nuclear power generators. The negative aura of nuclear energy is likely to prevent it from ever becoming something you can buy at Home Depot. But it's worth mentioning that the Lincoln Futura, which provided the visual and physical inspiration for the Batmobile, made its conceptual debut around the same time as the Nucleon, which may have inspired the Batmobile's power source. Yet despite achieving what Ford could not, Batman was humble in his assessment of this tech: in "The Greatest Mother of Them All," a sinister henchman of Ma Parker's commented on the Batmobile's engine; Batman's reply was simply, "It gets the job done."

But while the Batcave, the utility belt, and the Batmobile are Batman's most important technological marvels, the series also featured many others, some of them rather silly. Yet even these have some real-world resonance. Sometimes the best inspiration comes from the absurd.

For example, take the inflatable Batmobile, used to fool False Face in "Holy Rat Race." This fake Batmobile moved and sounded like the original. But even this silly piece of tech has real roots. During World War II, the Allied Forces wanted to similarly confuse their enemy. In order to convince Hitler that the D-Day invasion of Normandy was actually moving from a different part of England to a different part of France, the allies created inflatable tanks and other military vehicles and weapons. These looked real enough in photos taken from high-altitude reconnaissance planes. The plan was so successful that, when commanders in Normandy contacted Berlin about the invasion, German High Command dismissed the assault as a raid and delayed reinforcements. Newsreels after the invasion often showed these fake tanks, which looked perfectly convincing – until a soldier picked one up by himself. The Batman TV series used this idea slightly differently, but it worked both there and in real life.

Then there's Batman's famous Shark-Repellant Batspray, unveiled in the 1966 *Batman* feature film. He used it again in "Surf's Up! Joker's Under!" When a man-eating shark ventured too close, Batman sprayed the shark with this aerosol can, sending the shark on its way, and won his surfing contest with the Joker. This sounds like a silly extention of the various insect and pest repellants on the market, but one need only to watch "Shark Week" on the Discovery Channel to see some very real shark repellants. Some use electronic pulses, while others use chemical scents. Most are still in the developmental stages. Batman had the jump on this odd technology, perfecting it years before the general public saw it.

Batman and Robin also used Instant Unfolding Batcostumes. While being detained by Louie the Lilac, in "Louie's Lethal Lilac Time," Bruce Wayne needed only to look under his neckerchief to find these handy creations. A simple request for two warm cups of water allowed the Dynamic Duo to create full-sized costumes – complete with utility belts – to aid them in escape. Surprisingly, this is not too far removed from reality. A web search for "compressed cloth" will lead you to some products that are a close match. A Chinese T-shirt company sells products that resemble everyday items, like cell phones or soda bottles, but that expand in water into fully-sized, wearable T-shirts. But there's a twist: the directions instruct to put the product into water for *several* minutes for it to expand. Also, Batman's invention was about the size of a large pill, so it was considerably smaller than the current products, but it is remarkably similar.

Of course, all of this doesn't mean that *Batman* seriously pushed science forward, and there's no evidence that the writers ever did any scientific research. In the context of the technological 1960s, it was relatively easy for writers to borrow from a newly-forming dictionary of high-tech terms, constructing the illusion that *Batman* was on the cutting edge of gadgetry. The more one looks into the technology of the series, the more its techno terms seem just that: terms. Everything sounds great, but the true science behind the gadgets wasn't always used correctly – or at all. Entertainment, not technological prophecy, was the purpose. The series was never intended to predict the future or influence modern engineering. Many of the science-fiction shows and movies of the time, including *Star Trek*, are the same way.

That's not to say that *Batman* wasn't different, though not in a way that aids its technological realism. With *Star Trek*, one or two devices did many things, but with *Batman* it was the opposite. Each gadget served a single purpose. And this worked well with the show's campy style: each additional gadget meant another "bat" prefix, another addition to a seemingly infinite arsenal. This goes against the trend in technological development. Devices combine, adding to convenience and eliminating redundancy. The cell phone can do as much today as ten of Batman's gadgets in the 1960s.

Perhaps this doesn't matter, though. Gadgets aren't usually about realism, but they may inspire real invention. *Star Trek*'s technology wasn't hard science either, just a collection of ideas. Like any good science-fiction, *Batman* gives us a glimpse of technology that is perhaps only as far away as someone's imagination and determination. There will be no shortage of new tech (though you probably won't see a Batzooka on store shelves anytime soon). But you never know: far into the future, we may be driving atomic-powered cars and sliding down poles into Instant Clothing Changers.

Where the gadgetry of the 1960s show had a real impact was on the character of Batman. Indeed, the 1960s series has defined Batman on a technological level, cementing the role of gadgets as never before. Even as Batman has grown darker, he still bears the influence of the gadgetry that the 1960s demanded of the TV series.

Hollywood, in particular, has embraced this technological aspect of *Batman*. The 1989 film borrowed from the show by the sheer volume of gadgets that Batman used in it. Viewers may not realize it, but the various animated Batman series have also shown this influence. Even the Christopher Nolan films, known for their dark realism, embraced gadgetry.

And this added something to the character. In contrast with other super-heroes, Batman doesn't have super-powers. He does, however, have the wealth to buy his gadgets, and this lets him compensate. In this way, his gadgetry underlines his central story, which isn't about technology or equipment but about a man's decision to fight for justice in a world of crime.

Or, as the Joker famously put it in the 1989 film, "Where does he get those wonderful toys?"

Above all, from the 1960s TV series.

Theatre of the Absurd: The 1966 Batman Movie

by Robert G. Weiner

The 1966 Batman movie remains a milestone in the history of super-hero and sequential-art feature films. Unlike *Superman and the Mole Men* (1951), released as a feature film prior to the start of TV's *Adventures of Superman* (1952-1958), the 1966 Batman movie, filmed during May 1966, was released after the first season of the TV series had aired. When 20th Century-Fox released *Batman* (as the movie was simply titled, though it is sometimes known as *Batman: The Movie*), the series was already well-known to the American public. But the movie (which premiered on 30 July 1966 in Austin, Texas) helped solidify 1966 as the year of "Batmania" – and still remains one of the most fondly-remembered super-hero feature films.

The Batman mythos has been influenced by feature films from its very beginnings. In most depictions, when Thomas and Martha Wayne were gunned down, they were coming from seeing *The Mark of Zorro*. In fact, *The Mark of Zorro* (1920), starring Douglas Fairbanks, influenced Batman's co-creator Bob Kane, who was a big movie fan as a child. His early kid gang was called the "Crusading Zorros" (as he reports in his autobiography *Batman and Me*).

Another film that influenced him was *The Bat Whispers* (1930), which starred Chester Morris and was directed by Roland West, who also directed the original 1926 silent film, *The Bat*. The Bat was an arch-criminal who used people's fear of bats to strike terror into the hearts of those who might oppose him – to make innocent folks and the police so afraid that he could do his dastardly deeds without opposition. *The Bat Whispers* was a mystery film in which the villain was someone pretending to be a detective. This Bat's appearance helped determine the look of Batman. According to Kane:

> He wore a costume that looked a little like my early Batman's[,] with a black robe and a bat-shaped head. This made him look like a bat, very ominous. The film not only helped inspire Batman's costume, but it also it inspired the Batsignal, which appeared on the wall when the Bat announced his next victim.

In the film, the signal is referred to as "the Shadow of the Bat." Both *The Bat* and *The Bat Whispers* depict a city that looks an awful lot like shadowy Gotham. The Bat uses all sorts of gadgets, similar to those in the later caped crusader's utility belt. In fact, these films seem to have taken much of *their* inspiration from German Expressionism and movies like the *Cabinet of Caligari* (1919).

Other feature films which influenced Batman's creation include *The Black Pirate* (1926) and *Dracula* (1931). The pulp heroes like the Shadow, Doc Savage, and the Phantom also were influences, while Batman's major nemesis, the Joker, was based upon Conrad Veidt's performance as Gwynplaine in *The Man Who Laughs* (1928). Some of these influences are still felt in Adam West's portrayal of Batman, despite most of the character's darker aspects being replaced with a lighter approach. West's Batman remains a swashbuckling hero and a wealthy socialite like Zorro, but he also is a keen scientist and detective.

All these years later, West arguably still remains the most known and recognized of the actors to have donned the cowl of Batman. He can make a living going to conventions, talking with fans, writing books, and generally enjoying his status as a famous Batman. Michael Keaton, Val Kilmer, George Clooney, and Christian Bale have all worn the famous suit, though nowhere near as long as West. Even many not yet born when the series aired associate Adam him with Batman. As late as 2005, even the *Washington Times* argued that West was the *definitive* Batman.

Several critics have referred to West as a clown. To call Adam West's Batman a clown – even a heroic clown – is misleading because there are certain negative connotations that go with that description. Sure, West's Batman is fun, and he sometimes laughs – even at himself. But he is never a clown. Frank Gorshin quipped (on the *Adam West: Behind the Cowl* 2000 A&E special) that

West could have looked and acted "ridiculous" in the role of Batman, especially in the feature film, but he pulled it off beautifully.

When the first Tim Burton *Batman* movie came out in 1989, a huge revival of the Batman TV series and the original feature film followed. West wanted to reprise the role of the famous Caped Crusader, but the producers wanted nothing to do with him or Ward, and neither were invited to do a cameo (or West turned one down; there are conflicting reports). West was publicly hurt, angry, and disappointed, and some fans supported his sentiments. West had even himself written a script for a Batman film, but times had changed, and the Batman of 1989 was not the Batman of 1966. In *Back to the Batcave*, West said, "Burt Ward and I weren't asked to return[,] and even more painfully, our contribution to the legend was ignored, ridiculed, and denigrated by certain of the filmmakers... we certainly could have done the parts."

In 2003, when the TV movie *Return to the Batcave* aired, offering a semi-autobiographical account of the series and 1966 film with a little villainy thrown in, it garnered praise for keeping the pure, fun spirit of the show and film alive. *Return to the Batcave* only used footage from the feature film and not the series. Although Adam West and Burt Ward had aged, they fit into their old roles and routines as though they were well-worn shoes. The chemistry was still there.

As it was, above all, on the 1966 movie.

For Batman's turn on the silver screen, Producer William Dozier, director Leslie H. Martinson, and screenwriter Lorenzo Semple Jr. went all out, choosing to have Batman and Robin go up against four of the greatest, most dastardly Batvillains ever. None of the peripheral or "low rent," made-for-TV villains this time. Instead, the film showcased the Joker, the Riddler, Catwoman, and the Penguin, all together for the first time.

It was almost as if the film was made back in the old Universal horror days of the early 1940s (e.g., *Frankenstein Meets the Wolfman, House of Dracula, House of Frankenstein*), when the premise was that the more monsters in a film, the better. Tonally, the Batman film was more akin to the fun of *Abbott and Costello Meet Frankenstein* (1948), a film with many monsters that stands out as one of the comedy duo's finest outings. Its monsters are comical but not in an evil way – much the same as the villains in the Batman film.

All four villains were expertly portrayed, and it's worth contrasting them with their later movie incarnations. Cesar Romero's Joker is different from other, darker movie portrayals. While evil, he has a sense of whimsy that pervades everything he does. While given to pranks, they are not as mean and nasty as those of other Jokers. Romero's laugh is both funny and slightly creepy. He has style and panache – as do all the Batvillains in the movie – that other Jokers do not have. In 1968, toward the end of his Batdays, at age 61, Romero was called one of the "most beautiful men in the world" by *TV Guide*. Heath Ledger's Joker is an agent of chaos without any moral qualms, while Nicholson's Joker is simply malicious.

All the movie's villains had style, but the best-dressed character is Frank Gorshin's Riddler. His sports-coat costume, which first appeared in TV show's first episode, is perfectly styled. Jim Carrey's Riddler, in *Batman Forever*, had none of the charm of Gorshin's Riddler; devoid of magnetism, he seems flat by comparison (even though his costume was obviously patterned on Gorshin's).

Lee Meriwether, a former Miss America, portrays the film's Catwoman with charm and sultry good looks. In the skintight Cat-outfit (she had to be sewn into her costume), Meriwether is the temptress of all time, and her beauty shines through, especially when she portrays the Russian journalist, Kitka. She conveys an aura of sensuality. Series regular Catwoman, Julie Newmar, was unavailable at the time of the shooting; according to Burt Ward, she was working on *Mackenna's Gold* (1969). Although Meriwether was nervous, she could move and sound like a cat, so she got the part. Cesar Romero took her under his wing and helped her along during the filming. Many fans still prefer Newmar in the role, and Meriwether gets all too much flack for being a temporary Catwoman – but this usually comes down to simply *not being Julie Newmar*. But let's face it: who is? With her feline movements and cat-like utterances, Meriwether did a fine job filling the role. Playing Catwoman's alter ego Selina Kyle in *Batman Returns*, Michelle Pfeiffer seemed mousy and had little confidence, and her Catwoman was more about bondage than the sensual.

Burgess Meredith is stupendous as the Penguin, perhaps even more so than in the series. Meredith, who at the time of the filming was still at the top of his game, was a trained performer who had acted in many first-rate films, even directing one. With his large body of previous work, he is one of the few Bat-actors who did not become typecast and continued to act and garner praise after the show's demise. In his 1994 memoir, *So Far, So Good*, he said, "It's amazing how many people equate me with that one brief role. I still receive hundreds of requests for pictures... It never stops. Recently a newspaper qualified me as 'best known as the Penguin.'" While Meredith's Penguin did have *some* scruples, Danny DeVito's Penguin in *Batman Returns* was just plain weird, freaky, and without conscience.

To this day, the 1966 movie is the only time all four of the Dynamic Duo's arch-foes have appeared together in live-action. It's a wonder the screen could hold the combined personality and presence of Romero, Meredith, Gorshin, and Meriwether.

Advertising for the movie played up the sense of extravaganza, including the inclusion of four major villains: "The big screen gives us more space on land, sea, and in the air to challenge the most Batacylsmic collection of super-criminals ever: the more the merrier, 4 Batvillains as an UNHOLY QUARTET!" If the TV show was already overblown, the movie would be that squared.

"Some Days You Just Can't Get Rid of a Bomb"

The film opens with Batman and Robin acting on a tip and heading out to sea to help Commodore Schmidlapp – veteran actor Reginald Denny in his last film role – who may have a problem on his yacht and might be in danger. Batman calls the airport and orders someone to ready the Batcopter. When a group of policemen see Batman fly over, they all salute him, putting their hands over their hearts, and some townsfolk on a picnic comment, "Gives a fella a good feeling to know they're up there doing their job." It is as though just by seeing Batman and Robin, the world becomes a safer and better place.

One of the most iconic, famous, and controversial images in the film is of Batman fighting an exploding rubber shark. Of course, the Batcopter just *happens* to have a supply onboard of "Shark-repellent Batspray," along with Whale, Manta-Ray, and Barracuda varieties. Consistent with the weekly series, the right tools always seem to be on hand for whatever crisis Batman and Robin encounter. And in the movie, *everything* is labeled: machines, potions, weapons, and even objects in the villains' lair – as though the audience and cast members might need their help to find the appropriate tool for a job. This helps the audience feel included – and let in on the joke.

As it turns out, Batman and Robin were tricked into going to the ocean – the tip was a lure to obfuscate the villains' larger dastardly deeds.

In a press conference with Batman and Robin, Catwoman – disguised as Ms. Kitka, a reporter for the *Moscow Bugle* – asks Batman to remove his mask, as if that were a normal question. Of course, Batman cannot reveal his true identity, but when Kitka / Catwoman makes a comment about masked vigilantes in Western films, Robin says she should not be "put off" by the costumes.

Filming the submarine scenes from the 1966 *Batman* movie. Still from William Dozier's archives.   Copyright © Greenway Productions, DC Comics, and 20th Century-Fox.

"Underneath this garb, we are ordinary Americans." This is a cogent point: America was just beginning its official involvement in the Vietnam conflict and was still in the throes of the Cold War with Russia. Robin further reinforces the establishment, saying, "Support your police!" It's odd that Batman sees nothing unusual in Ms. Kitka's request for him to remove his mask – or that he doesn't recognize her from her previous arrests.

Batman tells Commissioner Gordon that there's more going on than meets the eye: Commodore Schmidlapp might have been kidnapped because he has invented a very important device that the villains want to use in their plans for world conquest. Batman and the Commissioner view a TV / computer screen to find out that the Penguin, the Joker, the Riddler, and Catwoman are still at large. Any of these could have set the decoy and sent the shark after Batman, but if these villains are working together, they could be all the more devious and dangerous. In a shotgun spray of presumption, the Dynamic Duo determines that must be the case.

Kitka / Catwoman goes to the villains' hideout on the docks, where the Joker is laughing wickedly. A sign in the background of the hideout states, "Today, Gotham City, Tomorrow the World, United Underworld," illustrating their goal of world conquest – if they can just get along with each other. It's a typical plot device in adventure stories that the villains can't get along, but here Catwoman reminds them that they have a bigger goal. The Clown Prince of Crime shakes hands with the Riddler and the Penguin, giving them a shock and exclaiming, "A joke a day keeps the gloom away!" (As Ward and West have pointed out, during some of the scenes with the crooks, the camera angles are purposely "crooked" to suggest that the "crooks were not on the level.")

Batman and Robin figure out that what they had seen was a "tricky projection of a yacht" from an unauthorized buoy, and they take their new Batboat to investigate. In his submarine, the Penguin launches torpedoes at the Batboat. Batman uses "reverse polarity" to divert them, but then the batteries run out. At the last moment, a porpoise comes to their rescue. Apparently, even the creatures of the sea know about Batman and Robin.

Batman contacts a Navy Admiral's office (in which the viewer sees some "Classified Waste" in the background) and learns that a war surplus, pre-atomic submarine has been sold to "P. N. Gwynne." In an obvious poke at the U.S. military, Batman is shocked that they would sell such a submarine to someone who only left a post office box and not a street address. Then a "Polaris" missile (seen in budget-friendly stock footage) is shot into the air, causing a riddle in the form of a joke to appear in the sky. The heroes thus figure out that the villains are working together, potentially endangering the whole world.

The Riddler comes up with an idea to lure Batman and Robin to the villains' hideout by kidnapping wealthy socialite Bruce Wayne; Batman would *surely* come to rescue a millionaire taken hostage. Using her charm, Kitka / Catwoman plans to lure Wayne into the trap. Batman / Wayne – who, true to character, still thinks of Ms. Kitka as an innocent – states that he has "rarely met a girl who's such a potent argument for international relations." When Batman learns that Kitka has gotten a message saying that some evil was to befall her, he states jealously that, if anyone harms Kitka, he will "bash him brutally." (Interestingly, on the DVD subtitles, the world "brutally" is left out, as if a little too unwholesome for Batman to utter.) West excels here and is actually the most suave of the all the movie Batman portrayals; he exudes a greater air of wealth, charm, and finesse than Keaton, Kilmer, Clooney, or Bale. There is no dark angst or brooding in West's delivery, and this adds to his James Bond-like charisma.

Robin and Alfred trail Wayne on his date with Kitka. This gives Alfred a chance to play the part of crime fighter, and he wears a Robin-style domino mask – as though no one would recognize Wayne's butler through such a flimsy disguise. Alfred and Robin have a device in the Batmobile with which they can peek in on Bruce and Kitka, but they turn it off during more intimate moments. In their horse-drawn carriage, the two would-be lovers pass a Benedict Arnold monument, which seems to foreshadow Kitka's impending "betrayal." When the Boy Wonder then asks Commissioner Gordon to flash the Batsignal as a ruse, Kitka sends her own "Cat-Signal" to tell the other villains to come and kidnap Wayne.

At her "borrowed penthouse apartment," Kitka serves Wayne some hot cocoa instead of alcohol – which sounds innocent but has an air of sensuality that foreshadows the kiss to come. Wayne is totally enchanted with her and begins to quote Edgar Allen Poe. Kitka / Catwoman is cool and collected. As Mark Reinhart notes in his 2005 *The Batman Filmography*, these scenes are far more "racy than anything the TV show could have ever depicted."

The Penguin's flying umbrellas take off to capture Wayne, and although Wayne fights with gusto in a madcap rumpus, he is overpowered. The movie gave Adam West more action scenes as Bruce Wayne than he ever got in the series. West's "only stipulation," as told in his *Back to the Batcave*, before agreeing to do the feature was to have "the chance to do many more scenes as Bruce Wayne."

Back at the villains' hideout, Wayne, who still doesn't understand what has transpired, threatens to kill the crooks if anything has happened to Kitka. Catwoman changes into Kitka, showing Bruce that she's okay. Knowing the villains are listening, he tells her he has a radio transmitter. Again showing the difference between East and West political and economic ideologies, he also tells her that he is a "good capitalist." The gruesome foursome cannot figure out why Batman has yet to come to rescue Wayne. Wayne fights his way out and escapes (no one notices that Wayne's fighting style is similar to Batman's). Back at Wayne Manor, he and Robin go down the poles to the Batcave and use the "Instant Costume Change Lever."

Back at the villains' den, the Penguin decides it's time to try out Commodore Schmidlapp's invention, which has the name "Big Ben Distillery Total Dehydrator" pasted on it in big, bold letters. The villains utilize five human guinea pigs (complete with shirts labled "GP" 1-5), who are more than willing to be experimented upon. The men are dehydrated and turned into a grainy powder. However, the villains prove themselves not totally evil when, as Catwoman is sweeping up their dehydrated goons, the Penguin notes, "Be careful – every one of them has a mother."

The Penguin plans to get into the Batcave by impersonating Commodore Schmidlapp. Apparently, the Batcave is common knowledge, but no one knows its location. Batman and Robin find the villains' hideout, which has now been abandoned. The neighborhood is not the best, but Robin cannot figure out why no one reported the criminals' whereabouts to the police. Batman replies that this is because most of the inhabitants have "alcoholic delusions" and are used to seeing odd people and odd things happening around them. Once again, this brings the audience in on the joke, pointing out the ridiculousness of costumed characters.

In the hideout, the duo finds a bomb waiting for them, and Batman courageously carries it off before it explodes. He runs around the neighborhood with it, but cannot ditch it because there are people and animals everywhere: lovers in a boat, a Salvation Army-type band, nuns, and ducks. This is probably one of the best and funniest scenes in the film. Some of the people are oblivious to the danger around them, as though it were a normal sight to see a man in a Batsuit trying to dispose of a bomb. In one of the greatest single lines ever committed to celluloid, Batman, quite obviously and uncharacteristically flustered, says, "Some days you just can't get rid of a bomb!" According to his DVD commentary, this is Adam West's favorite scene and line (and he states emphatically that the line was not a comment on the film itself being "a bomb"). After much stress, Batman finally succeeds in disposing of the bomb. When Robin asks why Batman would save the "riffraff" from the bar, Batman, ever hopeful, replies, "They may be drinkers, but they are also human, and they may be salvaged."

Batman and Robin meet the Penguin as Schimdlapp, but they aren't fooled one bit – ironic in a world in which no one recognizes them as Wayne and Grayson and they themselves do not identify Kitka as Catwoman. They suggest an ID test, a retinal eye scan – as if this was standard equipment in those days. Batman gives the Penguin knock-out Batgas so as not to disclose where the Batcave is located. Once at the Cave, the Penguin asks for some water because he wants to rehydrate the five guinea pigs so that they'll fight the Dynamic Duo. However, he accidentally adds atomic heavy water instead of soft drinking water, so that whenever Batman or Robin hits one of the five, they disappear into the ether, reduced to "anti-matter." (This scene recalls George Melies's 1902 *From Earth to Moon*, which features moon creatures who, battled by scientists, go "pop" and disappear.)

On their way back to town, Batman lets the Penguin go by pretending to be gassed by the Penguin's umbrella, and the Penguin takes off in the Batmobile. They just happen to be precisely where the Batcycle is parked, so Batman and Robin take it to head to the Batcopter. It's a particularly ludicrous coincidence, but this adds to the film's charisma because the audience sees that Batman always has a plan – even though it seems as if he's as lucky as thoughtful.

In the Batcopter, Batman and Robin get nicked by one of the Riddler's Polaris missiles and just happen to land on a sheet of foam rubber in front of Home Rubber's Wholesale Convention. A cryptic message from the Riddler's missile leads Batman and Robin to figure out the villains' plan to strike at the United World Organization (a thinly-veiled nod to the real-world United Nations) and its Security Council, dehydrating everyone there. Again, we see Batman and Robin running through the city with people around them acting as if this is a normal sight.

While the Council members are bickering amongst themselves about how to solve the world's problems, the villains make their way in and dehydrate the council members into different brightly-colored mounds of powder. Batman and Robin intercept the escaping criminals, but Catwoman plays the "Kitka will be harmed!" card, and the villains get away. Batman is stunned. The threat of violence to Kitka stops him in his tracks – but how Catwoman knew Batman would be interested in Kitka, aside from their meeting at the press conference, is one of the film's many little puzzles.

As it turns out, the four villains only want lots of money – a billion dollars, to be exact. It appears that they have no real political agenda and no plans for world conquest after all. But how they expect to spend the money and not be caught remains a mystery.

The Batboat approaches the Penguin's submarine and shoots a kind of depth charge at it to bring the sub to the surface. All the while, the vials which contain the Security Council members are on the verge of falling off the table, swerving back and forth to heighten the suspense. Batman and Robin finally board the submarine and fight the villains.

Here, for the first time, the audience finally gets to see the trademark "Pow," "Thwack," "Whap," and "Zwap" on the screen. Catwoman throws her cat at Batman, and Batman proceeds to fight villains while holding the cat, which is wonderfully hilarious. Never one to hurt animals, he finally sets the cat in a lifeboat and exclaims, "*Bon voyage*, Pussy" (perhaps a nod to James Bond's Pussy Galore from 1964's *Goldfinger*). Batman and Robin defeat the criminals and round them up in the water. Tripping, Catwoman falls and hits her head, losing her mask and revealing Kitka beneath. Batman's heart is broken; he is shocked and hurt, but he takes this revelation with grace, saying, "It's just one of those things in the life of a crime-fighter." The song "Plaisir d'Amour" plays over the scene, recalling Bruce's night of enchantment while dining with Ms. Kitka.

When Commodore Schmidlapp comes to see what all the fuss is about, he falls into Batman, who is holding the Security Council vials. The vials break, and the Commodore sneezes, sending the dust everywhere. The hope of the world now seems gone. But Batman happens to have a Molecular Dust Separator. The world waits with bated breath, as does a thinly-veiled President Lyndon Johnson, while Batman and Robin – dressed in doctor's garb – perform a different kind of surgery. When Robin suggests they might improve on what they're doing to make the world a better place, Batman admonishes, "It's not for us to tamper with nature's laws." They are, of course, successful in the separation, and back at the United World building, they rehydrate the council with blue-colored "light soft" water. The council goes back to their bickering, as though they were un-aware of their previous dire circumstances – though with their minds in the wrong bodies. The world has been saved, so Batman and Robin's job is done – as is the movie.

When the movie was released, the critics didn't really "get it." In the *Los Angeles Times*, Philip K. Scheuer's review called it "excruciatingly bad" and claimed it left him "numb" by the time he left the theatre. *The Christian Science Monitor* was more generous, calling the film a "lavish, entertaining, movie version of the comic-strip adventures of Batman and Robin... [with] good acting and directing." *The New York Times*, while not panning the film, felt it was a bit too long but also too much like a longer version of the show. (For his part, West maintains that the movie "plays different" from the series and that his performance in the film is not the same as on TV, as he says in his *Back to the Batcave*.) But a number of the reviews, even some that pan the film, talk about the film's successful cinematic look and color.

Reviews of the 2001 DVD release were mixed. Many critics praised the film, saying how superior the film looked in the DVD format. But a few regarded the movie as flawed through and through. *Entertainment Weekly* called it "Holy Uninspired," and gave it a grade of C+. *The Washington Times* commented that "newbies to the film will either walk away in disgust or giggle incessantly at the buffoonery." Not all of the reviews were this critical, however. Michael Idato's verdict in *The Sydney Morning Herald* was, "Holy DVD, Batman, this one's a winner," and *The Adelaide Advertiser* gave the film three stars out of four.

For the 2008 release of *The Dark Knight*, the 1966 movie was released on Blu-Ray and reissued on DVD around. Some felt the release and its advertising darkened the character to echo *The Dark Knight*. But there's no darkness to be found, beyond the noir-like credits at the film's beginning.

The 1966 Film's Influence

While there had been a number of serials and feature films that featured enhanced humans (e.g., Flash Gordon, Doc Savage, the Green Hornet, the Shadow, etc.), there had never been a full-length feature film that was made for the theater and featured a super-hero sequential-art character before *Superman and the Mole Men* (1951). There had been serials featuring Captain Marvel, Dick Tracy, Superman, Captain America, and Batman and Robin, and some had been cut and released as movies; however, there had never been an original, stand-alone movie that was intended to be a feature film. And there had never been a sequential-art feature film in color. Then the 1966 Batman movie came along and changed the landscape.

There's also a very short list of films based on TV series released while the show was still on the air. *Batman* wasn't the first to do that – that honor goes to, of all things, *McHale's Navy* (whose *two* theatrical films were released in 1964 and 1965). But it was fairly unique in this respect.

This film, along with the weekly TV series, helped fuel the Batman merchandising machine and made Batmania a mainstay for the summer and fall of 1966. Bat-merchandise was everywhere, and one could argue that this was an early precursor to the blockbuster merchandising of later years. More importantly, it would then be another 12 years before another comic-book feature, 1978's *Superman*, starring Christopher Reeve. Why the long gap? In part, it was because it was difficult to bring these characters to the screen with believable special effects and a good story. *Superman: The Movie* had many hurdles to overcome both in the effects department and with its story. The bottom line is that, from 1951 to 1978, a period of nearly 30 years, only three major sequential-art feature films were released to theatres, and two of them had the same main character.

The fascination with the 1966 Batman movie has never waned and, unlike the TV series, it has been available on all home video systems. People still talk fondly about it, and it continues to be shown occasionally on theatre screens (this author found a screening in New York as late as 2007). Part of its appeal and impact lies in the fact that the movie pokes fun at itself. Because it knows it's a fun ride and the audience can tell that the cast is having a good time, it never really comes across as silly, or even dated. With Ward, West, Meredith, Meriwether, Romero, and Gorshin, there was a type of chemistry that is hard to force, and this is an important reason the film still continues to amaze and entertain – it doesn't feel artificial. The interplay between the characters and all the clever one-liners still make audiences smile. In comparison, despite the fact that George Clooney looks great in the Batman costume, *Batman and Robin* (1998) just comes across as silly; its dialogue is bad, and frankly not much fun. The movie plods along with stiff dialogue that seems forced.

Although some of the elements of his original creation still remain, the 1966 movie offers a Batman who seems very different from his shadowy origins as a pulp-type hero. In the film, Batman is an ingrained part of the establishment of Gotham City; knowing he's there helps Gothamites sleep better at night. He and Robin are fully incorporated into the system as deputized officers, working with local police and federal and state authorities.

There is something reassuring about knowing that not all Batmen are dark and brooding. The 1966 movie thus fills the void that critically-acclaimed Batman movies (e.g. 1989's *Batman* and 2008's *The Dark Knight*) do not. Yes, those movies are good, and perhaps they are truer to the original spirit of the Batman in 1939, or the portrayal of Batman in classic graphic novels (like *Batman: The Killing Joke* and *The Dark Knight Returns*), but that doesn't necessarily make them better. Sometimes, people have an innate need for humor and amusement, and the 1966's *Batman* fills this need in a way that almost no other super-hero feature film has.

Despite those critics who would disdain the film's campy elements, one has to understand the film as a product of its time. By the mid-1960s, James Bond fever had hit the United States; gadgets, action, beautiful women, adventure, and crimes that needed solving were all the rage, as were series like *Get Smart*, movies like *Our Man Flint* (1966), and even the Bond parody *Casino Royale* (1967). *Batman* had all of these elements and more.

With the James Bond movies in full swing during the 1960s, gadget fever was in vogue, but one has to remember that these things had a precedent in the comic books long before Sean Connery's Bond was ingrained in the public consciousness. The 1966 Batman film had computers and technology that did not actually exist in 1966; all of the digital devices were far ahead of their time.

And let's face it: the Batcopter, Batboat, Batmobile, Batcycle, and all the other Batman gadgets of the feature film are just plain cool. Martinson's direction and Howard Schwartz's excellent point-of-view cinematography (especially the sky shots looking down on the various Batvehicles) give full breath to the majesty of those creations in a way the TV series never could. The Batcopter and Batboat were made especially for the film because it had a bigger budget than the TV series. And the movie is filled with all kinds of fun props too: cat signals, penguin periscopes, and giant flying umbrellas. In its review of the film, *The New York Times* acknowledged this by describing the film as, "a floating carnival of gadgetry and gaudy lights that looks nifty in color." In fact, in 1966 *The Wall Street Journal* reported that Bat-merchandising outsold 007's.

The film retains a coolness factor to this day. For example, designer George Barris's Batmobile is still the most famous film or TV car in the history of cinema, and after 40 years, it still looks great. Throughout the picture, Nelson Riddle's score sets the pacing and timing of the film to great effect. It fits the film's tone perfectly and still sounds unique today.

In 1966, *Batman* was one of the summer movies to see and to remember. Like most later blockbusters, the film had all the popular elements: explosions, adventure, suspense, kidnapping, villainy, romance, and a world crisis that needed to be solved. With its clever dialogue and fantastic one-liners, it is no wonder that the film was a hit.

Originally, the movie was going to be released before the series, as an advertisement for the show, but during the spring of 1966, the producers decided to go ahead with the series first – which, of course, was an unqualified hit. According to Adam West, they had already filmed 30-some episodes of the series before the movie, was ready to be released. Since the series was already a hit, the movie was used to feed the Batcraze that had spread throughout the U.S. For the overseas market, however, the film served as a way to sell the series, and it was very successful in doing just that. Ward and West visited over 39 theatres to meet fans and promote the movie. According to Burt Ward, the film, which was made with only a million dollars and took approximately a month to film, did indeed make a profit for the studio; even in 1966, a million-dollar budget was small by major studio feature-film standards. One might even call the film the first "Bat-blockbuster," since it was more than just a moderate success. The film even had a novelization tie-in, which is standard for feature films now but wasn't nearly as common in 1966: *Batman vs. the Fearsome Foursome* was published by Signet in August 1996 and written by Winston Lyon. When the film was shown on TV screens in the 1980s and released on videotape, it was again very successful.

The 1966 Batman movie remains a transitional film that helped pave the way for all the other sequential art features to follow. By the time Batman returned to theatres in 1989, many of Hollywood's writers and producers had grown up with Adam West. One only has to look at the influence of Adam West and the 1966 series on shows like *The Simpsons* or *Family Guy*. The film remains a mainstay of American history and its culture.

Perhaps because of the film's availability in home formats, unlike the series, a fair number of people below the age of 30 or so know Adam West's Batman only from the feature film. Ask them to say something about Batman, and there's a good chance they'll mention the shark repellent or the "Some days you just can't get rid of a bomb" line.

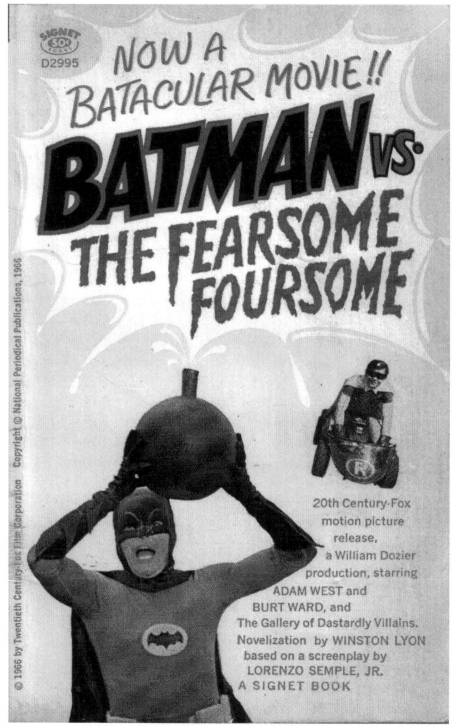

The official novelization of the *Batman* feature film (from Signet, August 1966).
Copyright © Greenway Productions, DC Comics, and 20th Century-Fox.

Holy Cow, Two Batwoman Movies!

Two bizarre movies were released to "cash in" on Batmania. Although they were not liscensed by DC Comics or tied to the characters from the Batman TV series, they used "Bat" in their titles and are relevant in 1966-68 culture. The first, *The Wild World of Batwoman* (1966), was directed by Jerry Warren (who also directed 1959's *Teenage Zombies* and 1965's *Creature of the Walking Dead*). The second, a Mexican knockoff named *Batwoman* (*La Mujer Murciélag*), was filmed in 1967, was released in early 1968 and directed by Rene Cardona (who also directed 1959's *Santa Claus* and 1971's *Santo and the Vengeance of the Mummy*).

The Wild World of Batwoman is just plain weird. It was released by Medallion TV Enterprises with an actual notice that it had no affiliation to National Periodical Publications. In fact, DC apparently sued director / producer / writer Jerry Warren, and for a time, the movie's title was changed to *She Was a Hippy Vampire*. It is a difficult movie to describe because it is so strange. The film has mad scientists (including one named Ratfink), a masked villain, dancing go-go girls (a staple of films during that time period), séances, action, really bad dialogue, romance, an Igor-like assistant to a mad scientist, and the requisite monsters (for which the film reuses footage from 1956's *The Mole People*).

In the film, Batwoman (Katherine Victor) has a cult of "Batgirls" (who are never in costume but have to take oaths), who follow her every whim. The whole thing seems very cult-like – and not in a good way. However, the Batgirls are dedicated to fighting evil, and they work with authorities to keep the world safe from Ratfink, who stole an atomic listening device with which he can listen in on any conversation, anywhere, from the AYJAX Corporation. Ratfink literally has a listening fetish, and Batwoman and her girls stop him to make the world safe for privacy, I guess. Batwoman outwits Ratfink at every turn, and the film ends with an explosion and a view of the Batgirls once again making their weird vow to Batwoman.

The Wild World of Batwoman has very little in common with the rest of Batculture, other than the use of the name Batwoman in the title. In the film, however, Batwoman does have a bat tattooed on her chest to signify that she is her minions' queen. This is the only thing Batfans will recognize as significant here. As an unmitigated mess of a movie that will leave most viewers scratching their heads, the film is not recommended viewing. In fact, currently the only way to see it is to watch the hilarious version of it released as a part of *Mystery Science Theatre 3000*.

Far more interesting is Rene Caradona's *Batwoman*, released by Cinematográfica Calderón S.A. and featuring Maura Monti in the role of the crime fighting Batwoman. Like Bruce Wayne, in her civilian guise Monti is beautiful, charming, and wealthy. She uses her money in a never-ending battle to fight crime and, like West's Batman, is ingrained in the system as a friend of police. She is an admirable athlete, skilled in all sports, but unlike Batman is also a professional wrestler who uses her Batwoman mask in the ring. Actually, she is a super-heroine combination of Batman and Santo, the wrestler who was very popular at the time and had his own movie series (in which he sometimes worked with other wrestler super-heroes like Blue Demon). Cardona had directed Santo movies, and *Batwoman* has the feel of a typical wrestling super-hero movie. However, Monti, as Batwoman, wears a costume that looks very much like a Batcostume. In her full action costume, she wears a skimpy, two piece Bat-bathing suit with a Bat-mask, a cape, boots, and gloves – and yes, she looks great in it. She uses a cell-phone-like device to keep in contact with her assistants and for surveillance purposes, and while her gadgets are not as extensive as those used by Batman, there is still a hint of advanced technology in the film.

The film's plot revolves around a mad scientist / doctor – complete with his own Igor – who is trying to create a race of gillmen by using pituitary glands and spinal fluids from wrestlers and combining them with a fish. He adds a little radiation, and a fish-man grows into an adult man-fish (in a rubber suit). In one scene, Batwoman throws acid in the doctor's face, and he becomes enraged and intent on revenge. He decides he wants to use Batwoman as a mate for the gillmen. Of course, Batwoman will have none of that, and like Batman, she outwits the villain, causes everything to blow up in a big bang, and saves the world – and the world of wrestling.

In this movie, the Batwoman character copies the style of West's Batman, and despite having no official ties to the series or DC / National Periodicals Publications, Monti's costume is recognizable to any Batfan. While not a great film, *Batwoman* is certainly an entertaining romp and worth at least a single viewing for those interested in 1960s Batculture. Those who love a kitschy movie that presents itself tongue-in-cheek will enjoy the film.

Both *Batwoman* and the *The Wild World of Batwoman* illustrate the way everything "Batty" had permeated the culture of the time. They were unlicensed attempts to cash in on a trend.

"To Fun Lovers Everywhere[,] This Picture is Respectively Dedicated"

The 1966 Batman movie helped solidify Batmania in the public consciousness, where Batman has remained ever since. The movie was not only for children but brought adults into the world of sequential art at a time when comic-book adaptations were considered simple throwaway fodder for kids. This is precisely why the film is pivotal in the annals of sequential-art-related features. The movie had great sets, notable effects for their time, illustrious colors, a clever script, great camera angles, and vehicles which are still the coolest ever put into a feature film. Even Lorenzo Semple, co-screenwriter of the great *Three Days of the Condor* (1975), *The Parallax View* (1974), and *Never Say Never Again* (1983, Sean Connery's last outing as Bond), says he is proudest of the 1966 movie (according to Warren Clements in his 2008 *The Globe and Mail* review).

In the words of Batfilm expert Mark Reinhart, "the good guys win, the bad guys lose, and a marvelous time is had by all along the way. With all the troubles in the world... [there is] nothing wrong with a screen Batman that can bring happiness to people of all ages." You've got to love a movie whose official poster screams, "Men Die! Women Sigh! Beneath That Batcape – He's All Man!"

Later Batfilms have at times gone back to the dark pulp origins of the Batman mythos, but the 1966 movie stands as a testament to a more amusing time in the history of film and sequential-art super-heroes. We need a lighter Batman, alongside the darker movie portrayals, to remind us that one should never lose sight of what the film's opening dedication refers to as the "fun lovers" within.

Jumping the Bat-Shark: The Demise of *Batman*

by Will Murray

Broadcast TV has always burned through talent and programming at a ferocious rate. Unlike its immediate predecessor, network radio, where a popular program could run for 20 years – supported only by familiar characters running through a simple, unvarying formula – audiences tire quickly of the typical TV show.

Batman was no exception. It exploded into the national consciousness with its January 1966 premiere (inciting a craze for all things Bat-centric, including more licensed memorabilia than James Bond at its height). But by September 1967, the once-popular program was limping. Ratings had declined over the course of its second season, and weak villains like the Minstrel and a Riddler knockoff called the Puzzler (along with the unexpected John Astin replacing the unavailable but irreplaceable Frank Gorshin as the real Riddler) had not helped hold onto viewers. Nor had the over-saturation of a full-length Batman feature film hitting theaters that October, just as the second season got underway.

Star Adam West blamed the deteriorating situation on the demands of shooting and producing that 1966 Bat-bomb over the summer hiatus, as well as Greenway Productions producer Bill Dozier's preoccupation with his jazzy new *Green Hornet* series. As West wrote in his 1994 memoir, *Back to the Batcave*:

> Frankly, we didn't leave ourselves enough time to hash out where we were going to go with the show in our sophomore year; as a result, it wasn't what it should have been. The villains were aimed at holding onto older

demographics – the product-buying public that sponsors wanted to reach – and the plots became formulaic so we'd be able to give younger viewers familiar thrills.

Scriptwriter Lorenzo Semple, Jr. had scripted the series opener and many top first-season episodes, yet he bailed from the series early in the second season. He confessed to *Cinefantastique*:

> It was too expensive to shoot. It got very sleazy. I thought it was produced horribly and very quickly. They didn't know they had a big hit. I think it steadily deteriorated, even the ones I worked on, because it sort of got wilder. They were straining harder. The great thing about the first few episodes is that they were amazingly unforced. They just seemed natural. Then people started with really silly characters.

The campy conceit of the show, so fresh in the beginning, was showing signs of fatigue. It became a repetitious ritual, like a Punch and Judy show. Industry wags quipped that ABC had become a two-car network – meaning the Batmobile and the Green Hornet's Black Beauty. No doubt ABC-TV brass were wincing from embarrassment in their Hollywood offices.

The phenomenon media pundits dubbed Batmania – coined as a riff on the Beatlemania then sweeping the nation – had clearly peaked.

As the producers prepared for *Batman*'s third season, all knew they faced a crucial make-or-break point for the fading TV show. In its wake, emulations and imitations – *The Green Hornet*, *Mr. Terrific*, and *Captain Nice* – had already come and gone, all one-season wonders. Plans to bring Wonder Woman and Captain Zero to TV never got past the pilot stage. Established series like *The Man from U. N. C. L. E.* and *The Wild, Wild West* attempted to "copybat" the more outrageous aspects of *Batman* with disastrous results.

Bill Dozier decided drastic measures were called for. As he explained to *The New York Times*, "Anybody with a series which has been on for a couple of years or more is making a serious mistake if they are complacent and don't keep adding sensible new ingredients to a show." He conferred with DC Comics, publishers of the Batman comic books. The situation demanded a rethinking of the faltering series. But the perennial problem with tinkering with a popular TV format was this: how do you fix a show without damaging the very elements that drew audiences? Because even in a ratings decline, *Batman* was faithfully followed by millions. The risks were great, but the rewards greater still.

Enter Batgirl.

Dozier asked long-time DC editor Julius Schwartz to create a new character, a female counterpart for Batman. Reportedly, the sexy success of Catwoman inspired their thinking. Attired in her glittery skintight Lurex costume, sexy Julie Newmar by herself was a huge ratings pull, whenever she appeared.

There was a delicious irony in Dozier's request. First, while the TV show drew mightily from the comic book, it harkened back to an earlier and cornier phase of the Caped Crusader's four-color adventures, an era of colorful costumed villains, gimmicky storylines, and insidious deathtraps. But after 25 years, Batman's comic sales had dipped to alarming lows. By 1960s standards, the art looked old-fashioned, and the stories were little more than plot puzzles. Characterization was perfunctory. Compared to the excitement being generated over at the resurgent Marvel Comics, Batman belonged to a less sophisticated era.

One aspect that had really hurt the Batman line was the proliferation of derivative supporting characters grafted onto the series in the 1950s in an effort to move the Caped Crusader away from the stigma of being a dark crime comic. This was in reaction to the 1954 Senate hearings on horror comics, which led to an industry pullback involving new anti-horror and anti-violence guidelines in the form of the Comics Code. First and foremost was the introduction of the motorcycle-riding Batwoman in 1955. Then came the magical other-dimensional imp, Bat-Mite. By 1961, Bat-Girl had joined the growing Bat-circus, which also included Ace, the Bat-Hound. She was the niece of Kathy Kane, Batwoman, and was clearly designed as a counterpart to Robin.

All of these Bat-concoctions were ruthlessly swept away when Julius Schwartz assumed editorial authority over the Batman magazine line in 1964. His "New Look" phased out the clunky old artistic style in favor of fan-favorite Carmine Infantino. Schwartz also dispensed with the tired old rogues gallery of super-villains like the Joker and Catwoman, replacing them with contemporary crime stories with ingenious mysteries, topped by the traditional but indispensable deathtraps. Schwartz told his writers, "Since Batman is sometimes called the world's greatest detective, let him act as a detective."

The makeover was so extreme that Alfred the butler was summarily killed off. (He and the old super-villains were hastily resurrected, soon after the TV show made them popular again.) Aunt Harriet was created to take his place, in part to address unfounded accusations of homosexual implications in the Bruce Wayne / Dick Grayson living arrangement.

Bill Dozier himself addressed this perception early in the show's phenomenal ratings climb when he told the *New York Times*, "There will be no doubt on TV that Batman and Robin like girls, even though they may be too busy fighting crime to have much time for them."

The last thing anyone involved with the updated Batman expected was the type of spin-off character who had previously undermined Batman's uniqueness, but that was exactly what Dozier wanted. Research had shown that Batman's audience was weak among young girls, and the producer was determined to fill that demographic hole.

Schwartz recounted the process of Batgirl's genesis in his 2000 autobiography, *Man of Two Worlds:*

> After the TV series had been on for about a year, Dozier decided that we needed to do something new to hype the program, and he asked if there was any way that we could add a young female as an ongoing cast member. I asked what kind of girl he had in mind, and as it turned out he had already worked out a possible scenario in his head whereby Commissioner Gordon had a daughter who decides to become Batgirl.

Artist Carmine Infantino recalled it differently, in *The Batcave Companion*:

> The *Batman* TV producer called Julie and said Catwoman was a hit, could we come up with more female characters? Julie called me and asked me to do that. I came up with Batgirl, Poison Ivy[,] and one I called the Grey Fox, which Julie didn't like as much. Bob Kane had had a Bat-Girl for about three stories in the '50s[,] but she had nothing to do with a bat. She was like a pesky girl version of Robin. I knew we could do a lot better, so Julie and I came up with the real Batgirl, who was so popular she almost got her own TV show.

Infantino worked up a concept sketch, then executed the now-classic cover design. He also gave Batgirl a Batbike – a customized motorscooter to get around on.

Schwartz then huddled with writer Gardner Fox, and together they brainstormed an origin and first story for the character, pitting her against an old Batman adversary known as Killer Moth. "The Million Dollar Debut of Batgirl" appeared in *Detective Comics* #359 (Jan 1967). Batgirl was an immediate hit with Batman readers. Soon she was appearing in stories of her own, independent of Batman and Robin.

The new Batgirl was a far cry from the old. The original character was painfully wholesome and girlish. On TV, she might have been played by Sally Field or Patty Duke. But the 1966 model was depicted as a sleek and sexy adult, well versed in the martial arts. In her secret identity of Barbara Gordon, head of the Gotham City Public Library, she was attractive in a stylish, intellectual way. Batgirl was not dubbed Batwoman for a simple but practical reason: to avoid potential confusion with Catwoman whenever an actor spoke the name.

Mary Ann Mobley was originally cast as Batgirl, but ABC had second thoughts. She had been the original April Dancer on *The Man from U.N.C.L.E.*, but when her character was spun off into her own series, Stephanie Powers assumed the role. In this case, ABC decided they preferred to reassign Mobley to their new Western, *Custer*.

Yvonne Craig was swiftly slotted in the role. A former ballet dancer, she had been transitioning from film to TV parts but had never done a regular series. Many of her TV roles involved exotic characters who danced on camera. In the small world of three-network TV, Craig had played the stepdaughter to Neil Hamilton, who would play her father on *Batman*, in an episode of *Perry Mason*. Producer Howie Horwitz had worked with her before and thought she would fill a Batsuit well – not to mention handle the choreographed fight scenes with aplomb. For *Starlog*, Craig recalled,

> [Dozier] called to ask if I would come in for an interview. When I got there, he said, "We're thinking of adding a new character to the Batman series – Batgirl. Would you be interested in doing it?" I said, "Very!" They were adding Batgirl to the show because they needed someone who could encourage an over-40 male audience and a prepubescent female audience. That's the real reason why they hired me!

A seven-minute Batgirl test pilot was shot with Tim Herbert playing Killer Moth, aided and abetted by his Mothmen. "In that 15-minute promo," Craig told *Starlog*, "Batgirl comes in and helps Batman and Robin solve a crime. Robin asks, 'Who is that masked girl?' And Batman says, 'I don't know, but I would like to know her!'" It was a loose adaptation of "The Million Dollar Debut of Batgirl" and included Carmine Infantino's transformation sequence in which Barbara converted her yellow skirt into a cape and donned a long red wig to become Batgirl. But it was never aired. Its sole purpose was to sell ABC on a third season of *Batman*. The network had been waffling.

After viewing the reel, network executives were on board. The thinking at that time was to give Batgirl her own show, which would lead into *Batman*, making a full hour of Bat-entertainment. The concept of two separate programs was illusionary, since the Batgirl storyline would carry over unresolved into *Batman*. Batgirl, presumably, would guest-star in the concluding half-hour. As an approach, a *Batgirl / Batman* hour was unworkable on its face and was wisely abandoned in favor retooling the Dynamic Duo into the Terrific Trio.

While the series was renewed, limitations were imposed. The budget was slashed. No longer would it be shown on consecutive nights. *Batman*'s tight seven-day shooting schedule was squeezed to nearly intolerable limits. "We shot an episode in three days," Craig told Bob Garcia in *Cinefantastique.* "We would start on Monday, finish it on Wednesday. Start another one on Thursday, finish it on Tuesday. Start another one on Wednesday, finish that on Friday. Start over again on Monday."

Gone were the signature Bat-climb cameo guest-star scenes. The two-part storylines, with their movie-serial cliffhanger bridge, were minimized in favor of self-contained episodes. To save money, only two directors – Oscar Rudolph and Unit Production Manager Sam Strangis – helmed the overwhelming majority of episodes. A trio of seasoned writers – Stanford Sherman, Charles Hoffman, and Stanley Ralph Ross – would produce virtually all of the scripts going forward.

All this was seen by the talent as problematic. "When Fox started to cut back on the costs," Adam West noted in *Cinefantastique*, "I fought it. They wanted to change it into a kiddie show, and that's when I knew it was over."

In a further irony, ABC had in 1966 cancelled the ratings hit *Honey West* in favor of a British import called *The Avengers* (which starred Diana Rigg as Emma Peel) because network executives thought there was no room on their schedule for two shows showcasing sexy leotard-clad action heroines. Now everyone concerned saw the salvation of *Batman* in a third such character.

Howie Horwitz put it this way to *TV Guide*: "I don't like to mess with success, but we think that adding a Batgirl freshens up the show. We figure we've always got the kids, boys and girls, up to 8. But girls over 8 need someone, a big girl, to identify with. So we give them Batgirl. I rather think the big boys will like to watch her too."

Batgirl was tweaked before the season began filming. Her form-fitting costume deviated very little from the original Infantino design, other than changing its midnight blue-black to scintillating lavender. Her headgear, however, proved to be too close for Craig's comfort. The mask element of her cowl came down in two batlike points. After shooting a scene, they left telltale indentations on her cheeks. "Basically," Craig explained, "when I took it off, it looked like I had been crying for weeks!" Once she pointed this out to costume co-designer Jan Kemp, alterations were swiftly made.

Another problem inhibited Batgirl's critical sex appeal, as Craig revealed to *Cinefantsatique*:

> The first time I put it on, it was made of an almost girdle-like fabric. It was not really as thick as neoprene but was somewhat constricting. Howie Horwitz took one look at me in it, and said to [co-designer] Pat [Barto,] "One of the reasons... no, actually, two of the reasons we hired her are being impeded by this costume. The fabric is just smooshing her down." Those were in the days of bullet bras, those pointy old things. So she cut it on the bias[,] and it became quite comfortable and looked good.

Her customized black motorcycle was reconfigured into the now-familiar purple Yamaha. As Craig recounted for Bob Garcia, "They said, 'You'll be riding this darling motorcycle, and it'll have this vanity mirror on the front, big batwings and a bow in the back and it'll look really frilly.' I said, 'Great,' not knowing that in order to customize it in that manner, you'd have to *take the shocks off*. Every time you went over a pebble it was like jumping off a table stiff-legged."

Finally, Batgirl's personality was tempered. Originally, Craig played her differently. "She was much more flirtatious," Craig recalled of her character. "And she had a lot more droll sense of humor than ever got written into the character on the show."

That was Dozier's decision. Horwitz had other objections. As Craig explained to Kyle Counts in *Starlog*, "Howie was a funny man. He had a wife and three daughters, and he wanted them all to be very feminine. So, he specifically said that Batgirl was not to do any karate, kung fu, any sort of martial arts-type stuff. That wasn't ladylike to him."

Between the two producers, the show's hoped-for savior was softened into a spunky, sparkling sex kitten.

The third-season opener, "Enter Batgirl, Exit Penguin," was telecast on 14 September 1967 and reintroduced Batman and Robin to Batgirl, ignoring the unseen test reel. For the villain, the producers fell back on the perennially popular Penguin, played by Burgess Meredith.

In her 2000 autobiography, *From Ballet to the Batcave and Beyond*, Craig singled it out as her favorite Batman premise: "It seems that the Penguin believes that it if he kidnaps and marries Barbara Gordon, he can continue his dastardly deeds without legal consequences due to the fact that this union makes him 'family' to Commissioner Gordon. Audacious!"

As a premise, it had been used before – in the Marsha, Queen of Diamonds episodes. And it would be recycled again before the season was over, a certain sign of faltering creative juices.

In the comic books, Barbara Gordon becomes Batgirl by accident. She wears a bat-costume to a masquerade party, where she's forced into action. Initially uncertain if she wants to continue, Barbara soon succumbs to the lure of crime-fighting. On TV, the character had her costume, secret room, and Batgirlcycle all ready for action when the Penguin tries to kidnap her. Her motivations are never explored, much less explained. Batgirl just *is*.

A corny touch was the addition of a parrot named Charlie, who lived in Barbara's apartment. Craig complained to *Starlog*:

> That bird was dreadful. They didn't want me looking like a lunatic – talking to myself to advance the plot – so instead of me walking around the room muttering, they said, "We'll give you a bird to talk to!" That would have been fine, except any time you approached his rotten little cage, Charlie would hop to the bottom and skulk down so you would be talking to an empty perch! After that scene, he would then make horrible squawking noises and ruin all the takes!

For the follow-up, "Ring Around the Riddler," Dozier snagged Frank Gorshin to reprise his infamous Riddler role. This time, he was allied with the seven-octave-range Siren, played by Joan Collins. It was another casting coup, but the episode was undercut by the network's need to lead with a familiar villain, so they bumped the Siren's debut episode, "The Wail of the Siren," into the following week. As a result, audiences were confused.

It fell to Stanley Ralph Ross to conceptualize her. "They said we have other guys who can do the comic characters," Ross explained to *Cinefantastique*. "We need you for originals. So that's why I kept coming up with originals... when they told me they had Joan Collins, they said create a character for her. I thought Siren was perfect for Joan."

"Ring Around the Riddler" was the last and lamest face-off between Batman and whom Adam West considered his edgiest, most vicious foe. As West related in *Adam West Remembers Batman*, "I always sensed in Frank's characterization, while the other bad guys were more interested in taunting Batman, Riddler was the only one who might actually get violent – he was living dangerously close to the edge."

But no more. The spectacle of Batman, wearing boxing gloves with regulation prizefighter trunks over his costume, squaring off against a similarly-attired Riddler in the ring, signaled worse buffoonery ahead.

When Bruce Wayne falls under the hypnotic spell of the Siren and is ordered to jump off a tall building to his death, Batgirl and Robin team up to save him, simultaneously fighting off henchmen while keeping "Mr. Wayne" from walking over the edge. Even played for laughs, it was more inventive than the typical Bat-fight. Sadly, "The Wail of the Siren" was the last episode directed by George Waggner, whom West praised because he "knew the essence and code of the show."

The Penguin returned for a two-parter, "The Sport of Penguins" and "A Horse of Another Color." Batgirl stumbles across his latest skullduggery and calls in Batman and Robin to foil them. Set in the world of horse racing, the Penguin coats the Batmobile with a prototype super-glue, trapping the Dynamic Duo. A handy, anti-climactic Bat-solvent frees them.

The tried and true King Tut appeared next in a single episode, the show's 100th. "The Unkindest Tut of All" was one of the better conceived episodes, although it fell back on a classic comic-book formula: Tut bugs the Batmobile and tracks it back to Wayne Manor. He puts two and two together and challenges Bruce Wayne to prove he isn't Batman. The story was based on a couple of vintage comic-book stories, neither of which originally featured Tut, who was the most successful Batvillain created for TV.

The true decline of Batman might be said to begin with comedian Milton Berle's turn as another original villain, Louis the Lilac, in the episode of that same name. It's remembered as the notorious hippie show. Any episode that opens with Batman painting flowers on the Batmobile can't possibly end well. And it doesn't. Louis' scheme involves cornering the flower market, which throws Gotham's flower children into confusion. Batman to the inevitable rescue. After the Dynamic Duo escape Louis' carnivorous Brazilian lilacs, the closing credits were a relief.

Lisa Seagram, who played henchgirl Lila, once recalled to *Starlog*, "I really enjoyed my scene alone with Batman and Robin, where I trap them. They wake up being eaten by a giant plant, which was hilarious! Yvonne Craig's Batgirl was in the last scene, but she didn't really have anything to do with us in that episode."

This became a problem with Batgirl as the season wore on: a lack of scenes. The producers doggedly shoehorned her into every episode – regardless of whether or not she fit. Since neither of the Dynamic Duo knew her secret identity, she rarely interacted with other regular cast members –

with the exception of her father and Alfred, who learned her identity in the course of her first appearance but was sworn to secrecy.

Vincent Price returned as Egghead, another Bat-foe created for TV and one of the few who returned repeatedly, in what was planned as the season's first three-parter. But concern over the TV audience's short attention span caused the producers to hold back and run part three as a standalone episode. It was an omen of problems to come.

"My absolute favorite villain would have to be Egghead, because I loved Vincent Price!" Craig remarked in *Starlog.* "I found him to be a fascinating man – bright, witty, urbane, nice-looking and just wonderful! I also ran him over with my Batcycle, and he *wasn't* even mad about it."

"The Ogg and I" and "How to Hatch a Dinosaur" teamed Egghead with Olga, Queen of the Cossacks, played by Anne Baxter. Their joint attempt to hatch an ancient dinosaur egg – the better to terrorize Gotham City – ends in silly travesty. Batman, dressed in a clunky creature costume borrowed from the prop department of *Lost in Space,* ultimately springs roaring from the cracking egg to turn the tables.

"*Batman* was starved for quality and crucified for its costs," Burt Ward reminisced in his autobiography, *Boy Wonder: My Life in Tights.* "In its third season, episode by episode, the series that I loved with all my heart died a slow, painful death."

It seemed that *Batman* couldn't sink any lower. But it did.

A generation before the phrase "jump the shark" entered the cultural lexicon and ten years before the 1977 *Happy Days* episode that inspired the term, *Batman* became the first TV show to truly fling itself over the cliff of self-parody.

Radio personality Jon Hein coined the famous phase as code for when a TV series goes off the deep end, usually in response to sagging ratings. It was inspired by the ludicrous spectacle of Henry Winkler's character, Fonzie, wearing swim trunks and his trademark leather jacket while water-skiing over a live shark.

In "Surf's Up! Joker's Under!", Batman battles the Joker for control of Gotham Beach. As part of his plot, the Clown Prince of Crime has siphoned the surfing ability of a champion surfer. The two adversaries settle their dispute via a surfing contest, with Batman wearing superfluous canary-yellow swim trunks over his Batcostume.

The Caped Crusader sinks the ship while sporting shark-jumping shorts on top of his costume, in the third season's "Surf's Up! Joker's Under!" Publicity still (1967). Copyright © Greenway Productions, DC Comics, and 20th Century-Fox.

"Surfing in the Batsuit was a low point for me," Adam West later lamented in *The Official Batman Bat-Book*. "We crossed the line between parody and stupidity in this show, I fear."

Batman had jumped the shark.

An on-set mishap became a metaphor for the decline of *Batman*. Carrying his surfboard atop his cowl, West accidentally squashed one bat-ear out of shape. It never stuck up properly in any of the remaining episodes, and no one seemed to care enough to fix it properly. Finally, the other ear was bent in a lame attempt at symmetry.

Things only got worse from there. A three-parter set in London – a blatant attempt to evoke the 1960s appeal of "Swinging London" – followed. The first episode was called, farcically, "The Londinium Larcenies." In it, Batman, Robin, Alfred, Commissioner, Barbara Gordon, *and* the Batmobile all travel to England to protect the crown jewels. It was a desperate attempt to freshen the formula, but all the producers accomplished was to relocate the snowballing inanities.

In the ultimate cliffhanger, Robin is subjected to the fatal stings of the African death bee. When he miraculously survives, the Boy Wonder resorts to what had long ago become a tired Bat-cliché: the ridiculous ruse. "I was down to my last African death bee antidote pill," he chirped.

Although Frank Gorshin had come back as the manic Riddler, Julie Newmar was out as Catwoman – she was filming *MacKenna's Gold*. What should have been a disaster was redeemed by a clever bit of stunt casting, when chanteuse Eartha Kitt was given a shot at playing the coveted role.

"We felt it was a very provocative idea," recalled Charles FitzSimons in *Starlog*. "She was a cat woman before we ever cast her as Catwoman. She had a cat-like style. Her eyes were cat-like and her singing was like a meow. This came as a wonderful off-beat idea to do it with a black woman."

Everyone involved seemed to enjoy Kitt's turn in the role. As Yvonne Craig related in her autobiography, she was delighted to square off against the new Catwoman: "The reason was not that I admired her feline abilities (I did, of course), but that she was smaller than I was[,] and in the fight scenes I could convincingly beat her up!" Generously, original Catwoman Newmar concurred: "She had the most perfect 'purr-r-fect.' She was wonderful. That voice of hers was heaven."

"Catwoman's Dressed to Kill" was written by Stanley Ralph Ross, who penned the majority of Catwoman episodes. Inevitably, Catwoman captures Batgirl and holds her hostage to keep the Dynamic Duo from thwarting the villain's further schemes against the fashion industry.

The dangling final segment of Egghead's three-parter followed. In "The Ogg Couple," Egghead and Olga are reduced to more mundane criminal enterprises: looting Gotham's much-plundered city bank and museum.

In this episode, a trussed Batgirl is forced to dance the Cossack saber dance, hopping on bound legs as several swordsmen flail away at her with frosted blades. Here as before, Craig's dance background was crucial to the fight scenes. Watching one unfold on-set, a *TV Guide* reporter described it as being "as meticulously choreographed as a rumble in *West Side Story*, as stylized as *Swan Lake*." Yet they fit the surreal Bat-milieu without a jar.

"I used to put her on top of a table or a pedestal, and have the villains come to her, instead of her going to the villains," stuntman Victor Paul told *Cinefantastique* of the Dominoed Dare-Doll. "I would dream up stuff where I would grab her by the waist and throw her to [stunt coordinator] Hubie [Kerns], and as she goes through the air she'd kick a guy. It was ballet or an *adagio* fight."

"I was allowed to kick the bad guys in a sort of high-kick, ballet manner," Craig revealed to *Starlog*, "or spin into them and waste them, but I was supposed to be able to sneak out of their grasp before any punches were thrown. Consequently, I had an easier time talking Howie [Horwitz] into letting me do my own stunts."

Eartha Kitt wiggled back into the Lurex costume to team up with Cesar Romero's Joker for a two-parter, but the cliffhanger first-chapter ending was edited out to create two separate but related episodes. When the Joker is paroled, Catwoman enlists him in another mindlessly repetitive crime: looting the Federal Depository. Along the way, Batgirl is trapped by strangling "Cat Whiskers," and the Dynamic Duo escape an exploding lighthouse trap using convenient Anti-Blast Bat-powder. An editing lapse at the beginning of "The Joke's on Catwoman," referring to the already-resolved escape, was broadcast uncut.

Even though Kitt's first turn as Catwoman stirred up no affiliate complaints, racial issues continued to concern ABC. In one sequence, a forced marriage between Batman and Catwoman reared its head – a first-season episode premise recycled with different characters. This led to alarm over the interracial ramifications of such a union. For *Cinefantastique*, Stanley Ralph Ross recalled the confrontation: "I said, 'Don't be ridiculous! This is Gotham City. This isn't New York. They're never going to culminate their marriage. She's going to be captured in the end.'"

Disappointingly, Milton Berle returned for a second outing in "Louis the Lilac's Lethal Lilac Time." This time, he kidnaps Bruce and Dick, giving Batgirl the majority of the action screen time. The Dynamic Duo finally enters the picture when Bruce activates what is certainly the most ridiculous example of Bat-paraphernalia of the entire series: Instant Expanding Batman and Robin Costumes. Just add warm water and they swell up to the correct size.

The third season's Catmobile: more shark-jumping? Publicity still (1967). Still from William Dozier's archives. Copyright © Greenway Productions, DC Comics, and 20ᵗʰ Century-Fox.

It was a far cry from the days of the first season, when Bill Dozier assured the *New York Times*, "We can't have any comedians on this show. If any actor plays it for laughs, he goes. He's got to act as if he's deciding whether to drop a bomb on Hanoi."

Square-jawed satire had devolved into bald-faced farce and silly slapstick. "I became extremely frustrated and unhappy, and wanted out," Adam West admitted to *Starlog*. "There was nothing I could do to convince the producers or the studio to make improvements. I was just a hired hand."

As the season wound down, forgettable femme fatales predominated. "Nora Clavicle and Her Ladies' Crime Club" showed just how low a TV show can stoop under budgetary pressures. Barbara Rush played the title character, who takes over as Commissioner of Police and promptly replaces the entire force with liberated ladies. It's all a cover for a crime spree involving robbing city banks with the help of exploding mechanical mice.

If wind-up novelty-shop mice weren't cheap enough, this episode's diabolical deathtrap was priceless – that is, it cost the producers nothing. As June Wilkinson, who played Evilina, recalled for *Starlog*: "Barbara Rush orders me and another henchwoman to tie Batman, Robin[,] and Batgirl into a human knot, which, of course, we do! It was an unusual way to get rid of Batman!" The stunt, which required all three actors to sit in a complicated pretzel entanglement, pretending that one wrong move would strangle them all, enabled the production to skip the obligatory Bat-fight for once.

"We had a horrible time getting into it," complained Yvonne Craig of the infamous Terrific Siamese Human Knot, "because Burt is inflexible. They would say, get closer, get closer guys. We had to stay that way for rather a long time[,] and he was complaining that it hurt. I said, 'It's supposed to hurt.'" Ward dryly recalled in his autobiography, "Yvonne had no problem with tight muscles because of her ballet training and conditioning."

The preposterous spectacle has since spawned websites and YouTube clips galore.

The overabundance of original female villains in the third season can be attributed to several imperatives. For one, Batgirl provided a continuing Bat-protagonist to tackle them physically – Batman being too much of a gentleman to lay hands on a lady, of course.

Also, budgetary concerns mandated fewer elaborate costumes. Subordinate female villains such as Ethel Merman's Lola Lasagne and Nobu McCarthy's Lotus could be costumed straight from wardrobe at low cost. Thus, West's lobbying for exotic comic-book creations like Two-Face and Cat-Man went unheeded by Dozier.

Strangely, one of Carmine Infantino's most popular new Bat-foes was missing in action. As a deliciously evil vixen who lusted after Batman, Poison Ivy took comics by storm in her 1966 debut. Dozier ultimately spurned her. The complexity of her ivy costume may explain why.

"As Batman's Unit Production Manager," Sam Strangis explained to *Starlog*,

> I was in charge of the crews, putting the episodes together and making sure they were done for the money that Fox gave me. It wasn't much money, and because we were trying to do a live-action comic book with action and effects, sometimes we went a little over. But not as over as we could have been."

Burgess Meredith played the Penguin for the last time in "Penguin's Clean Sweep." This time, he was assisted by B-movie actress Monique Van Vooren as Miss Clean. His final scheme is at least worthy of him: he contaminates all the money in the Gotham Mint with deadly germs, then sics diseased flies on Batman and Robin.

Arguably, this was the final classic episode of *Batman* – thanks in part to Meredith's scenery-chewing approach to his character. No Batman villain was better loved by TV audiences than the Penguin, and every effort was made to accommodate the actor so that the character never suffered the fates of the multiple Riddlers and Catwomen. "On *Batman*," Meredith told *The Twilight Zone* magazine, "they ultimately kept a script always ready for me[,] so that when I would be in Los Angeles, they'd have a show all set to go."

The series's final two-part cliffhanger brought back Cliff Robertson as the cracked cowboy, Shame. Both episode titles, "The Great Escape" and "The Great Train Robbery", were nods to classic films.

Shame was the creation of Stanley Ralph Ross, who considered him a favorite Bat-antagonist. "A lot of times the casting was not what we had imagined," recalled Ross in *The Official Batman Batbook*. "I would just write the scripts and then find out Cliff Robertson was playing the part of Shame. I would have loved to have seen it played by Clint Eastwood, and he was a TV actor at the time."

Robertson relished the role. "I've never had so much *fun* in all my life," he told *Starlog*. "They gave me complete freedom, and it was a ball. The whole idea was to play Shame as a dumb cowboy who took himself very seriously. I loved that character."

Robertson's wife, Dina Merrill, played Calamity Jane. The storyline focused on the usual hijinks, with colorful clues pointing to bizarre but convoluted crimes. Batgirl pitches in to help solve the proceedings and — predictably — has to be rescued from captivity yet again.

Ross scripted the next episode, "I'll Be a Mummy's Uncle," in which King Tut discovers the Batcave while searching for a new wonder metal. He thus again stumbles upon Bruce Wayne's secret identity, which probably left viewers vaguely suspecting they were watching a repeat. At the end, a falling roof stuns Tut back to his normal, timid alter ego — the only character-arc closure a recurring Batman villain ever enjoyed.

"The Joker's Flying Saucer" was a sad farewell for the Clown Prince of Crime. By this time, slapstick silliness was the rule rather than the exception. In this heavy-handed lunatic romp, the Joker is out to build a flying saucer with which to conquer the planet — an implausibly out-of-character ambition that never would have cleared DC editors. Mistaking Alfred the butler for a scientist, the Joker forces him to construct the craft.

This was another of Charles Hoffman's many cheesy misfires. In *Boy Wonder: My Life in Tights*, Burt Ward placed some of the blame for the show's decline in quality on the 70-year-old *Batman* story editor, who was scripting to save precious budget money. "I am surprised that Charlie was able to turn out the volume of scripts that he did," Ward wrote. "Unfortunately, for all of us, it didn't matter. The net result was still the same. *Batman* was sinking fast into uncreative quicksand."

"The Entrancing Dr. Cassandra" introduced alchemist Dr. Cassandra Spellcraft in a gimmicky rollercoaster of a show. Played by Ida Lupino (with husband Howard Duff as her henchman Cabala), the villainess becomes invisible, turns the Terrific Trio into two-dimensional paper dolls, and then over-ambitiously springs several of Batman's worst foes from the pen.

"That was what we call a 'bottle show,' where you have to shoot an episode and don't have any money," director Sam Strangis informed *Starlog*. "You take a show that has to be shot in six days, and find a way to do it in four. Usually, you have no locations or money left and use flashbacks to pad it out for no money. Bottle shows are always tricky to write, but you save money, which is why all series do them. For the jailbreak, we had look-alikes for the Joker, Catwoman[,] and King Tut. And we saved money by having the screen go dark when Batman battles them. We just put up 'POW!' and 'KRASH!' on a black screen."

Everyone seemed to remember this one – although not necessarily with fondness. As Stanley Ralph Ross related, "The producers ran over budget on this episode, and they could not afford to take the two days necessary to block and shoot the fight scenes. So, I wrote this episode in such a way that the fight was in the dark; therefore, the episode was shot in less time."

Ross wanted to call Cassandra's weapon a Ronald ray-gun. "This was the only time they really censored me," recalled Ross. "The weapon took the third dimension out of them and made them into cardboard cutouts. At the time[,] Reagan was our governor." He renamed it the Alvino ray-gun, after obscure 1940s big-band leader Rey Alvino.

The final episode, "Minerva, Mayhem and Millionaires" was written by Charles Hoffman and directed by Sam Strangis. Zsa Zsa Gabor played Minerva, whose scheme revolved around mind-reading machines doubling as hair dryers at her health spa. Gabor stood in for unavailable first-choice Mae West. She described her character on the 1984 TV special, *Celebrities, Where Are They Now?*:

> Those hair dryers got all of the spy stories out of the people's brains and I could find out what they were thinking. One person for example was a

jewelry salesman[,] and I could find out the combination of his safe. I opened that safe and diamonds kept on falling all over me. I loved it.

The final unimaginative deathtrap: a giant pressure cooker. Variations of this conceit had plagued the entire third season. It was easier and cheaper to employ dry ice and bee-smoke to simulate steam than it was to construct an elaborate mechanical device.

Adam West said it best in *Back to the Batcave*: "One of our weaker shows, and a sad way to go-go."

Ratings had slipped but not sufficiently to guarantee cancellation. In fact, *Batman* still led its time slot. For a time, there was talk of a fourth season. The studio was open to the possibility, provided the budget was further slashed, lesser characters cut, and other cost-saving measures implemented. Madge Blake had barely appeared in the third season, so Aunt Harriet's departure was a foregone conclusion. There was also talk of eliminating Chief O'Hara.

"I was willing to do it," West wrote in *Back to Batcave*, "provided we could get good scripts. We had a meeting where there was talk of eliminating Batgirl, though some executives were in favor of eliminating Robin and making Yvonne my sidekick. As fond as I'd grown of Yvonne, I thought that would be a mistake, not to mention unfair to Burt. I suggested she could guest star, perhaps even alternate with Robin."

West also wanted to direct some episodes and shoot the show in foreign locales like London or Paris, where he envisioned the Caped Crusader encountering European super-heroes. "The Batman comic book had done that, teaming him with the Knight and the Squire in England, the Legionnaire in Rome, and the Musketeer in France," West pointed out in *Back to the Batcave.* "I'd have loved to put them on the air, involve them all with new and old villains. And I think audiences would have enjoyed it, too."

Bill Dozier, focused on his planned *Dick Tracy* series at the time and not wanting to compromise any further on *Batman,* was reportedly reluctant to brook any further budget cuts.

In the end, Dozier's concerns were not decisive. Audience demographics had skewed too young. Surveys showed that *Batman* had its biggest following among youngsters, but the adult segment of the audience had tuned the show out in droves. Adult viewers had sunk from three-quarters to one tenth of measurable viewers. Since they controlled the household purse strings, this meant Batman was not reaching the critical spending public. It was a fatal flaw.

"The show became too expensive for the time period," Dozier asserted in *The Official Batman BatBook*. "It was a very expensive show to do because of all the special effects. It became too expensive for the number of people who were watching at that time – the right kind of people, the people who spend money on the sponsor's product." As Dozier observed elsewhere, "This is a merchandising medium, not an entertainment medium."

Add to that the fact that the former ratings powerhouse was no longer attracting new affiliates to the ABC-TV network, and *Batman* was doomed. At least, from a network point of view. In fact, a syndication offer was already on the table, one of the most lucrative deals ever floated at that time. In the strange world of broadcast TV, it made more economic sense to halt production on the show and go straight into syndication.

"When ABC did not pick up its option, the syndication deal was immediately closed," asserted FitzSimons in *Starlog*. "Afterwards, there was some kind of ire on the part of ABC. They basically said, 'But we didn't cancel the show.' And the reply was of course, 'But you didn't pick it up either.' Apparently[,] there was indecision and it went by default."

Bill Dozier was sanguine about this in the *New York Times*. "Well, we had a good three-year run. That's not bad for what was essentially a novelty show. You've got to be realistic about such series. They can't last too long. In fact, I was surprised that it went a third season."

Yet *Batman* almost made it to a fourth.

"When we were cancelled by ABC," Yvonne Craig related in *The Official Batman Batbook*, "they wondered if we could get on another network. When it looked like we couldn't, they came with a bulldozer and bulldozed the whole set – the Batcave and all of that. Then, two weeks later, NBC said, 'Listen, we'd like to take a shot at *Batman*, if you still have the set.' They didn't want to start from scratch and build them because the set was $800,000. So, it was too late, and nothing came of it."

West recalled that NBC offered to return to *Batman*'s first-season roots, and that he and Ward and Dozier were open to the switch. NBC had hoped to build a night out of TV out of a Friday block of *Tarzan* and *Star Trek,* presumably with an hour-long *Batman* leading off the evening.

But it was never to be.

The cancellation was announced in January 1968. The show went off-air in March. It had been a long, strange bat-trip. When *Batman* first premiered to astonishing ratings in January 1966, industry insiders derided it as "a hula-hoop hit." In other words, a fad. They proved to be correct, but only in the short-term. Ratings made *Batman*, but demographics really killed the series. Two hectic years after it had begun, Batmania was done. Critics at the time said that *Batman* was a victim of its own out-of-control success, which had led to excess. But it was a spoof that grew into a cultural phenomenon, and like all fads and phenomena, it had simply run its course.

In reality, it was a mercy killing.

Newsweek saw *Batman*'s demise in '60s cultural terms: "But alas, the fad had to fade. As the pop revolution moved beyond its comic-book fetish, adults grew bored with the Caped Crusader and the Boy Wonder and left the show to flicker in the playroom as a baby-sitter."

Why did *Batman* crash? Those involved with the show expressed wildly divergent opinions.

"Eventually[,] I lost all interest because I felt the series was being neglected," Adam West complained to Steve Swires in *Starlog*. "They weren't spending the money they should have[,] and we weren't getting the scripts we deserved. I didn't want any part of that kind of situation any more. I was tired of fighting for better shows. The program I wanted to do was no longer possible."

"The writing and directing had become hackwork," Ward concurred. "I tried to fight to preserve the quality, because the show meant so much to me, but I had no influence over such matters. I was labeled a'troublemaker.' I was told, 'Don't ask so many questions. Just go *do* it.'"

Even the scripters acknowledged it. As one told *Newsweek* anonymously, "Everyone has a certain amount of guilt about *Batman*. It was so fantastically easy."

From the beginning, Yvonne Craig felt that something was missing from her character: an unexplored potential that might well have grabbed a bigger audience and lifted sagging ratings. "There was something happening between her and Batman, that got lost in the shuffle," she explained. "She ended up being this cute little bland character, when she could have been more in the style of Katherine Hepburn." She elaborated to *Starlog*, "She wasn't exactly condescending to Batman, but she had an 'I'm better able to do things than you are' attitude, treating him as if he were less than capable and finding it amusing. He was also somewhat sexy; he appealed to her... My relationship with Batman became more one-dimensional, which was OK, since it was a comic book."

The addition of Batgirl was not the solution to Batman's production woes but neither was she the central problem. Behind the scenes, her value was seen very differently by those involved.

"Yvonne was an important addition to the show," Sam Strangis claimed to *Starlog*. "She gave the crew another person to shoot. We could film her while Adam and Burt were resting or off with another unit shooting a different episode."

"There was a possibility of her spinning off into her own show," Charles FitzSimons related, "but she never did. The real emphasis was Batman, so let's face it, she was a subsidiary character."

But as Stanley Ralph Ross enumerated in *Cinefantastique,* the problems went beyond Batgirl:

> When the show got cut to just half hour episodes, and they added Batgirl, it became extremely difficult to write. In every show[,] you had to have Bruce Wayne and Batman, Robin and Dick, Commissioner Gordon, O'Hara, and you had to have Barbara and Batgirl. Now, you had to introduce eight characters before you even got to the villain. The villain always had to have two assistants[,] and that made 11 contractually obligated speaking parts before you got to the plot. And the whole thing had to be done in twenty-four minutes and twenty seconds.

The true problems were more fundamental and went right to the creative core of the TV production: scripts. The formula established in the first season failed to sustain itself, especially when the cliffhanger was excised. Half-hour dramatic shows were on the wane. The limited timeslot is widely believed to have killed Dozier's *Green Hornet*. The only way forward on *Batman* was to push the mock-heroic humor envelope as far as possible. But doing so demolished all suspension of disbelief.

Lorenzo Semple, Jr. seemed to have predicted *Batman*'s inevitable downfall back in the first season, when he responded to comic fan complaints that he camped up their hero beyond reason. "Things that are really camp are never intended to be so," he admitted to *TV Guide*. "So it is true. Ours is a synthetic form of art at best. Perhaps we should have thought to make it *really* atrocious."

As for the characters, colorful as they were, they had no human dimension, no personal lives, no life objectives, and therefore nowhere to go. The villains kept returning, as if Gotham Prison had a revolving door. Consequently, they became mere ritual puppets – variations on a super-villain stereotype rather than distinct menaces. Nothing was ever truly at stake, and so viewers became bored.

As scriptwriter Ellis St. Joseph observed in *The Official Batman Batbook*, "There is a delicate balance between comic or camp and suspense, and if you listen to the critics too much about the camp, you become totally comic and lose suspense. I think that kids as well as grown-ups want a little suspense along with the comedy, but they had lost it."

Actor Alan Napier said it more succinctly to *The Official Batman Bat-Book*: "Of course, we didn't go on and on forever. It ran out of characters and situations."

Yet *Batman* enjoyed a second, far longer posterity off-network. Charles FitzSimons admitted that this had been the plan all along. "Dozier and I knew that once we had 53 episodes, we had something that would live forever and go right into syndication." In fact, 120 episodes were produced.

"There's always a new crop of children growing up," Dozier explained to *The Toronto Telegram* in response to the show's demise.

Batman went into worldwide syndication in September 1968. And never stopped.

The enduring appeal of *Batman* shocked the talent behind the masks. "I just can't believe people are still watching it over 30 years later," Yvonne Craig marveled in 1989. "I really didn't think we were making *Gone with the Wind* — just an episodic TV series that would be over when it was over and then it would never rerun again. I've been told that *Batman* has apparently never stopped rerunning somewhere in the world. That blows my mind!"

"*Batman* reruns will still be playing long after you and I are gone," Adam West predicted in *Batman & Me*. There is every reason to think posterity will not contradict him.

But *Batman* went beyond reruns. 20 years after the TV show, the character was resurrected for a major motion picture in 1989. Charles FitzSimons saw this as the perfect window of opportunity for a Batman TV revival. As he related to *Starlog*:

> When Warner Bros. was going to make the first one, I approached them because I wanted to do a new Batman movie for TV. I had a wonderful idea. I wanted to do Gotham City 20 years later, when Batman was 20 years older and paunchier, as Adam was, and all the villains like Cesar Romero were alive. The basis was that all the villains were paroled on the same night, so they get together and there's a new outbreak of crime.

Commissioner Gordon's replacement gets out the Bat Signal and you have an older Adam West hear the phone ring – it's covered with cobwebs – and Batman and Robin have to go back to work. The Batmobile's out of shape and they burn their crotches on the Bat-poles. It would have been wonderful, but Warner Bros. said, "No, we're going to do our own Batman movie and make it seriously!" I thought, "Oh, that's the end of that."

Yvonne Craig recognized the basic incompatibility between the two incarnations when she joked to Kyle Counts, "If, however, they *were* going to make it a laughy, campy, jokey movie, they might have used us in cameo roles – like me as a meter maid... Or if they wanted to touch on the women's lib angle, I could have been a lady police commissioner, since I used to be the commissioner's daughter. It would have been fun."

West, who reportedly turned down a cameo as Bruce Wayne's father in Tim Burton's *Batman*, had definite ideas on what he'd do if given another shot at the Caped Crusader. As he told *Comics Scene* in 1987:

My Batman film would focus on his beginnings, but would be presented as a flashback. The picture would open with Bruce Wayne today – the hard-driving chief executive officer of Wayne Industries – in retirement as Batman, because Gotham City has been pretty well cleaned up. Then, an event would occur which would be so nefarious that he would be forced to consider coming out of retirement. He would visit the Batcave, see his costume suspended with platinum wires in a Lucite box under a spotlight. And remember how it began. Batman is obsessed. He is a multi-faceted person, and this must be brought out more than we did in the TV series.

Contrarily, Lorenzo Semple, Jr. expressed only studied disinterest to *Variety*: "I am often asked what I think of the string of Batman features which has followed. My answer disappoints. Truth is, I think only rarely about Warner's big screen charades, for they are related to our antique effort in little beyond the eponymous title."

40 years later, a new cycle of Batman films is in full cry, depicting a vision so bleak and dark that Semple's words sound like an absurdist understatement. Batman endures. It's unlikely that his worldwide fame would be a fraction of what it is in the 21st century were it not for a quirky, risky TV show that happened along in an experimental decade when audiences were open to it. That is the legacy of *Batman*.

But the ultimate assessment should go to the two men whose opinions most matter – the creators of Batman, artist Bob Kane and writer Bill Finger.

"The costumes were great," Finger told interviewer Robert Porfirio in 1973.

It wasn't that the scripts were terrible – although I wrote one myself – it's just that they were a lampoon, a burlesque of Batman. They camped it up.

And they camped it up to the point where they did themselves out of a series that might have gone on longer. I felt that there were times where it could have been a little more, not grim, but a little more evil. With multitudinous villains you got overwhelmed. It was boring. It was always just one villain after another. They should have done some stories with interesting characters. And still burlesqued it if they wanted to. Certainly – within limits. Again, it was a caricature of a caricature of a caricature. And you can't go on like that. You just can't.

Interviewed by *Starlog* at the time of Tim Burton's first Batman film, Kane took the long view:

Batman's still a classic. It's unique. It will stand forever on what it is. It's camp. It's a comedy for the older folks, and the kids took it seriously when it came out. It's on two levels. And the villains! My God, you'll never in your life again see an array of villains with the name stars in cameos. I loved it right off. It was a comic book come to life. It will go on forever.

"Some Days You Just Can't Get Rid of a Bomb": The Legacy of *Batman*

by Paul Kupperberg

When the first episode of *Batman* aired on 12 January 1966, I was ten and one-half years old. I was already a hardcore comic-book reader and something of an accumulator (if not quite yet a collector). I was the ideal audience for that show – eager, no, *dying* to see another of my four-color heroes come to life on the TV screen, following *The Adventures of Superman*, which aired 104 episodes between 1952 and 1958 and continued in daytime syndication during my childhood.

Pow! Zap! Bam!

Yes, I recognized they were making fun of Batman, but so what? Grown-ups always made fun of comic books. My father, himself a reader of the pulps, nonetheless called the four-color pamphlets "Popeyes" – as in Popeye the Sailor Man, whose name became the noun for all comic books. "You left a pile of your Popeyes in the car," he would say. "When you're finished reading your Popeyes, would you take out the garbage?" Most adults just called them "funny books."

Even in the ghetto of pop culture, comic books were the lowest of the kid stuff. Dangerous, even, if one believed the doomsayers of the 1950s witch-hunts against the evils of comic books and their damaging effect on young minds. And certainly disposable. To later collectors with Mylar bags sealed between slabs of plastic, the notion that a comic book was rolled up and stuck in the back pocket of a kid's jeans is sacrilegious, but that was exactly what we did.

Comics did not get respect before *Batman* and, aside from the *recognition* of comics during the run of the show, were no better off after than before. Respect was too much to ask of a funny book.

By the 1960s, the comics had been effectively neutered and were unlikely to feature anything capable of offending anybody. Senator Kefauver's Congressional hearings into the link between comics, juvenile delinquency, and childhood emotional problems were only a decade in the past. These hearings were inconclusive and came up with no result, other than the creation of the industry's self-policing agency, the Comics Code Authority of America. A bad taste had nonetheless been left behind in everybody's mouths and, in their memory of the hearings, comics had been officially stamped "garbage" by the U.S. government. What other proof did they need?

Pow! Zap! Bam!

When it came to picking from this heap, Hollywood had not always approached it with such trepidation. In the 1940s, super-heroes were successful on the radio (Superman had a three-times-a-week program on the Mutual Network) and on the big screen as serialized adventures (ten or twelve 15-minute weekly shorts, each with a cliffhanger ending to draw the kids back to the theater to see how the hero gets out of *this* one). Superman, Batman, Captain Marvel, Captain America, Blackhawk, and others from the comics were made into serials, while a series of Superman cartoon shorts produced by the Fleischer Studios – creators of Popeye and Betty Boop before the Man of Steel – for Paramount are still considered classics of animation. *The Adventures of Superman* starring George Reeves was, despite the nostalgic chuckles it elicits today, a very faithful and, for the most part, straight adaptation of the Superman then in the comic books, scaled down from his skyscraper-lifting level of four-color power to a syndicated TV program's budget. But of course, the program was produced by DC Comics, its stories overseen by comic-book editors-turned-producers Whitney Ellsworth and Mort Weisinger. They were company men playing with company toys, and they were *very* careful not to break anything.

The one thing all of the above have in common is that they were created as and always intended to be *for kids*. Serials were shown on Saturday mornings, along cartoons and other kids' stuff. *The Adventures of Superman* radio program ran for 11-years in a late afternoon timeslot. *The Adventures of Superman* TV show, though its first two black-and-white seasons are darker and more serious than the later color seasons, was always a kids show, right down to its sponsorship by Kellogg's cereals.

Comics only started getting into on-screen trouble when someone decided to do a TV show for grown-ups without first getting over their embarrassment at what they were doing.

One always has to start from the premise that the people adapting comics to the screen, big or little, do not have any respect for the material – certainly not then and (comics' overall public relations progress to the contrary) not still.

The people who make movies and TV shows, who stage Broadway shows and publish literature, are embarrassed by the source material, whether they will admit to it or not. They voice a love and admiration for this true American art form, but if what has hit the movie and TV screens is the result of love, hate me, please. Even the best of them can not help metaphorically winking uncomfortably in acknowledgment of the source. The subtext may be Shakespearean in scope, but the brilliance is clad in primary-colored spandex that overwhelms even the strongest message. These same dramatists forget that Shakespeare himself was little more than a TV writer of his time, the legends and tales of the era serving as the source material for his plays, themselves pandering to the lowest common denominator in the cheap seats.

But no message, as it turned out, would ever be stronger than this:

Pow! Zap! Bam!

It *made* the show. It was, the first time it hit the screen that January night in 1966, a self-announcing visual punch in the nose. It made Mom and Dad laugh. It was kitschy, campy, and in tune with the Pop Art movement popularized by such commercial artists as Andy Warhol and Roy Lichtenstein, both influenced by comic art. Lichtenstein had lifted without credit or remuneration entire panels from romance and war comics to recreate as such paintings as *Drowning Girl*. Marvel Comics even went so far as to change its corner symbol identifying their titles as "Marvel Pop Art Productions" for four or five months during 1965, riding the wave of a trend their existence helped to set rolling.

"Pow! Zap! Bam!" was brilliant, an inclusive nod to the source material. Sound effects have long been a vital part of comics' vocabulary. A picture of a fist in the vicinity of a chin is only half the story. The "WHAM!" of the knock-out punch or the "whoosh!" of the fist sailing past its target tells the rest. Hand-lettered onomatopoeia came straight out of the newspaper comic strips and comic books the chuckling adults had read as children. It was self-referential and precious, and it was exactly the right touch of gentle mockery to catapult *Batman* into a full-blown, two-year-long bona fide fad.

The only problem was, even after *Batman* was gone from the airwaves, it left *"Pow! Zap! Bam!"* behind.

My ten-year-old ears heard the dry delivery of Adam West and the over-the-top cartoon dialogue that razzed the conventions from which it sprang, but beggars can't be choosers and when it came to live-action super-heroes. *Batman* was, hands down, better than nothing. Batman, Robin, Commissioner Gordon, the Riddler, and the rest of the comic-book characters looked as they were supposed to look, acting more or less as they were supposed to act. This was enough to satisfy my preadolescent sensibilities. I would have liked a little respect, sure, but a *Batman* that took itself seriously likely would not have lasted, much less caught on and become a cultural phenomenon embraced by tens of millions of viewers. These viewers wouldn't have dreamed of picking up an issue of the *Batman* or *Detective Comics*, no matter how much they loved the TV program.

Comic books had always been a niche market, and that niche has been shrinking steadily since its peak during World War II, when titles such as Superman and Captain Marvel sold a million-plus copies per issue and every kid, it seemed, read comic books. TV undeniably took a chunk out of this audience, but those numbers were in decline long before TVs were in enough homes to make a difference. Were post-war children growing too sophisticated for comics, or had they just been a fad that had begun to lose steam? The slide in circulation still continues today, when 10-15,000 copies of a title is considered sustainable and anything above 100,000 is a runaway success.

Around 1964, with sales hovering around the low side of half a million copies an issue, *Batman* was in danger of being cancelled.

I discovered Batman in the waning days of Jack Schiff's editorial reign. Under his stewardship, Batman and Robin were forever going up against aliens and monsters and weird manifestations of science gone wrong. They were surrounded by Batwoman and Bat-Girl, owned Ace the masked Bat-Hound, and were constantly bedeviled by Bat-Mite, an other-dimensional imp with magical powers whose attempts to help the Dynamic Duo usually caused near-disastrous results. Covers were fantastical displays pitting Batman and / or Robin against scaly aliens, strange creatures, or unexplainable manifestations of themselves or their friends.

What I didn't know was that those stories were completely absurd. Not in the good "absurdly fun" way but, in context of the character of Batman, just plain as far off the creative mark as could be. They were to the core concept of Batman as a box of Captain Crunch is to nutrition.

I had no way of knowing at the time that this wasn't *really* Batman.

The real deal was created by Bob Kane – with heaping helpings of creative input by writer Bill Finger and writer / artist Jerry Robinson – as a shadowy, avenging creature of the night. His earliest adventures were dark and atmospheric, inspired by the pulp magazines and the black-and-white horror and suspense films of the 1930s.

Only later was a conscious effort made to soften the character, beginning with the introduction of Robin, the Boy Wonder, and a gradual turn towards a Batman who not only appeared routinely in broad daylight but also held press conferences and seemed to be the grand marshal for every parade Gotham City ever had. How he turned from this sunny, smiling hero with a kid sidekick and no residual trauma to a science-fiction character could probably be explained by the popularity of that genre in the mid-to-late-1950s. Science-fiction movies were the rage and, though made on shoestring budgets, also popular on TV, from the aforementioned *Superman* and *Captain Video* for kids to *Outer Limits* and *Twilight Zone* for their parents.

By 1964, Batman was a Dark Knight out of his noir.

His editors had done what the Joker and Catwoman had failed to do. "They were planning," according to Bob Kane, as quoted in Les Daniels's *Batman: The Complete History*, "to kill Batman off altogether." Daniels writes: "Today's fans often look back with affection at the sheer zaniness of the stories from the late 1950s and early 1960s, but the seemingly endless array of stunts designed to prop up the hero had nearly done him in. There was no core character left, just a hollow man being battered from place to place by whatever gimmick could be concocted, and sales were dropping drastically. Things looked bad."

Jack Schiff's successor, Julius Schwartz, set about getting the Caped Crusader back on track. Schwartz had been behind the revival of super-hero comics, beginning with the 1955 revival of the Flash, soon followed by Green

Lantern, the Atom, the Justice League of America, and many others. While admitting to having no knowledge of Batman and no feel for the character (his true interest lay with the science fiction titles he edited), he did, according to his 2000 memoir, *Man of Two Worlds: My Life in Science Fiction and Comics*, recognize that "Batman in the years prior to my tenure had strayed away from the original roots of the character."

Schwartz discarded the giant-headed aliens and science-fiction trappings and made a 180-degree turn, taking the character back to his "dark-mystery roots" and reviving the death-traps that writer Bill Finger had used so successfully in the Dark Knight's earlier, grittier days. Schwartz brought in his top writers, John Broome and Gardner Fox, and his most cutting-edge penciller, Carmine Infantino, and put them to work redefining the creaky old bat. The result was the "New Look" Batman, and "to set off for history the start of my term as editor on the title, I had them incorporate an oval around the bat emblem on Batman's chest, so there would never be any question as to when the Julie Schwartz *Batman* came into being."

Schwartz can be forgiven his ego because he delivered. *His* Batman was the real deal. And we noticed. This was a much better comic book, far more in line with the times and exploring, ever so cautiously, the fringes of the more "mature" (i.e. aimed at college students instead of sixth graders) storytelling developing under Stan Lee at Marvel. Storylines continued across several issues, long-range plots were allowed to develop over time, and characters tried, at least, to relate to one another as human beings and not just as springboards to explain and further the plot. Had something resembling those stories been translated to TV, it would have come closer to Christopher Nolan's *The Dark Knight* than the Saturday morning cartoons with which Schwartz's Batman self-consciously shied away from identifying.

But William Dozier seems to have been reading the older, goofy Batman edited by Jack Schiff. He likely would have been predisposed to take the tongue-in-cheek road regardless of what version of Batman he first saw. The subject was comic books, and comic books, after all, were not to be taken too seriously.

William Dozier was a Hollywood veteran with Paramount and RKO before his move, in 1951, to TV to become CBS's executive producer of dramatic programming. In 1959, he became vice president in charge of Columbia Picture's TV division, Screen Gems. In 1964, he left that position to form

Greenway Productions, his own production company. ABC had acquired the rights to Batman from DC Comics and offered it to Dozier to develop.

Dozier and the smash hit he created from that offer were the subjects of a 1966 episode of the Canadian Broadcasting Company's news and interview program *Telescope With Fletcher Merkle*. On it, the executive producer of *Batman* discussed the program's genesis, but before he could have his say, host Fletcher Merkle introduced the piece by observing,

> Suddenly a few years ago, pop went the easel of many a North American painter. Then, snapping at the heels of Pop Art and crackling with novelty, pop went mass culture all over the continent and beyond the seas. Batman is part of pop, though neither art nor culture. If it's the worst program on the air these days, and some say it is, at least it is bad on purpose.

Merkle went on to point out that the associated "Bat-merchandise" was worth "a gross in the tens, if not hundreds, of millions," and, without any further ado – "Zap! Pow! Blam!" – he introduced the self-proclaimed "super Bat-chief" of this phenomenon, Dozier.

The report is far gentler than one would expect from a so obviously biased reporter, but Merkle was not the only voice expressing distate, if not contempt, for the source material.

"I had never had a Batman comic book in my hands," Dozier told Merkle. "I of course was aware there was such a thing, but I had never read one. When they first came out in 1938, '39, I had an eight, nine-year-old son, and I was busy making a living for him and his mother and myself." What had Dozier been weaned on? "When I was growing up, I read *David Copperfield*, *Great Expectations*, and the things you are supposed to read."

After meeting with ABC executives, Dozier hunted up some back issues – "it took quite a bit of doing to get some of the older ones; they cost three, four dollars apiece" – and proceeded to do his research:

> I took them on the plane with me and flew back to Hollywood. I was sitting in an aisle seat doing my homework, with five or six copies in my lap and reading one, not thinking how this would look to somebody and, sure enough, a friend of mine in the ad agency business in New York was on the same flight. He tapped me on the shoulder and he said, "Well, I guess those scripts do get dull after a while." I couldn't tell him why I had a lap full of comic books, because it was a big secret.

In another telling of the same story, as related in Joel Eisner's *The Official Batman Batbook*, Dozier added, "I felt a little bit like an idiot."

Embarrassed even to be seen in the company of comic books, Dozier took the bold step of embracing everything he *thought* a comic book was and laid that down as his foundation. "The fairly obvious idea – it seems obvious now, at least," Dozier told the *Telescope* audience, "to make it so square and so serious and so cliché-ridden and so overdone and yet do it with a certain elegance and style that it would be funny. That it would be so corny and so bad that it would be funny. That appealed to me and I began to enjoy it."

What better way to get around the perception of the material than to make the perception into the joke and laugh at it before the audience has a chance to laugh at you?

"I knew kids would go for the derring-do, the adventure, but the trick would be to find adults who would either watch it with their kids or, to hell with the kids – and watch it anyway," Dozier said in *The Official Batman Batbook*. "And the biggest wink and nod to the grown-up viewers who were, after all, the ones with the money to spend on the products to be advertised on *Batman*, was 'ZAP' and 'POW.'"

Dozier recalled pitching his concept of *Batman* to the ABC executives, explaining how young Bruce Wayne had been orphaned and taken an oath to fight crime to avenge their deaths:

> They looked at me and they thought I was a little crazy. I said, "That gentlemen, is his motivation, and he dedicated his life to fighting crime." Then I explained how we were going to do it – that we were going to have "ZAP" and "POW." And I remember Leonard Goldenson – president of ABC – said, "We are going to have, right on the screen, 'ZAP' and 'POW'?" I said, "Yeah, and a lot more, Leonard." "Oh, my," he said.

Oh, my, indeed.

In *Batman: The Complete History*, Les Daniels said "the idea that something could be amusing because it was corny or ridiculous was essential to Pop and its allied aesthetic, camp."

Batman was corny.

Batman was ridiculous and, Fletcher Merkle aside, was not only Pop Art but *high* art that evolved into the poster child for the camp movement. Suddenly, everything was camp... even staid Archie Comics offered poorly-done re-launches of their stable of 1940s super-heroes as "High Camp Super-Heroes" (an unfortunately too apt description of well-intended but poorly-executed material). Camp was appealing or collectible for its bad taste and ironic value; it offered a reverse snobbery appeal by being deliberately pretentious and artfully naïve, like pink plastic lawn flamingoes. Camp originated in the early 20th century as a term for exaggerated and affected homosexual behavior: bad boys in ostentatious drag that informed everything from Liberace to John Waters's *Hairspray*. This exaggeration and ostentation lived on in *Batman*, which flaunted its lowbrow origins by wearing them openly while sashaying down Main Street at the head of the parade.

Laughing with it or laughing at it, everybody was watching – an estimated 30 million viewers a week. In an almost unprecedented arrangement, Batman aired *twice* a week, one-half hour each on Wednesday and Thursday evenings, with a 1940s-movie-serial-style cliffhanger between them to draw you back for the second part. Viewers responded. So did Hollywood. It became a symbol of an actor's hipness to appear on Batman, either as a guest villain ("Even Eli Wallach phoned me up," recalled Dozier in a 1968 interview with the *Toronto Telegram*. "He said he was a flop with his grandchildren because he'd never been on *Batman*.") or in a cameo, sticking their head out a window and making a quip as Batman and Robin climb past on their Bat-rope. The latter attracted the likes of Edward G. Robinson, Howard Duff, Jerry Lewis, and Don Ho. It was a free-for-all, a campy romp that knew no boundaries and made everything into a "Bat-something," with only the Beatles (and maybe *The Man From U.N.C.L.E.*) in competition for most over-exposed craze of the 1960s.

And the biggest joke, of course, was that this total disrespecting of the core of Batman, produced by a man who "felt a little bit like an idiot" when caught reading comic books by another adult... Well, this is precisely what saved Batman's comics from possible extinction. Even as it provided comic books with a handy-dandy short-hand label that says, "no matter what we say, this is kid stuff that you don't have to take seriously."

Pow! Zap! Bam!

The reaction was immediate and, in retrospect, predictable. The media loves a label that conveys not only a name or brand but a value judgment as well. The campy, childish splash of colorful words across the TV every time a punch was thrown summed it all up and was, on top of everything else, too clever for its own good.

Pow! Zap! Bam! and its sidekick, Robin's breathless exclamation of "Holy fill-in-the-blank!" became shorthand for comics. And comics were, as we all knew, the province of morons.

In 1955's *Artists And Models*, a Dean Martin and Jerry Lewis comedy set in the world of comic books, uses the theme that comics were a corrupting influence on impressionable children. In the film, simple-minded, nine-year-old-acting Jerry is addicted to the four-color drug, which causes him to have nightmares – the outlandish stories of which his partner sells to the comic-book publisher.

Watch the 1960s bucolicomedy *The Andy Griffith Show*: simple, good ol' boys Goober and Gomer could often be seen reading comic books while sitting around the filling station between customers.

The 1992 film *The Lawnmower Man*, marginally based on a Stephen King short story, features a mentally-retarded man who is made smarter through a series of virtual-reality experiments. To symbolize his growing intelligence, he is shown giving away his comic books.

In *A Few Good Men*, Aaron Sorkin's 1992 military courtroom drama, one of the Marines on trial for a hazing death is revealed to be simple-minded. One of the visual clues to his low intelligence is that he reads comics.

To paraphrase Rodney Dangerfield, comics don't get no respect – especially in Hollywood. The embarrassment at being affiliated with such lowbrow material is certainly a factor. The temptation to "fix" the sillier conventions of comic-book storytelling is always there for moviemakers, both to elevate the material to loftier levels and because they always have to show the *creators* of the comics how to do it *right*. Sure, it's arrogant, but Hollywood holds the card that trumps both common and creative sense: money. A comic book costs maybe $20,000 to produce. Even a low-budget syndicated TV show costs millions, and forget about the upwards of a quarter of a *billion* dollars it can now sometimes cost to produce an epic super-hero special-effect flick. A thing's only true value in Hollywood is its monetary value; ergo, cheaply-produced comics lose to even direct-to-video trash.

The list of movies and TV programs based on comic books done correctly is miniscule – and, I admit, entirely subjective. A movie like *Iron Man*, which treats the source material as an intelligent jumping-off point, finds that it doesn't need to jump too far from the comic-book character on which it's based. The filmmakers recognized that all the elements for a successful story were in the comics, and they merely needed to tweak things here and there in order to adjust for the difference in the media. The result was a rare case of a comic-book movie that appealed to a mass audience – its highest priority – yet satisfied comic-book fans by remaining faithful and respectful to the source – its lowest priority. There is really no percentage in pandering overmuch to fan sensibilities; their numbers, ranging at most around a hundred thousand, are not enough to make or break a movie at the box office. And the dirty little secret of fandom is that fans will go see a movie based on a comic book no matter how bad it is, if only so they can have an excuse to complain about it.

Even when one of comics' own got the chance to write and direct a major motion picture based on a comic-book character, it can be a disaster. *The Spirit*, based on the character created by Will Eisner in the 1940s, is unanimously hailed as a classic of the medium. Eisner, whose career spanned the entire history of the industry until his death in 2005, when he was still creating graphic novels, was considered one of the handful of geniuses the art form has given rise to. Yet Frank Miller, a comic-book writer and artist of some fame himself (whose own *The Dark Knight Returns* reads like a post-apocalyptic, postmodern version of the *Batman* TV show), whose own comic creations *Sin City* and *300* had been made into stylized but *faithfully adapted* successful films, could not help but *fix* Eisner's classic creation for the big screen. The end result was closer to Miller's *Sin City* than Eisner's *Spirit*, leaving one to wonder if Miller is just a one-trick pony or if Hollywood budgets exert such weight that even a man who would have screamed out against the corruption of one of his own comic-book creations thinks nothing of corrupting another man's work.

Batman gave the mass media the slug line it needed. From then on, it was a sure bet that anytime a newspaper or magazine story appeared or some unctuous local TV news anchor did the lead-in to a story that had anything at all to do with comic books or the people who created or read them, we would be treated to a "Holy this!" or a "Pow! Zap! Bam!" in one form or another.

Batman had not even made it onto the air yet on 9 January 1966 when the *New York Times* ran an article about William Dozier – or the "Caped Crusader of Camp," as he is called. "I hate the word camp," Dozier says in the piece. "It sounds so faggy and funsies." The reporter explained, "It is not for nothing that the Caped Crusader is called upon time and again by Police Commissioner Gordon, powerful antagonist of jaywalkers and litterbugs when evil is a-foot in Gotham City. WHAM! WOW! ZUP! BAM!" All it took was a single screening of the premiere episode for this critic to latch onto it, but being the first, he can at least be given points for originality.

And homophobia seems to abound in this piece, perhaps due to camp's associations. Besides Dozier's crack, several paragraphs are devoted to the old charge that "Batman and Robin, cozily ensconced in Wayne manor... is like a wish dream of homosexuals living together," which is then followed by the producer's assurance that our heroes' sexuality will *not* be in question. This is topped off by Adam West chuckling over the pseudo-Freudian interpretations of his character: "With the number of homosexuals in this country, if we get that large audience, fine. Just add 'em to the Nielsen ratings."

Which begs the question: was there *anything* about the concept of Batman that Dozier *was* comfortable with?

The condescension his discomfort spawned was everywhere.

In 1968, an article in *The Toronto Telegram* about the just-announced cancellation of Batman carried the headline, "Krunch! There Goes Batman!"

An article in the 2 January 1972 *New York Sunday News* magazine section about a producer who hoped to leverage the popularity of Marvel Comics into a multimedia powerhouse began, "In the fantasy world of comic books, muscle-bound super-heroes such as Spider-Man, Thor[,] and Captain America strong arm their way through life with nothing more than a few well-chosen WHRRR-RAMS! BA-LANGS! and KA-BLOMS! What can you do against a KA-BLOM! anyway?" In the same article, Stan Lee is quoted as saying,

> Most people feel you must necessarily be a moron to read comic books. They regard them in the same light as those published in the [']40s. In those days, dialogue was corny and story lines concerned monsters taking over the earth. Comic books are totally different nowadays. There's a definite sense of reality running through all stories.

Un-huh. Tell that to the hopeful producer who, the article tells us in closing, "certainly has plenty of PZAP FTAM! and ZASSK!"

An 11 April 1972 *New York Post* review of an exhibition, at the city's prestigious Graham Galleries on Madison Avenue, of political and comic-book art from Thomas Nast through the underground comics, managed to get through a few hundred words without a hint of condescension. That is, until the very last line: "The exhibition goes over with a bang. And a voom. And maybe even a Zap."

A blurb in a 1973 issue of *Playboy* starts off sounding like maybe someone was taking comic fans seriously, but even the sophisticates at the Playboy Mansion had to take a last little dig:

> Anyone who still considers comic collecting kid stuff should drop by Manhattan's Commodore Hotel July 4-8 and dig the Sixth Annual Comic Art Convention that will be in progress. Hundreds of collectors will be there to swap and sell their wares, along with guest speakers... plus films, seminars, parties, lectures, art exhibits and MUCH, MUCH MORE! POW!"

An earlier adaptation of Will Eisner's *Spirit* appeared as an ABC made-for-TV movie in 1987. It was lower budget than the later feature film, and while not good in any sense of the word, it at least resembled the source material. *The*

New York Times started its review by explaining some of the character's back story before adding, "Actually, none of that matters; remember that this is from a comic book." The reviewer goes on to try and write about the lead character but, "Not being familiar with Mr. Eisner's creation... this viewer does not know how faithfully the actor Sam Jones captures [the Spirit], or even if there is anything to capture." One can't imagine *The New York Times* not even bothering to do its research, let alone dismissing the need to do so, for anything but a comic-book adaptation.

Yet examples abound in *The New York Times* alone. Serious financial woes that nearly sunk Marvel Comics in the 1990s were reported as "Pow! The Punches that Left Marvel Reeling." In the TV Notes section of 4 October 2000, an article on World Wrestling Entertainment is entitled "Bam! Pow! Zap! Do Not Underestimate the Lure of Professional Wrestling." The cartoonish nature of the James Bond franchise is quickly established in this capsule movie review from 29 December 2006: "The latest James Bond vehicle finds the British spy leaner, meaner[,] and now played by an attractive piece of blond rough named Daniel Craig. Zap, pow, ka-ching!"

Especially after Art Spiegelman's *Maus* (a graphic memoir of his father's experiences as a Jew under Hitler) won the Pulitzer Prize in 1992, many serious critics and scholars began cautiously taking comics seriously. By the 1990s, a slew of creators were telling individual and unique stories whose only resemblance to an issue of *Superman* was that they consisted of drawings and word balloons printed on paper and shared a common visual and storytelling vocabulary.

But even when taking the topic seriously, *The Times* can't help throwing in that little jab – *Pow!* A report on a January 1999 University of Massachusetts seminar on the graphic novel (a fancy term someone in comic books came up with to make long-form comic-book storytelling sound legitimate) was headlined "Meeting of Comic Minds but No Bam! Splat! Zap!" The article posed the question everyone reading it (but none of the people participating in the seminar) would have asked: "Do comic books really deserve such sober treatment?"

Holy stereotypes, Batman!

When *Batman* hit the airwaves, it sparked an interest in comics that did little to improve sales but dramatically heightened public awareness of their existence, if not their current quality. "Oh, are those still being published?" grown-ups would say. Comics were a part of childhood, a happy memory that had been momentarily resurrected, and the adult TV viewer was unlikely to have seen any difference between *Batman* and other adventure series, like *Star Trek* or *The Man From U.N.C.L.E.*, both of which possessed all the qualities the general public perceived as belonging to comic books.

And comic books remained kids stuff, at least in the minds of that public and certainly to the press, who now had "Pow! Zap! Bam!" to fall back on so they didn't have to look at what was actually going on but could continue to give the reader the message they expected to hear.

Batman's onomatopoeia and Robin's exclaimed "Holy"s were brands seared into the hide of comic books. 41 years after *Batman*'s last new episode was broadcast, it is the show's legacy, a knee-jerk response to the mere mention of comic books.

Batman was originally broadcast at 7:30 p.m., in a time-slot known as "family hour," reserved for kid-friendly fare. The program also spawned a theatrical film in the summer of 1966 that cleaned up at the box office but only reinforced the show's patent ridiculousness and originated such well-remembered clichés as "Shark-repellent Batspray" and the infamous line, spoken by Batman after spending several moments trying to dispose of a cartoonish bomb in a heavily trafficked area, "Some days you just can't get rid of a bomb." After the program's 120 episodes aired on first-run network TV, it went into daytime syndication, exposing it to subsequent generations of viewers, fewer and fewer of whom would ever read a Batman comic book and knew him only through the reruns and such Saturday morning cartoon shows as *Super Friends*.

Batmania, the media and merchandising craze resulting from the show, gave legs to the attention being received by Stan Lee over at Marvel Comics. Spider-Man's teenaged existential angst and the Fantastic Four's ever-exploding nuclear family had the intelligentsia *thinking* about comics. *Batman* wasn't so much about thought as it was about nostalgia for the critics and grown-ups who gave any thought to it at all. Nostalgia, however, has a way of infantilizing its subject, and *Batman* and its dated image of comic books has remained the public perception of the media ever since.

All this has done nothing to damage the commercial viability of Batman the *product*. As early as 29 March 1966, two months after *Batman* debuted – and on the eve of the opening of the Broadway musical comedy based on another DC Comics property, *It's a Bird… It's a Plane… It's Superman* – *The New York Times* was reporting that Pop Art was taking over "the cultural, subcultural and pseudocultural scene... Just now the principle pop focus is on the comic strip, which, in more forms than one can keep track of, is turning into the biggest bonanza of all." Batman alone was pulling in an estimated $75 million a year in sales; Superman was expected to exceed that figure.

In the years since, Batman has never failed to provide his share of the rent money to DC Comics and its later parent company, Warner Communications – later Time-Warner, later Time-AOL, and currently back to Warner Bros. *Batman* reruns ran for years, although they have been missing from American airwaves for the last decade or so. Rumors that this is because Warner Bros was embarrassed by the program and did not want its campy goofiness tarnishing its later blockbuster movie franchises are false. The show is available for syndication but has simply had little to no takers in the domestic market – it does run in several overseas markets. In the words of a Warner Bros. executive, "we enjoy cashing checks on [*Batman*]." Rather, the Fox Corporation, the primary rights holder on the show, and Warner Bros. have thus far been unable to work out an agreement that will allow the show to be released on DVD.

Batman has led to a succession of successful, some even critically acclaimed (others deservedly bashed) movies, TV shows, and animated programs: *The Adventures of Batman* (animated TV series, 1967-1970), *Super Friends* (1973-1986), *The New Adventures of Batman* (animated TV series, 1977-1981), *Batman* (1989), *Batman Returns* (1992), *Batman: The Animated Series* (1992-1999), *Batman: Mask of the Phantasm* (animated feature, 1993), *Batman Forever* (1995), *Batman and Robin* (1997), *Batman & Mr. Freeze: SubZero* (direct-to-video animated feature, 1998), *Batman Beyond* (animated TV series, 1999-2001), *Batman Beyond: Return of the Joker* (direct-to-video animated feature, 2000), *Justice League* (animated TV series featuring Batman, 2001-2004), *Birds of Prey* (TV series, 2002-2003), *Teen Titans* (animated TV series featuring Robin, 2003-2006), *Batman: Mystery of the Batwoman* (direct-to-video animated feature, 2003), *Catwoman* (2004), *The Batman* (animated TV series, 2004-2008), *Justice League Unlimited* (animated TV series featuring Batman, 2005-2006), *Batman Begins* (2005), *The Batman Versus Dracula* (direct-to-video animated feature, 2005), *Batman: Gotham Knight* (direct-to-video animated feature, 2008), *The Dark Knight* (2008), *Justice League: The New Frontier* (direct-to-video animated feature, 2008), *Batman: The Brave and the Bold* (animated TV series, 2008-present), *Superman / Batman: Public Enemies* (direct-to-video animated feature, 2009), *Justice League: Crisis on Two Earths* (direct-to-video animated feature, 2010), *Batman: Under the Red Hood* (direct-to-video animated feature, 2010), and *Superman / Batman: Apocalypse* (direct-to-video animated feature, 2010). Finding a day since 1966 when Batman did not appear in some shape or incarnation on an American TV screen might prove to be an impossible task. Batman is one of the very few most recognizable fictional characters in the world. One does not have to wonder how the Caped Crusader made it to this list.

Commercially, *Batman*'s legacy can be counted in the *tens of billions* of dollars.

It was the right program hitting the airwaves at the right time with just the right attitude to tap into the American gestalt. It was quirky and irreverent, at once celebrating the country's strength and righteousness – it was, let's not forget, the height of the Cold War with the evil Soviet empire – and mocking of its authority figures. The Man couldn't handle the insanity of the bizarre criminals created in reaction to the old, authoritarian state, so he had to call in the costumed outsider to save him. Batman didn't need a badge, just the knowledge that he was on the side of good and justice. Batman was a kinder, gentler anti-hero, a primetime Children's Hour version of Marlon Brando or James Dean.

Batman also made it possible for every super-hero movie and TV show that followed. It proved that super-heroes could be successful network fare (the 1950s *Adventures of Superman* had been a syndicated program), even if the networks still didn't quite get what a super-hero program should be. NBC responded to *Batman* in January 1967 with *Captain Nice*, a spoof created by Buck Henry (co-creator with Mel Brooks of *Get Smart*) and starring William Daniels as a bumbling police chemist who accidentally creates a formula which gives him super-powers. CBS was right there that same month (in fact, the same night) with *Mister Terrific*, wherein bumbling gas station attendant Stanley Beamish secretly fights crime for a government organization with the one hour of super-powers supplied him by a secret "power pill." In both efforts, hilarity did not ensue, and after 17 episodes each, they sunk into well-deserved oblivion. Batman caught the right tone to make it Pop Art; *Captain Nice* and *Mister Terrific* just missed the point.

Still, the list of TV shows and major motion pictures made possible by the success of *Batman* is nothing short of amazing, with more than a few movies holding box-office records among the highest grossing films of all time. And ticket sales are only the tip of the monetary iceberg. If *The Dark Knight* grossed half a billion dollars in tickets, it likely quadrupled that number in licensing and merchandising revenues. Multiply those numbers by half a dozen successful Batman, Superman, X-Men, Spider-Man, and other franchises, add in licensing fees and revenue from DVDs and soundtracks, throw in animated shows that run for several years before going into syndication and being released on video... And we haven't even gotten to the Underoos, the lunchboxes, T-shirts, backpacks, sneakers, nightlights, belt buckles, car floor mats, electric toothbrushes, coffee mugs, mouse pads, costume jewelry, and pool cues, among the hundreds of licensed items available. The licensing department at DC Comics receives thousands of requests a year for deals, even without a movie or TV show driving interest. Batman, Superman, and Wonder Woman are what the licensing business calls perennials or evergreens: the whole world knows who these characters are, and they sell, year after year, on the strength of their own brand.

Much of this, one can argue, is thanks to *Batman*.

Of course, there was the "Pow! Zap! Bam!" price to pay for comics' newfound acceptance. Yes, the popular kids in mass media finally recognized comic books and invited them to sit at the cool table with them in the lunchroom... but not out of friendship. It was so they would have a whipping boy close at hand to make fun of and slap around. News stories connected to comic books, whether about a new movie, the attendance at a convention, the record price paid for an old comic, or a creator, will not fail to reference *Batman* in one way or another.

One can't blame the show for all of this. It did, after all, get the essence of Batman himself correct: a serious, sober man and the world's greatest detective, finding and analyzing clues like nobody's business and escaping cunning deathtraps. It played off his seriousness to create the comedy and used the pop culture of the moment for its style and tone. And if not for the pop sensibilities and Warholian irony, *Batman* would have been just another failed sitcom with a goofy angle like *Captain Nice* or *Mister Terrific*. The only difference was that Batman had a rabid fan base to complain about the injury done to the object of their affection – people who, as a whole, tend to be unable to separate what is going on in the comic books, their medium of preference, from events or approaches to the material in other medium.

Except for some of the carry-over from the TV show to the comics at the time, William Dozier's version has done little to the character itself. That damage has been done on that front, by writers raised on *Batman* who subsequently offered bad interpretations of the Dark Knight, is undeniable, but

At left, Homer Simpson embraces the show's legacy, albeit in a mocking manner. From *Simpsons Comics* #164 (March 2010). Art by Jason Ho and Mike Rote. Copyright © Bongo Entertainment. At right, artist and Bat-fan Michael Allred claims that DC made him alter this artwork for fear of likeness issues. It was later used on the back cover for *Solo* #7 (Dec 2005), the front cover of which featured Wonder Girl doing the Batusi. Copyright © DC Comics.

blaming *Batman* for that would be like holding the manufacturer of velvet responsible for the bad paintings of Elvis people have done on pieces of their cloth. The true culprit (and culprits there have to be in a tale about super-heroes) is mass media, the lazy reporters, and writers and editors whose imaginations are not equal to the task of headlining the imaginations of others.

A Google search of "pow zap bam" yielded 191,000 results. It's probably easier to find a reporter who can tell you what the initials of Captain Marvel's "SHAZAM" stand for than one who has not used the sound effect gimmick in a story about, however peripherally, comics. I wouldn't be surprised if many writers have resisted the temptation, only to have the words inserted by editors after the fact. Why take the time to research a story when you can produce one that meets the expectations of your readers with canned phrases and pop references?

But the producers of comic-book movies and TV are also to blame for providing the source of the clichés by creating material which often seems like just another string of them. They are embarrassed to be associated with this kid's stuff, but can't walk away from all the money to be made from it. Isn't there a word for that practice? They are purveyors of pop culture, although, like athletes who demand their fans not view them as role models, they see no responsibility as coming with their job. Only in rare cases (*Iron Man* and *Batman Begins* spring immediately to mind) do filmmakers get through an entire movie without feeling the need to wink at the audience and slip in the self-referential moment that lets you know that *they* know that this stuff isn't really to be taken seriously.

In interviews, Adam West was quick to point out that the mere act of putting on the cape and cowl took the performance to a different level, essentially to a world in which things like a man putting on a costume to go into the night and fight crime actually happen. "The trick," he told an interviewer in 1966, "is to let the costume work for you." In other words, the costume inhabit the world the way the actor inhabits the costume. Treat it as real and with respect because, for the purposes of this fiction, it *is* real.

West found the element that made his Batman believable and was able to give a performance free of any sign that he was embarrassed to be playing the role.

Holy Hollywood! Why is that so hard for the rest of them to figure out?

Afterword

by Jeff Rovin

If you're here, I don't need to sell you on the *Batman* TV series. You know the show wasn't a celebration of "*the* Batman" or "the Dark Knight." You understand that the show's operative word is "fun," as it was for the Batman comics of the 1950s and early '60s, in which it is rooted. You recognize that many of us cherish that simplicity and sense of wonder. Indeed, a few of us prefer it. Passionately.

The show helped to save the Batman comic book (which was in newsstand free-fall), but it had larger media ramifications. *Batman* (along with *Star Trek*) boosted the sale of color TVs. It also gave stature to ABC, which had consistently been third among the top three networks.

Still, not everyone in comics fandom family loves the Batman show. Unlike *The Adventures of Superman* or *The Lone Ranger*, it seemed to be making fun of our hero.

It wasn't, though. Not the same way that *Honey West* joyously dumped on the conventions of detective fiction, or *The Man from U.N.C.L.E.* and *Get Smart* perforated the spy genre to different degrees, or virtually every screen Tarzan until Gordon Scott devolved Edgar Rice Burroughs' articulate Englishman into a Cro-Magnon. No, *Batman* was a blend of the deadpan and the *outré*, done so artfully that if you looked at it with an adult sensibility, it just wasn't serious any more. That was unique, and it was genius.

Think about it. The TV series *Captain Nice* and *Mr. Terrific*, which debuted (and quickly departed) a few months after *Batman*, were respectively clever-funny and stupid-funny, but no one remembers them much. *The Green Hornet* had a lot going for it: Bruce Lee, the racing Al Hirt theme song, the seductive Black Beauty, the lovely Wende Wagner, and Van Williams looking sharp as the crime fighter, but it was kind of plodding and self-important.

Not *Batman*.

When the show debuted, many of us kids ignored the adults who laughed at it. And I didn't share the pique of fans who resented the "holy" this or the "bat" that. I mean, Batarang and Batmobile were okay, but "super-fine Bat-grain" film wasn't? "Pow" was acceptable in a comic book but not on TV? Holy hypocrisy!

We enjoyed the energy, the high production values, and the villainy so extreme and impractical that it could only make sense to characters who purred like a cat or waddled like a penguin or had a head shaped like an egg. Then there was the enthusiasm of Burt Ward, the dignity of Alan Napier and Neil Hamilton, and of course, the singular poise, conviction, and mesmeric delivery of Adam West.

(Speaking of Adam, whom I've known for over a quarter-century, when my son resisted potty-training, I had Adam call him. "You need to master this," Adam said in his best underlining-a-life-lesson-for-Dick voice. "And I know what I'm talking about. My initials *are* B.M.")

For those of you too young to remember, Batmania excited, daunted, puzzled, and pervaded our society in 1966. That's not an overstatement. It was the culmination of a three-year pop-culture boom that threaded from the Beatles through Bond to the Batcave.

Nor was it unprecedented: Disney had created similar crazes in the 1950s with Davy Crockett and Zorro (though those were not perceived in quite the same way), as part of a larger pop-culture upheaval of society. That parade pretty much ended with the Caped Crusader, as American innocence was consumed in the counter-culture / anti-war blaze that followed.

Batmania also elevated, then discarded, the man at the center of the craze: a former Hawaiian TV personality and Warner Bros. contract player born Bill Anderson. Over a dozen years ago, when I worked with Adam West on his memoir *Back to the Batcave*, I was startled to find that the most telling memory he had of the era was that he had relatively few memories of the era. He was working on two, sometimes three episodes at a time (shooting the scenes for one or more shows in the Batcave, rehearsing new scripts) and often slept in his studio dressing room to get an early start the next day. There were also interviews, personal appearances, and filming the feature-length film. Understandable how it all ran together.

I had first broached the idea of Adam's memoirs around 1982, when I was writing a film column for *Omni*. Adam didn't know me then, but he knew the magazine. He was living just outside of Hollywood and agreed to meet at a restaurant on Sunset Boulevard. Adam was still grumpy about the whole thing. The show had used and chucked him. He couldn't get work despite the fact (or because of the fact) that when he called information every phone operator on the planet recognized his voice. I wouldn't call it regret, but he was certainly second-guessing the fact that he had abandoned the Clint Eastwood Spaghetti Western route in order to do *Batman*. He didn't even have the "if you can't beat 'em, join 'em" option; Mike Uslan had been conventioneering and talking up a new Batman movie that would leave the "camp" approach behind.

That wasn't the article I wanted to write, and didn't. Instead, I had another suggestion. I was publishing a magazine at the time, *Videogaming Illustrated*, and invited Adam to co-host an awards presentation at an industry convention in Chicago in 1983 (along with Bob Shayne, Inspector Henderson of TV's *The Adventures of Superman* – a meeting of crime-busting titans). Adam was charming and people loved him. I asked him to attend a fundraiser at my son's school in Connecticut; before agreeing, Adam first made sure the young man was toilet-trained. The event was modestly advertised but drew a large, adoring crowd. Adam felt good, and after working on a few things that didn't pan out (a film version of the Phantom which would have been shot in Mexico City had King Features not wanted too much money for the rights; a new super-hero called Devil Bat; and an animated, all-rabbit epic called *Ben Hare*), we agreed to pursue the memoir.

But there was the real problem of big, gaping holes in his memory. Happily, over many years of doing celebrity interviews for magazines like *Omni* and *Ladies Home Journal,* I had met a number of his *Batman* co-stars like Vincent Price, Cliff Robertson, Otto Preminger, and Burgess Meredith. Eartha Kitt, whom I didn't know, once dialed a wrong number and got me – I kid you not – so we talked. When I worked for DC in the early 1970s, I chatted with Bob Kane. Their memories triggered Adam's memories. I had met producer Cubby Broccoli in 1979 and asked if it were true that Adam had been a finalist to replace Connery as James Bond (it was). The saga was a helluva story, and we were gratified that we got to set it all down. Adam was particularly moved when he showed up at a Barnes & Noble signing on tony Fifth Avenue in New

Adam West and Bob Shayne (Gotham's Bruce Wayne and Metropolis's Inspector Henderson) co-host an industry awards presentation in Chicago in 1983.

York City to find a long, long line that stretched well outside the store. It seemed a transformative moment. Adam had seen a new Batman, Michael Keaton, don the cowl... but he hadn't been forgotten as he once thought. The fans remembered.

And clearly, you remember still.

Appendix: Episode Guide

by Joseph F. Berenato

For easy reference, each episode's annotation begins with the name of its villain(s). Interesting notes and factoids are provided in italics at the end of the annotation.

First Season (1966)
1. "Hi Diddle Riddle" (12 January 1966)
2. "Smack in the Middle" (13 January 1966)
The Riddler sues Batman. His moll, Molly, infiltrates the Batcave disguised as Robin. Batman then tracks the villain to the Moldavian Pavilion at the Gotham City World's Fair. *This is the only episode featuring the death of a major character.*
3. "Fine Feathered Finks" (19 January 1966
4. "The Penguin's a Jinx" (20 January 1966)
The Penguin sets out to snare Batman in his latest scheme but nets Bruce Wayne instead. In turn, Batman plans to trap the Penguin using a beautiful actress as bait. *This episode was based on "Partners in Plunder," from Batman #169 (Feb 1965).*
5. "The Joker is Wild" (26 January 1966)
6. "Batman is Riled" (27 January 1966)
The Joker, after repeatedly being foiled by the contents of Batman's utility belt, creates one of his own. Batman then gets wise to Joker's plans and lies in wait to capture him. *Cesar Romero was actually the third actor considered to play the Joker after Jose Ferrer and Gig Young.*
7. "Instant Freeze" (2 February 1966)
8. "Rats Like Cheese" (3 February 1966)
Mr. Freeze, seeking revenge on Batman for causing his condition, begins a series of crimes involving diamonds. He captures Batman and Robin and plans to put them on ice – literally and figuratively. *Based in part on "The Ice Crimes of Mr. Zero" from Batman #121 (Feb 1959).*
9. "Zelda the Great" (9 February 1966)

10. "A Death Worse Than Fate" [10 February 1966]

Zelda the Great, renowned escape artist, robs Gotham's First National Bank to pay a "mad Albanian genius" for escape tricks for her act. The Albanian's invention? An inescapable doom-trap meant for Batman and Robin. *Based on "Batman's Inescapable Doom-Trap!" from* Detective Comics *#346 (Dec 1965) – though the villain was changed from the Great Canardo to Zelda the Great, in an effort to add more femme fatales to the show.*

11. "A Riddle a Day Keeps the Riddler Away" [16 February 1966]

12. "When the Rat's Away, the Mice Will Play" [17 February 1966]

The Riddler returns. European potentate King Boris comes to Gotham bearing a monument meant for the city's museum, but the Riddler swaps out the king's gift with a bomb. Batman must solve the Riddler's clues and do some swapping of his own before it's too late. *The final TV appearance for actor Reginald Denny, who portrays King Boris.*

13. "The Thirteenth Hat" [23 February 1966]

14. "Batman Stands Pat" [24 February 1966]

The Mad Hatter begins abducting the hats of the jurors (and the jurors themselves) who sent him to jail after his last crime spree. He also targets Batman, whose testimony ensured the guilty verdict. *Based in part on "The New Crimes of the Mad Hatter" from* Batman *#161, Feb. 1964.*

15. "The Joker Goes to School" [2 March 1966]

16. "He Meets His Match, the Grisly Ghoul" [3 March 1966]

The Joker has started to recruit students from Woodrow Roosevelt High School (which Dick Grayson attends) into his Bad Pennies Gang. Batman and Robin convince one of Dick's cheerleader classmates to help them bring the gang down. *Donna Loren (Susie the Cheerleader) was chosen in 1963 to be the first and only Dr. Pepper Girl – a title she held for five years.*

17. "True or False-Face" [9 March 1966]

18. "Holy Rat Race" [10 March 1966]

False-Face, master of disguise, begins a robbery spree by stealing the Mergenberg Crown and replacing it with a forgery, right under the eyes of the local police. Nothing is as it seems as Batman and Robin follow false leads and false clues. *False-Face (whom many believe to have been created for the TV series) had only one comic-book appearance, in "The Menace of False Face!" from* Batman *#113 (Feb 1958).*

19. "The Purr-fect Crime" [16 March 1966]

20. "Better Luck Next Time" [17 March 1966]

Catwoman is on the prowl in Gotham, stealing artifacts to help her locate a lost pirate's treasure. Batman and Robin battle tigers and minefields before cornering her near a bottomless ravine. *Julie Newmar, who portrayed Catwoman for much of the series, designed and sewed her own costume for the show.*

21. "The Penguin Goes Straight" [23 March 1966]

22. "Not Yet, He Ain't" [24 March 1966]

The Penguin, appearing to have given up crime, manages to frame the Dynamic Duo for robbery. Batman and Robin fake their own deaths in order to flush out the Penguin's true intentions. *This episode introduces the Batcycle.*

23. "The Ring of Wax" [30 March 1966]

24. "Give 'Em the Axe" [31 March 1966]

The Riddler steals a rare book to learn the location of the Lost Treasure of the Incas. The Caped Crusaders pursue him to a museum where the Riddler stands ready to destroy priceless artifacts to find the treasure. *Joe E. Tata (Tallow, the*

Riddler's henchman) is better known as Nat, the owner of the Peach Pit on Beverly Hills, 90210.
25. "The Joker Trumps an Ace" (6 April 1966)
26. "Batman Sets the Pace" (7 April 1966)
The Joker commits a series of robberies that make no sense to anyone but him. Batman believes the Joker is going to steal the Maharajah of Nimpah's solid-gold golf clubs, but the Joker instead kidnaps the Maharajah himself, holding him for a $500,000 ransom. *Inspired by the story "A Hairpin, a Hoe, a Hacksaw, a Hole in the Ground" from Batman #53 (June-July 1949).*
27. "The Curse of Tut" (13 April 1966)
28. "The Pharaoh's in a Rut" (14 April 1966)
King Tut is created when a respected Yale University professor of Egyptology receives a blow to the head. Batman must stop the criminal from carrying out his plans, which include the kidnapping of Bruce Wayne. *King Tut was the first villain created for the show with no counterpart in the Batman comics.*
29. "The Bookwork Turns" (20 April 1966)
30. "While Gotham City Burns" (21 April 1966)
The Bookworm uses pilfered book plots to plan his crimes. Things heat up for Batman and Robin as they attempt to stop his robbery spree. *This was the first episode to feature the famous window cameos; the guest was Jerry Lewis.*
31. "Death in Slow Motion" (27 April 1966)
32. "The Riddler's False Notion" (28 April 1966)
The Riddler commits (and films) a series of crimes in the style of classic silent movies. Batman must come to the aid of a silent-era film star who has crossed the Riddler's path. *This was originally a Joker story in the comics, "The Joker's Comedy Capers!" from Detective Comics #341 (July, 1965).*
33. "Fine Finny Fiends" (4 May 1966)
34. "Batman Makes the Scenes" (5 May 1966)
The Penguin kidnaps Alfred to learn the location of Bruce Wayne's Multimillionaires' Annual Award Dinner. He crashes the party and gasses everyone – including Batman and Robin. *Victor Lundin, who pays the Penguin's henchman Octopus, also played Star Trek's first-ever on-screen Klingon, in 1966's "Errand of Mercy."*

The Movie (1966)

With the series a hit, 20th Century-Fox agreed to make a feature film, at a budget of almost $1.4 million. Filming took place after the first season had wrapped, from 25 April to 31 May, and the movie was in theatres in July, before the second season began. At 105 minutes, longer than four episodes, it remains the longest single story in the show's history.
Batman (20 July 1966)
The Joker, the Penguin, the Riddler, and Catwoman, together comprising the United Underworld, marshal their forces in a bid to take over not only Gotham City but also the world. When they kidnap and dehydrate the nine members of the United World Security Council, Batman and Robin must endure exploding sharks, torpedo attacks, Batcave infiltrators, and more in order to save the world.
This was the final film appearance for Reginald Denny, who played Commodore Schmidlapp. The voice of President Lyndon B. Johnson was done by Van Williams, better known to audiences as the Green Hornet. This film was the final film appearance of Madge Blake, who played Aunt Harriet Cooper.

Second Season (1966-1967)

This season contained the show's first two three-parters, in the season's second half, but was otherwise comprised (like the entire first season) of two-parters.

35. "Shoot a Crooked Arrow" (7 September 1966)
36. "Walk the Straight and Narrow" (8 September 1966)
The Archer and his men rob from the rich – including Bruce Wayne – and give to the poor, winning the hearts of Gothamites. Batman and Robin must expose him for the fraud they believe he is. *This episode's window cameo was Dick Clark.*

37. "Hot Off the Griddle" (14 September 1966)
38. "The Cat and the Fiddle" (15 September 1966)
Catwoman returns with a school for cat burglars and a string of cat-themed robberies. Batman sets a trap for her using Robin and two violins as bait. *This episode is the first of three appearances by actor James Brolin; he plays driver Ralph Staphylococcus.*

39. "The Minstrel's Shakedown" (21 September 1966)
40. "Barbecued Batman" (22 September 1966)
The Minstrel uses his music-based electronic gizmos to send the Gotham Stock Exchange into a panic. Batman and Robin must stop him from shattering the market – and the Exchange itself. *Comedienne Phyllis Diller has a cameo as a scrubwoman.*

41. "The Spell of Tut" (28 September 1966)
42. "Tut's Case is Shut" (29 September 1966)
King Tut's latest plans involve an ancient beetle. Batman must overcome mind-control to stop the villain's nefarious scheme. *This episode's window cameo featured Van Williams as the Green Hornet and Bruce Lee as Kato.*

43. "The Greatest Mother of Them All" (5 October 1966)
44. "Ma Parker" (6 October 1966)
Ma Parker and her family of gangsters get arrested by Batman and Robin, but that plays right into her plans. She and her cronies take over the prison, and it's up to the Dynamic Duo to stop them. *Julie Newmar makes a brief cameo as Catwoman.*

45. "The Clock King's Crazy Crimes" (12 October 1966)
46. "The Clock King Gets Crowned" (13 October 1966)
The Clock King springs into Gotham, committing a series of time-themed crimes, including the theft of valuable artwork. Clues lead Batman and Robin on a race against time to Gotham's Clock Tower. *Popping out of a window in this episode is Sammy Davis Jr.*

47. "An Egg Grows in Gotham" (19 October 1966)
48. "The Yegg Foes in Gotham" (20 October 1966)
Egghead takes control of the city, exploiting a little-known clause in the Gotham City charter. When he legally banishes Batman and Robin, they must try to find another clause in the charter to scramble Egghead's plans. *Bill Dana appeared as Jose Jimenez, a popular TV character of the time, for this episode's window cameo.*

49. "The Devil's Fingers" (26 October 1966)
50. "The Dead Ringers" (27 October 1966)
Chandell, a famous pianist, comes to Gotham with plans to marry Aunt Harriet, get rid of Bruce and Dick, and thus win the entire Wayne fortune. Batman must come to the rescue, but things become discordant when Chandell's twin gets involved. *These two episodes were the highest-rated in the show's history.*

51. "Hizzonner the Penguin" (2 November 1966)
52. "Dizzoner the Penguin" (3 November 1966)

The Penguin, again claiming to have gone straight, waddles his way into running for Mayor of Gotham City. Batman must not only stop him from winning but also from committing crimes all over the city. *The appearance by Paul Revere and the Raiders in this episode marks the first time a rock band appeared on a sitcom.*

53. "Green Ice" (9 November 1966)

54. "Deep Freeze" (10 November 1966)

Mr. Freeze, after escaping from prison, kidnaps Miss Iceland and begins plans to discredit the Dynamic Duo. Freeze holds the city ransom for one billion dollars, and Batman and Robin must infiltrate his lair to defeat him. *This episode's eccentrically-named director, George WaGGner (not a typo), helmed the classic 1941 Universal horror film, The Wolf Man.*

55. "The Impractical Joker" (16 November 1966)

56. "The Joker's Provokers" (17 November 1966)

The Joker is back in Gotham City, this time performing a series of key-themed crimes with the help of a mysterious box. When he reveals that his box allows him to control time, it's up to Batman and Robin to trap him before it's too late. *Actor Howard Duff provides this episode's window cameo. He would later appear in the third-season episode, "The Entrancing Dr. Cassandra."*

57. "Marsha, Queen of Diamonds" (23 November 1966)

58. "Marsha's Scheme of Diamonds" (24 November 1966)

Marsha, the Queen of Diamonds, puts Commissioner Gordon, Chief O'Hara, and the Boy Wonder under her spell with a love potion. Meanwhile, she schemes to get the Bat-Diamond, which powers the Bat-Computer. Batman must resist her charms – and her marriage proposal – to put her away for good. *Carolyn Jones (Marsha) is best-remembered for starring as Morticia Addams in The Addams Family (1964-1966).*

59. "Come Back, Shame" (30 November 1966)

60. "It's the Way You Play the Game" (31 November 1966)

Shame, a crime cowboy, and his gang have been stealing car parts to build a truck that can outrun the Batmobile. When the Dynamic Duo fails to stop his many capers, they are forced to use their powers of deduction to determine his whereabouts. *Cliff Robertson (Shame) is much better known for his portrayal, decades layer, of Uncle Ben Parker in the Spider-Man trilogy of feature films.*

61. "The Penguin's Nest" (7 December 1966)

62. "The Bird's Last Jest" (8 December 1966)

The Penguin has been collecting handwriting samples from wealthy Gothamites, hoping to have his cellblock buddy use them to forge checks. Batman, Robin, and the entire judicial system make it their mission to keep him out of jail. *Ted Cassidy is this episode's window cameo, appearing as Lurch from The Addams Family.*

63. "The Cat's Meow" (14 December 1966)

64. "The Bat's Kow Tow" (15 December 1966)

Catwoman has a new toy – a Voice Eraser – and uses it on Commissioner Gordon, talk-show host Allen Stevens, and British rock singers Chad and Jeremy. She holds the rockers' voices for a hefty ransom, and Batman must find her to restore the voices. *Real-life talk-show host Steve Allen portrays fictional talk-show host Allen Stevens.*

65. "The Puzzles are Coming" (21 December 1966)

66. "The Duo is Slumming" (22 December 1966)

The Puzzler has set his sights on the world of multimillionaire Artemus Knab, from the jewels of his party guests to his new supersonic jet. He is no match for Batman and Robin, as they solve his puzzles and confront him at the jet's hangar.

This episode was originally slated to spotlight the Riddler but was altered when Frank Gorshin declined to reprise the role.

67. "The Sandman Cometh" (28 December 1966)
68. "A Stitch in Time / The Catwoman Goeth" (29 December 1966)
Catwoman and Sandman, a European criminal, team up to steal the fortune of J. Pauline Spaghetti. When they kidnap Robin, Batman must rescue him, Ms. Spaghetti, *and* her fortune. *Burlesque queen Gypsy Rose Lee, upon whose life the musical Gypsy is based, makes a cameo as a newscaster.*

69. "The Contaminated Cowl" (4 January 1967)
70. "The Mad Hatter Runs Afoul" (5 January 1967)
The Mad Hatter, after escaping from prison, irradiates Batman's cowl and plans to swipe it when it is removed for decontamination. Little does he know there's a homing beacon inside of it, which Batman and Robin use to their advantage. *Based on "The Mad Hatter of Gotham City!" from Detective Comics #230 (April, 1956).*

71. "The Zodiac Crimes" (11 January 1967)
72. "The Joker's Hard Times" (12 January 1967)
73. "The Penguin Declines" (18 January 1967)
The Joker and the Penguin team up to plan a series of crimes inspired by the Zodiac. Joker's moll becomes disillusioned with him and switches allegiances to aid Batman and Robin. Penguin takes advantage of that switch, and the Dynamic Duo must overcome both his and Joker's chicanery. *Look for a very young Rob Reiner as a delivery boy.*

74. "That Darn Catwoman" (19 January 1967)
75. "Scat! Darn Catwoman" (25 January 1967)
Catwoman's assistant, Pussycat, drugs Robin and is able to enlist his help in their crimes. Batman is later drugged, but his anonymous calls to the police help in the arrest of Catwoman's gang members. *Pussycat was played by pop singer Lesley Gore, the niece of producer Howie Horwitz.*

76. "Penguin is a Girl's Best Friend" (26 January 1967)
77. "Penguin Sets a Trend" (1 February 1967)
78. "Penguin's Disastrous End" (2 February 1967)
The Penguin and Marsha, Queen of Diamonds team up when the Penguin starts a movie company and coerces Batman and Robin to sign contracts to appear in a movie with Marsha. Naturally the company is a front for Penguin's latest robbery plans, and the Dynamic Duo find themselves in mortal peril. *Guest-star Alan Reed (General MacGruder in "Penguin Sets a Trend") is best known as the voice of Fred Flintstone.*

79. "Batman's Anniversary" (8 February 1967)
80. "A Riddling Controversy" (9 February 1967)
The Riddler crashes a party for Batman's crime-fighting anniversary and makes off with the donations. After a few more robberies, he buys a De-Molecularizer, holds the city hostage and Batman must curtail his plan. *John Astin, best known as Gomez from The Addams Family, appeared as the Riddler because of a contract dispute with Frank Gorshin.*

81. "The Joker's Last Laugh" (15 February 1967)
82. "The Joker's Epitaph" (16 February 1967)
The Joker is distributing funny money via a robot teller at Gotham National Bank. A plan by Batman to uncover the fraud makes Joker the bank's vice-president, which subsequently results in Bruce Wayne being declared insane. *Lawrence Montaigne (Mr. Glee) is best known as Stonn from the classic 1967 Star Trek episode "Amok Time."*

83. "Catwoman Goes to College" (22 February 1967)
84. "Batman Displays His Knowledge" (23 February 1967)
Catwoman, a new criminology student at Gotham City University, steals a life-sized statue of Batman so she can make a costume replica for one of her cronies. Her plan lands Batman in prison, leaving her free to commit her crimes... or does it? *Sheldon Allman (Catwoman's henchman Penn) wrote the theme song for George of the Jungle.*

85. "A Piece of the Action" (1 March 1967)
86. "Batman's Satisfaction" (2 March 1967)
Colonel Gumm arrives in Gotham with his counterfeit stamps, spurring his adversaries Green Hornet and Kato to follow. Batman and Robin believe the two are villains, leaving Col. Gumm free to go after both pairs of crime fighters. *Edward G. Robinson provides the window cameo for this episode.*

87. "King Tut's Coup" (8 March 1967)
88. "Batman's Waterloo" (9 March 1967)
King Tut returns after yet another blow to the head. He kidnaps a wealthy socialite's daughter, believing her to be Cleopatra. Batman must not only rescue her but also Robin, whom Tut is going to boil in oil. *Grace Lee Whitney, who portrays Tut's queen Neila, released her autobiography, The Longest Trek: My Tour of the Galaxy, in 1998.*

89. "Black Widow Strikes Again" (15 March 1967)
90. "Caught in the Spider's Den" (16 March 1967)
Black Widow perpetrates a string of alphabetical bank robberies, but Batman and Robin are hot on her trail, leading to their inevitable capture. Batman soon falls under her power, however, and Robin must come to his aid. *While under the Widow's spell, Batman croons a tune from Gilbert & Sullivan's H.M.S. Pinafore.*

91. "Pop Goes the Joker" (22 March 1967)
92. "Flop Goes the Joker" (23 March 1967)
The Joker opens an art school for millionaires (including Bruce Wayne), and kidnaps them instead. Later he holds priceless paintings for ransom, and Batman and Robin – and Alfred – help put the criminal in his place. *Look for actor Fritz Feld, better known as the mouth-popping Mr. Zumdish on Lost in Space.*

93. "Ice Spy" (29 March 1967)
94. "The Duo Defy" (30 March 1967)
Mr. Freeze, with the help of figure skater Glacia Glaze, kidnaps an Icelandic scientist in order to extract his formula for instant ice. He then starts to freeze parts of Gotham, and Batman must track him down and put him on ice. *The final window cameo of the series was by the Carpet King, a carpet mogul who reportedly snared it by selling Persian rugs to series producer William Dozier.*

Third Season (1967-1968)

Airing only once weekly, the third season contained many single-episode stories (a first for the series), along with several two-parters and one three-parter. The multi-part stories did not retain the rhyming titles of past seasons, however.

95. "Enter Batgirl, Exit Penguin" (14 September 1967)
The Penguin, hoping to gain immunity to the law, kidnaps and plans to marry Commissioner Gordon's daughter Barbara, unaware she is actually Batgirl. Alfred, posing as a preacher, learns her double identity. *Dick Grayson finally gets his driver's license in this episode and is legally allowed to drive the Batmobile.*

96. "Ring Around the Riddler" (21 September 1967)
The Riddler is back in town, this time with the intent of controlling prizefighting in Gotham. He challenges Batman to a bout in the ring. *Ill health and a smaller*

budget forced Madge Blake to deliver only two cameos as Aunt Harriet in the third season; this episode is the first.

97. "The Wail of the Siren" – (28 September 1967)

The Siren, a.k.a. Lorelei Circe, is able to mesmerize men with her voice and does so to both Commissioner Gordon and Bruce Wayne. She orders Bruce to sign over all of his holdings to her, and Batgirl and Robin rush to stop her. *The character of The Siren was created specifically for actress Joan Collins.*

98. "The Sport of Penguins" (5 October 1967)

99. "A Horse of Another Color" (12 October 1967)

The Penguin and Lola Lasagne team up after he steals her parasol, unaware she is an old acquaintance of his. The two team up to make a killing at the race track, but a late horse entry by Bruce Wayne puts the kibosh on their plans. *Herbert Anderson (the Racing Secretary) is best known as Henry Mitchell, the title character's father in* Dennis the Menace *(1959-1963).*

100. "The Unkindest Tut of All" (19 October 1967)

King Tut is brought back by a brick to the head, and he begins to predict crimes for the police (and secretly carry them out to gain the police's confidence). A false prediction leads the police in the wrong direction, allowing Tut to steal an ancient artifact. *James Gammon (Osiris) is better known to modern audiences as Coach Lou Brown from* Major League *and* Major League II.

101. "Louie, the Lilac" (26 October 1967)

Louie the Lilac, a gangster, has kidnapped the leader of a flower-in and hopes to control the minds of Gotham's flower children. A battle with a man-eating plant leaves the Dynamic Duo hoping for a rescue from Batgirl. *Lyrics to Batgirl's theme song were used for the second and last time in this episode.*

102. "The Ogg and I" (2 November 1967)

103. "How to Hatch a Dinosaur" (9 November 1967)

Egghead and Olga, Queen of the Cossacks, kidnap Commissioner Gordon and hold him for ransom, issuing a series of demands. They steal a 40-million-year-old egg and some radium, with plans to hatch it on an unsuspecting city. *Alan Hale Jr. has a cameo as a character named Gilligan, a riff on his just-completed three-year run as "Skipper" Jonas Grumby on* Gilligan's Island.

104. "Surf's Up! Joker's Under!" (16 November 1967)

The Joker kidnaps surfer Skip Parker and uses a device to steal his knowledge, hoping to become the king of surfing. Batman challenges him to a surfing contest, with Dick Grayson as a judge. *This episode features a musical cameo by Johnny Green and the Greenmen.*

105. "The Londinium Larcenies" (23 November 1967)

106. "The Foggiest Notion" (30 November 1967)

107. "The Bloody Tower" (7 December 1967)

Lord Ffogg and Lady Peasoup are the villains of this three-parter, in which a series of baffling robberies leads Commissioner Gordon, his daughter Barbara, and Bruce and Dick to far-off "Londinium." There, Batman and Robin discover that Lord Ffogg and Lady Peasoup are running a girls' school for thievery. *This is Madge Blake's last appearance as Aunt Harriet Cooper.*

108. "Catwoman's Dressed to Kill" (14 December 1967)

Catwoman captures Batgirl during an attack on a fashion show. If Batman saves her, however, he leaves the target of Catwoman's next attack vulnerable to her whims. *This is Eartha Kitt's first appearance as Catwoman; series regular Julie Newmar was unavailable for the season.*

109. "The Ogg Couple" (21 December 1967)

Egghead and Olga, Queen of the Cossacks, are at it again, this time with several thefts from the Gotham Museum, as well as a heist involving 500 pounds of caviar. Batgirl convinces Egghead to turn on Olga, but her plans get scrambled when he leads her into a trap. *Originally intended to air in between "The Ogg and I" and "How to Hatch a Dinosaur."*

110. "The Funny Feline Felonies" (28 December 1967)
111. "The Joke's on Catwoman" (4 January 1968)
The Joker and Catwoman team up after the Joker is paroled, and the two begin following clues to a hidden cache of gunpowder. The villains are arrested and put on trial, but it doesn't exactly go as Batman – who is acting as prosecutor – had planned. *Pierre Salinger, White House press secretary under both Kennedy and Johnson, plays Catwoman's defense attorney.*

112. "Louie's Lethal Lilac Time" (11 January 1968)
Louie the Lilac, intent on cornering the market on perfume, kidnaps Bruce and Dick, coercing Bruce (an animal expert) into removing scent glands from several animals. When Bruce refuses, Louie coerces him by threatening to kill a captured Batgirl. *Nobu McCarthy (Lotus), who was once Miss Tokyo, is perhaps better known for her portrayal of Yukie, Mr. Miyagi's old flame in The Karate Kid, Part II.*

113. "Nora Clavicle and the Ladies' Crime Club" (18 January 1968)
Nora Clavicle, a women's rights activist, becomes police commissioner after Mayor Linseed removes Gordon. When Clavicle deposes Batman and begins her scheme to blow up Gotham, it is up to the Terrific Trio to stop her. *This was the only episode that did not feature a Bat-fight.*

114. "Penguin's Clean Sweep" (25 January 1968)
The Penguin infects money from the Gotham Mint with a deadly sleeping sickness, causing Gothamites to dump all of their cash into the street and into the Penguin's clutches. A worldwide warning issued by Bruce Wayne puts the Penguin's plans in jeopardy, and the umbrella-obsessed villain must retaliate. *Burgess Meredith's final appearance as The Penguin.*

115. "The Great Escape" (1 February 1968)
116. "The Great Train Robbery" (8 February 1968)
Shame, the crime cowboy, returns when his fiancée Calamity Jan helps him break out of prison. Two proceed to rob the Gotham City Opera House. After successfully robbing a train, Shame finds himself challenged to a duel – by Batman. *Dina Merrill (Calamity Jan) was, at the time, married to Cliff Robertson (Shame).*

117. "I'll Be a Mummy's Uncle" (22 February 1968)
King Tut goes drilling under Wayne Manor in search of the world's strongest metal, but his drilling leads him right into the Batcave. *Comedian Henny Youngman has a cameo as Manny the Mesopotamian.*

118. "The Joker's Flying Saucer" (29 February 1968)
The Joker, bent on world domination, creates a flying saucer scare, all the while planning to steal the necessary metals to construct a real saucer. He captures Batgirl and Alfred, incapacitates the Dynamic Duo and begins to issue demands from space. *Guest-star Ellen Corby (Mrs. Green) is best known as Grandma Esther Walton from The Waltons (1972-1980).*

119. "The Entrancing Dr. Cassandra" (7 March 1968)
Dr. Cassandra Spellcraft and Cabala, her husband, perpetrate a series of invisible robberies using camouflage pills. The evil duo dispatches Batman, Robin and Batgirl, and sets about their master plan: to release all the super-villains from prison. *This episode's Bat-fight occurred in the dark (i.e. off-screen) – a result of the producers running over their budget.*

120. "Minerva, Mayhem and Millionaires" (14 March 1968)
Minerva, unbeknownst to her millionaire clientele (including Bruce Wayne), has been using a device at her spa to find out where they keep their valuables. Alfred goes undercover but is exposed, and the Dynamic Duo must spring into action. *Producers William Dozier and Howie Horwitz make cameos as two of Minerva's millionaire victims.*

Appendix: A Bat-Discography

by *Michael S. Miller*

The following is a track-by-track discography of the major musical spin-offs and side-projects inspired by the series. For more general information on music and the series, please see my essay.

Neal Hefti, *Batman Theme and 19 Hefti Bat Songs* (1966)

1. "Batman Theme" (2:19). The classic theme, stretched to almost three times its TV length. Still energetic, especially with Hal Blaine's go-for-broke drumming, and a relatively roomy exploration of Neal Hefti's masterpiece. The already speedy tempo increases as the record progresses, becoming more urgent, but never reckless, as it builds to its crescendo. While the TV version seems to climax with "na-na-na-na-na-na-na-na-na," this version clearly ends with a series of "ba-ba-ba-ba-ba-ba-ba-ba-ba" syllables that burst into its final "Batman" cry, evoking the then just months-old stutter on The Who's "My Generation." Maybe that's why the band returned the compliment by recording the "Batman Theme" for its 1966 EP "Ready Steady Who."

2. "Evil Plot to Blow Up Batman" (2:05). An even faster tear through the basic "Batman Theme" riff, propelled by fuzzy guitar, cymbals and brass. It's a breathless, insistent song that offers no clues to the mechanics of the "Evil Plot," but one can envision a feverish Joker ordering a roomful of henchmen around to the hyperkinetic beat.

3. "Sewer Lady" (2:13). A loping, almost whimsical interlude, with slow drum patter, a bluesy harmonica-like trumpet and finger-popping-out-of-a-cheek water bubble dripping sounds that evoke the title reference's atmosphere.

4. "The Mafista" (2:52). More fuzz guitar with a clean guitar-plucked note riding over a bed of brass and ominous xylophone hits. The most dangerous-sounding composition Neal Hefti wrote for the "Batman" project.

5. "Holy Diploma, Batman – Straight A's" (1:43). A regal and respectful march to no doubt accompany young Dick Grayson's cap and gown moment. If you did

not know this came from a *Batman* soundtrack, you might think you had stumbled upon a lost attempt to seriously expand the "Pomp and Circumstance" genre.

6. "Eivol Ekdol, the Albanian Genius" (2:05). A theme for the minor villain Ekdol, as played by Jack Kruschen in two episodes. It starts as an ethnic dance number and drives that feeling all the way through its two minutes, incorporating handclaps, horn charts and tambourine. An actual footstomper, and again, if you approached this music without the prejudice of knowing its origins, you might think you'd found an actual traditional festival song.

7. "The Batusi" (2:15). One of those harmless yet insistent secondary tangents that a massively popular phenomenon manages to propagate, like *Star Wars* with its bounty hunter Boba Fett, or Beatles' fans obsession with Paul McCartney's "death." "The Batusi" features the leathery slapping of batwings over an innocuous "Watusi" beat shuffled by Hal Blaine, accented with enthusiastic horns and the fad dance craze's stop-start beat.

8. "Just a Simple Millionaire" (2:00). A foray into Austin Powers territory, a swingin' lightweight ode to Batman's public persona, Bruce Wayne. The song features a contextually odd country-western twang that gives way to an organ riff. One of the least memorable tracks in the Neal Hefti "Batman" oeuvre.

9. "My Fine Feathered Finks" (2:29). Music for waddling super-criminals, with clunky drums and a bass line that pays respect to Burgess Meredith's memorably graceful take on Oswald Cobblepot.

10. "Mr. Freeze" (2:24). Fuzztone guitar brushed with icicle-chime percussion and an appropriately cold and clinical melody. Three different actors played Victor Fries – George Sanders, Otto Preminger and Eli Wallach – so it's handy to have a unifying theme for the villain.

11. "Jervis" (2:07). Strangely conventional for Mad Hatter music; there is no hint of madness or instability in this pleasant stroll of a theme.

12. "Batman Chase" (1:53). The main theme recycled with more emphasis on the Duane Eddy twang and more '60s organ to add to the urgency of a good chase scene. During the last 20 seconds, the female chorus reappears with a few enthusiastic "Batman" chants.

13. "Gotham City Municipal Swing Band" (2:37). The follow-up single to "Batman Theme" offers a prescient take on the New Vaudeville Band's "Winchester Cathedral," which dominated the charts in late 1966. "Gotham City Municipal Swing Band" was co-opted as the "Creature Features" theme for a 1960s San Francisco TV show.

14. "Señorita Boo Bam" (2:34). More Duane Eddy rock, with about as much authentic Spanish flavor as a Taco Bell burrito. Nice echoey guitar and a fleeting trumpet reference to Henry Mancini's "Peter Gunn" theme, though.

15. "Honorable Batman" (2:11). If Batman were a cowboy policeman misplaced in a city landscape – kind of like *McCloud* – this would be his opening title theme. Driving bass book-ended by a gong sets a tone that would not be totally out of place in an early Clint Eastwood cop movie.

16. "Robin's Egg Blues" (2:05). The junior varsity version of the main theme, bouncier and just as kinetic, but lacking the magical gravity of the main theme.

17. "King Tut's Tomb" (2:10). Dark, halting music for the nine episodes in which Victor Buono played the Egyptian villain. There is no world music current flowing through the theme, but it effectively haunts.

18. "Mother Gotham" (2:27). A few years after *Batman*, Neal Hefti would write the theme for *The Odd Couple*, which must not have been as challenging for

him as the "Batman Theme," because he'd already written and recorded the riff here, right down to the prissy, percolating organ.

19. "Fingers" (2:56). The longest track Neal Hefti recorded for his "Batman" work, this jaunty, organ-driven track is the least melody-driven work in the collection.

20. "Soul City" (2:30). Ironically, the least soulful track in this set, with a wordless background chorus following the trumpet to nowhere. An anti-climactic to an otherwise imaginative project.

Nelson Riddle, *Batman Original TV Soundtrack* (1966)

1. "Batman Theme" (2:34). An even longer version than on Neal Hefti's album, with a much more jazzy, flute-accompanied take, featuring a "do-do-do" chorus; there are long stretches of this tune that bear no resemblance to the famous theme. When it finally kicks in, it does rock, but what it gains in seconds it loses in intensity.

2. "Batman Riddles the Riddler," or "Hi Diddle Riddle!" (1:41). A saxophone-led trifle featuring a riddle passed between Frank Gorshin's Riddler – "There are three men on a boat and four cigarettes, but no matches. How did they manage to smoke?" – and Burt Ward's Robin – "They threw one cigarette overboard and made the boat a cigarette lighter!"

3. "Batusi-A-Go-Go" (1:35). A much faster take on the dance version of the main theme than on Neal Hefti's album, but with the bonus of a great snippet of dialogue as Batman, in full cape and cowl, enters a club: "Ringside table, Batman?" "Just looking, thanks, I'll stand at the bar. I shouldn't wish to attract attention."

4. "Two Perfectly Ordinary People" (0:44). Batman and Robin aid an overwhelmed fan, as Robin assures her that behind the masks, they are just "two perfectly ordinary people." Then the track bursts inexplicably into "Stars and Stripes Forever." It must have made sense on the show.

5. "Holy Hole in the Doughnut" or "Robin, You've Done It Again!" (1:54). A sleepy lounge track underscores a series of Robin's more esoteric exclamations: "Holy Blizzard!"; "Holy Schizophrenia!"; "Leaping Lumbago!"; "Holy Haberdashery!"

6. "Batman Pows The Penguin" or "Aha, My Fine-Feathered Finks!" (1:46). Neal Hefti's theme evokes waddling, but Nelson Riddle's track takes a more aviary approach, with bird-like woodwinds. Contains dialogue between a cuckoo (penguin) clock and a clench-jawed Burgess Meredith, plus spoken-word readings of "pow" and "crunch" as the fight ensues.

7. "To the Batmobile" (2:15). We hear "Atomic batteries to power... turbines to speed..." and then another rendition of the "Batman Theme," with spacey instrumentation – is that a Theremin? – weaving around engine sounds and abrupt segues into incidental music.

8. "Batman Blues" (1:44). More jazz, late-night mopery for an overwhelmed super-hero trying to make his way in the world.

9. "Holy Flypaper" (2:59). At three minutes, this is the Grateful Dead jam of Nelson Riddle's Batman music, a wandering tour through stringy guitar, 1-2-3 drums, saxophone and Burt Ward book-ending the enterprise with the title outburst.

10. "Batman Thaws Mr. Freeze" or "That's The Way the Ice-Cube Crumbles!" (2:00). A sad, lilting piano elegy that, independent of a Batman project, could have found life as a simple love ballad. Unfortunately, the track's every second is buried under dialogue between George Sanders (as Mr. Freeze) and Adam

West. This gives way to a joke about Bat thermal underwear that leads to a brief "Batman Theme" reprise.

11. "Gotham City" [2:01]. Not the complex theme such a city deserves, but another 3am New York gin joint slice of jazz.

12. "Zelda Tempts Batman" or "Must He Go It Alone?" [2:27]. Jack Kruschen's Eivol Ekdol arranges a contract on Batman's life and Anne Baxter's Zelda attempts seduction in a smoky wind-down to the album.

The Marketts, *The Batman Theme Played by the Marketts* (1966)

1. "Batman Theme" [2:42]. An even longer version of the theme, much more of a rocker, by the group that took its *Twilight Zone*-themed "Out of Limits" instrumental to the top of the charts. This charted as a Top 20 single, even higher than Neal Hefti's version. It borrows its background "oooh oooh ooooohs" from the Four Tops' "Baby I Need Your Loving."

2. "The Bat Cave" [2:26]. More borrowing, this time from the band's own "Out of Limits." Much more Bond than Batman, but it does offer a nice ominous chorus of "ba-ba-ba-ba-ba-Batman" as bat wings flap across the speakers.

3. "Robin the Boy Wonder" [2:11]. Further plundering, as the track kicks off with a direct lift of Hal Blaine's classic intro from "Be My Baby," which it repeats between a chorus chanting the title track. But that's forgiven, as Blaine recorded with the Markettes and said he probably played on this track.

4. "The Bat Signal" [2:09]. Guitar twang, bursts of brass, and a background chorus mixed way in the back move this jaunty track along. The twang never takes over, but a cheesy organ pipes in and keeps the whole thing cooking, albeit on low heat.

5. "The Batmobile" [2:44]. Not just evocative of James Bond, but an actual swipe of the slow-build Bond theme trumpet over jittery guitar and that omnipresent chorus.

6. "The Joker" [2:21]. Finally, a track about the Clown Prince of Crime. It kicks off with an appropriately awed, hushed "The Joker!" before a cackling laugh and then a brass theme with great big cymbal splashes and dueling bass and organ. Powered by a hopping drumbeat, and directly connected to the guitar line of the Batman theme. It's insightful, as the Joker is most often seen as another half of the Batman; tying their themes together shows that someone in the Marketts was paying attention to more than just which riffs to steal from the radio hits of the day.

7. "The Penguin" [2:33]. Less descriptive than the Neal Hefti and Nelson Riddle themes, but with a great acoustic guitar flourish, handclaps and a shouted "Hey!" that keeps up with anything Def Leppard or Bon Jovi ever recorded.

8. "The Bat (Dance)" [2:18]. Incorporates elements of "The Batusi" and "Batman Theme," wrapped around a large borrowed section of Chuck Berry's "Memphis." A glaringly obvious section, but at least the Marketts consistently stole from the best.

9. "Doctor Death" [2:19]. Despite the gllomy title, the Marketts jam like they're celebrating the Easter Bunny. At one point, a "da-da-da-da" refrain fools the listener into thinking they are about to break out in a joyous "da-da-da-da-Dahctor Death!", – but at the last second, they dissolve into more rounds of "da-da-da-da."

10. "The Riddler" [2:35]. Another variation on the "Batman Theme," though not as consciously evocative as the Joker's music. Whoever the women in the chorus were, they must have been big Frank Gorshin fans; their lusty cry of "The Riddler!" is the most enthusiastic thing on the album.

11. "Bat Cape" (2:18). If Herb Alpert did not cover this, he should have. Although it is possible, given the Marketts' tendencies, that some Alpert variation came first.
12. "The Cat Woman" (2:22). Given the sexy Julie Newmar and Eartha Kitt embodiments of this character, which neither Neal Hefti nor Nelson Riddle honored in song, you might expect a slinky, seductive theme. And while the cut swings, it has all the feline sex appeal of week-old kitty litter.

Dan & Dale, *Batman and Robin – The Sensational Guitars of Dan & Dale* (1966)

Dan & Dale was a studio name for a group that included the centers of Sun Ra's Arkestra and Al Kooper's Blues Project. Unlike the cash-in kids projects of the era that this was meant to be, this is music that could almost be described as experimental, in its quest to incorporate as many styles as possible.

1. "Batman Theme" (2:16). This version rides on a flat chorus chanting the hero's name and an oom-pa-pa chugging beat that is implied in Neal Hefti's version but is brought to the forefront here.
2. "Batman's Batmorang" (2:51). A Latin-tinged groove perfect for dancing the Batusi. Note: the official spelling is "batarang."
3. "Batman and Robin Over the Roofs" (6:50). Nearly seven minutes of bass-driven, jazzy groove, which, like many of the Dynamic Duo's foes, just keeps going and going ...
4. "The Penguin Chase" (2:44). An organ-led romp that actually does help one envision the Penguin waddling as fast as he can from Batman, although it is doubtful he could keep his breath as long as the musicians do here.
5. "Flight of the Batman" (2:09). Saxophone and an Odd Couple-like melody propelled along with sirens and a perky guitar line. And slide whistles. And pig-like squeals. And creaking doors. And haunted house sound effects. And mad laughter.
6. "Joker is Wild" (1:09). Harmonica kicks off this subdued, surf-music tribute to the Harlequin of Hate.
7. "Robin's Theme" (3:05). The only track in this set with lyrics, sparse as they are. An unidentified female wails "Robin, yeah, I say Robin!" over a riff of the "Batman Theme" as a guitar plays a faster and faster tempo.
8. "Penguin's Umbrella" (3:05). Al Kooper's organ zips this one along with a circus feel, foreshadowing Tim Burton's take on the character 25 years later.
9. "Batman and Robin Swing" (2:43). More Batusi music but with a deeper groove than usual.
10. "Batmobile Wheels" (2:09). The horn riff is a direct lift from the 1964 Toys' record "A Lover's Concerto," but since *they* lifted it from Johann Sebastian Bach, the offense may be forgiven. The tune bounces along nicely, albeit without a single moment that evokes the Batmobile.
11. "The Riddler's Retreat" (2:12). Traditional rock-and-roll beat with more surf music guitar and the riff, atmosphere and changes taken directly from the Beatles' "She Loves You." It even ends with the "yeah, yeah, yeah" chords.
12. "The Bat Cave" (2:47). Slow, dragging saxophone over a strolling backbeat – yet another excuse to Batusi, if you need one.

The Dynamic Batmen, *Batman Theme* (1966)

Another album in the vein of *Batman and Robin – The Sensational Guitars of Dan & Dale*, this one is of little or no distinction, sloppy even by garage-band standards.

There is an eerie Joker laugh that presages Johnny Rotten and a Fats Domino-inspired saxophone that pops up, but this is the nadir of the instrumental albums.
1. "Batman TV Theme" (2:37)
2. "The Joker Laughs" (3:03)
3. "Riddle, Riddle, Riddle" (2:42)
4. "Take Off Wheels" (3:29)
5. "Robin the Bird" (1:59)
6. "ZAP" (2:28). Features an annoying, constant electrical sound effect.
7. "POW" (3:06). Features an annoying, constant yell of "Pow!"
8. "Bats Away" (4:53)
9. "The Penguin's Walk" (1:46)

Jan and Dean, Jan and Dean Meet Batman (1966)

1. "Batman" (2:45). The Beach Boys backbenchers might not break any musical ground with this project, but they win big points for knowing the source material. In this "We need the Batman" song based on Neal Hefti's "Batman Theme," they sing, "Criminals are a superstitious, cowardly lot / So my disguise must be able to strike terror into their hearts" and "I must be a creature of the night; black, terrible ... a bat! That's it! It's an omen! I shall become a bat!"
2. Narration: "The Origin of Captain Jan and Dean the Boy Blunder" (2:28). A recording studio mishap, channeled through the Little Old Lady from Pasadena, turns Jan and Dean into quasi-super-heroes. By singing her name, they turn into caped, well, you know.
3. "Robin the Boy Wonder" (2:28). A respectful ode to the colorful sidekick, complete with interjections of "Holy..." Say this for Jan and Dean: when they jump in, they jump in all the way.
4. Narration: "A Vit-A-Min a Day" (3:48). A mad scientist and his wife, the obedient Hypo, plan to poison the Surf City water supply "to destroy these war-mongering imperialists once and for all." Notable for its portrayal of the chief of police as a bumbling fool, and for the answer he receives when he asks his "deputies," a group of kids, who could possibly save the day: "The Beach Boys!" they yell. Ends with a cliffhanger, in the best tradition of the TV show.
5. "Mr. Freeze" (2:54). A brassy, swinging instrumental powered by castanets and organ.
6. Narration: "The Doctor's Dilemma" (2:36). The conclusion to the Vit-A-Min saga; the bad doctor sounds distractingly like Adam Sandler at his dopiest, until he dissolves into a dangerously-close-to-racist approximation of Vietnamese.
7. Narration: "A Stench in Time" (2:57). A new episode begins, as the "Titanic Twosome" take on the Garbage Man. Another cliffhanger closes the A-side of the record, as the heroes are dumped into a garbage pit.
8. "Batman Theme" (2:24). A high-energy take on the TV theme, with powerful surf-driven guitars and liquid drumming that rivals Hal Blaine's work – unless this *is* Hal Blaine playing. Jan and Dean chant Batman's name, passing the lead to an organ before it all wraps up.
9. Narration: "A Hank of Hair and a Banana Peel" (2:59). Sound effects to rival old-time radio plays illustrate once again that Jan and Dean might be goofing around, but they take this project seriously. Mostly.
10. Narration: "The Fireman's Flaming Flourish" (3:52). A Cleveland concert by Jan and Dean is interrupted by the Fireman, leading to a stolen-tiger circus

cliffhanger of sorts, as the Boy Blunder takes a wrong turn and gets the team lost in Jersey City.

11. "The Joker is Wild" (3:10). Since neither Hefti nor Riddle gave the Joker a theme on their respective albums, Jan and Dean do their best to fill in, with manic laughter, a skipping drumbeat and some quasi-demonic wailing.

12. Narration: "Tiger, Tiger, Burning" (2:48). The boys climb into their "atomic-powered Woody" and find the Fireman at the Torch Club. Another cliffhanger, as the heroes are plummeted into a flaming pit. "Holy Campfire Girls!" indeed.

13. "Flight of the Batmobile" (3:14). Beach Boys-like studio power segues into an ode to Batman's crime-fighting equipment. Sloppy, kind of funny, and derivative. In other words, quintessential Jan and Dean.

14. Narration: "A Hot Time in the Old Town Tonight" (2:39). The conclusion of the Fireman story, as the duo jails their enemy, and the Boy Blunder marvels at the difficulty of writing plot intricacies into a two-minute script.

Various Artists, Batmania: Songs Inspired By the Batman TV Series (1997)

A collection of theme recordings and novelty records of the era.

1. "Batman Theme" by Neal Hefti (2:18). The original album version.

2. "The Story of Batman" by Adam West (2:40). In the fine tradition of William Shatner and Lorne Greene recording pop songs, this West "Bat-disc" features a piano and brass take on the Batman theme, describing Batman as "king of all the heroes." Between choruses, West describes step-by-step how listeners can use the disc as camouflage, although he does not explain how that can be accomplished while the disc is playing. This track was reportedly recorded in the mid-1970s, long after the show left its twice-weekly run. To West's credit, he speaks the lyrics and does not try to sing.

3. "The Capture" by Burgess Meredith (2:26). "He's the Penguin," a female chorus intones, over a slow, jazzy trumpet and drum track, as Meredith, also to his credit, speaks the lyrics and does not try to sing. Features several fine Meredith "quacks."

4. "Batman to the Rescue," by LaVern Baker (2:23). Baker, a Rock and Roll Hall of Fame vocalist, adapts her "Jim Dandy" classic to honor the Caped Crusader, as a funky guitar and trumpets blast over such shouts as "Swing, on, Batman!" and "Don't lose your cool Robin!" Manages to work in the Batmobile, Batplane, the Joker, Mr. Freeze, and even "biff!" and "pow!" This should be embarrassing for a blues shouter of Baker's caliber, but she brings such enthusiasm and life to her vocal, and the record works, even if it can't explain why "Batman is on his way to Maine."

5. "Batman Theme" by Al Hirt (2:13). Trumpeter and band leader Hirt manages to shave a few seconds off the Neal Hefti recording, but offers one of the best non-Neal Hefti versions, with a careening guitar and drum foundation under his charts. A real rocker.

6. "Ratman and Bobin in the Clipper Caper" by the Brothers Four (4:05). This B-side uses the guitar riff from "Batman Theme" over a bizarre tale of a master criminal, the Mad Barber, who is cutting off rock stars' hair – "He's reduced the Rolling Stones to the Smooth Pebbles!" Ratman and Bobin rescue the Beatles from the Mad Barber, after working in Sonny and Cher, Dracula and Lawrence Welk. "Take him away, Commissioner," indeed.

7. "Batman a Go-Go" by the Combo Kings (2:21). A saxophone and R&B vocal take on the "Batman Theme," meant to be a dance floor raver. Wicked tambourine and repeated frat-house shouts of "Batman!" set the tone.
8. "Miranda" by Adam West (2:48). All that credit West built up by not singing earlier on the album is squandered here, as West does his best Pat Boone imitation, singing as Batman. Worth listening to for such hilarious innuendo as "Would you like to see me make my muscles dance?" and "Come over and take a teeny-weeny peek."
9. "That Man" by Peggy Lee (2:04). The singing legend is clearly referring to Batman, although such lyrics as "he goes through walls and he walks through space" stretch things a bit. Points for a series of sung "biffs!", "pows!", and "zows!" Ends with the singer letting listeners know she is stowed away in the Batmobile's trunk.
10. "Batman Theme" by Davie Allan & the Arrows (2:48). A grungy, guitar-driven version that displays muscle but is played at a slower tempo that drags the disc down. Improves with repeated listenings.
11. "The Joker is Wild" by Jan and Dean (3:12). Details on this track are listed with the entry on the album *Jan and Dean Meet Batman*.
12. "The Riddler" by Frank Gorshin (2:10). Written and arranged by Mel Torme (of "The Christmas Song (Chestnuts roasting on an open fire...)" fame), this is a fun kids recording featuring a series of progressively bad riddles giggled over a percussion-crazy track and a back-and-forth annoying female chorus. Gorshin, when he's not squealing his helium-fueled laughter, actually acquits himself well as a vocalist.
13. "The Escape" by Burgess Meredith (2:25). This B-side to "The Capture" features the exact music and vocal backing track, over a tale of The Penguin's big escape from jail. Refers to the Dynamic Duo as "Mud Hens," a slice of trivia for Toledo minor league baseball fans.
14. "Batman and Robin" by Adam West (3:17). This, the B-side of "The Story of Batman," earns West some points back as he reverts to speaking his way through a caper with the Tickler.
15. "Batman Theme" by Joel McNeely and the Royal Scottish National Orchestra (2:28). String-laden arrangement starts with the Danny Elfman theme from the Tim Burton films, then leaps into the Neal Hefti theme, complete with brass accents for the punches. Manages to mash together both themes by the close of the brief recording.

Other LPs

60sgaragebands.com lists these additional LPs as having been inspired by Hefti's theme. All are from 1966.
1. 5th Avenue Buses, *Trip to Gotham City*
2. Bat Boys, *Batman Theme*
3. Merriettes, *Children's Treasury of Batman Musical Stories*
4. Revengers, *Batman & Other Supermen*
5. Spacemen, *Music for Batman & Robin*
6. Ventures, *Batman Theme*

Other Singles

60sgaragebands.com lists these singles as having been inspired by Hefti's theme. All are from 1966.
1.. Astronauts: "Batman Theme"

2. Avengers: "Batman" / "Batarang"
3. The Bats: "Batmobile" / "Batusi"
4. Batmen with the Phantom Band: "Linda" / "Just You Don't Know It"
5. Batt Man & The Boy Wonders: "You Wouldn't Listen" / "I'll Keep Searching"
6. Buddies: "Duckman Pt.1 & Pt. 2"
7. Campers: "Ballad of Batman" / "Batmobile"
8. Cartoons: "Batusi" / "Big Bad Batusi"
9. Ronnie Cole Trio: "Batman"
10. Wade Denning & the Port Washingtons: "Batman"
11. Esquires: "Batman Theme"
12. Falling Stars: "The Real Batman" / "Batman"
13. Four of Us: "Batman"
14. Gallants: "Batman Theme" / "Robin's Blues"
15. Dickie Goodman: "Batman and His Grandmother"
16. Gotham City Crimefighters: "Who Stole the Batmobile?"
17. Gotham City Teens: "(Holy Holy) Ravioli" / "Ravioli"
18. Invisible Burgundy Bullfrog: "Batman Rides Again"
19. Jon & Lee & The Checkmates: "Batman Theme" / "Batman 2 (The Batusi)"
20. Bob Kuban & In-Men: "Batman Theme"
21. Madd, Inc.: "Batman" / "Batman A-Go-Go"
22. Scotty McKay: "Here Comes Batman"
23. Merriettes: "It's the Batman" / "Look Out for the Batman"
24. Merriettes: "There Goes Robin" / "The Wonderful Boy Wonder"
25. Merriettes: "Here Comes The Batmobile" / "The Battiest Car Around"
26. Merriettes: "The Joker gets Trumped" / "Ho Ho Ho The Joker's Wild"
27. Merriettes: "The Penguin" / "A Penguin Caper"
28. Paniks: "I Can Beat Him Up"
29. Pacers: "Big Batman" / "Gotham City"
30. Plunderers: "Batman"
31. Revengers: "Batman Theme"
32. Riddlers: "Batman Theme"
33. Robin & The Batmen: "Batskinner"
34. Robins: "Batman" / "Batarang"
35. Rocky & The Riddlers: "Batman"
36. Scaffold: "Goodbat Nightman"
37. Seeds of Euphoria: "Let's Send Batman to Viet Nam"
38. Spotlights: "Batman and Robin"
39. Squires: "Batmobile"
40. Standells: "Batman Theme"
41. Ventures: "Batman Theme"
42. Gate Wesley & Band: "Do the Batman"
43. Link Wray & The Raymen: "Batman Theme"

About the Contributors

Becky Beard earns her living primarily as a professional musician. An Appalachian dulcimist by trade, she is also a writer, poet, interviewer, and folktale / fairytale enthusiast. A keen follower of pop culture, her tastes in film and TV tend towards the quirky.

Jim Beard, a native of Toledo, Ohio, is a comic-book writer, historian, and journalist. His credits include work for DC, Dark Horse, IDW, and TwoMorrows, and he currently provides weekly content for Marvel.com. His second favorite comic-book character is Shelly Mayer's Ma Hunkel, the original Golden Age Red Tornado.

Joseph F. Berenato claims to have lived a very "bat-saturated life." After obtaining a B.A. in English Literature, he spent several years as a mild-mannered reporter before returning to his roots and working on his family's blueberry farm. He can currently be found writing for CriticalMess.net under his alter ego, "coffeejoe."

Timothy Callahan is a comics scholar, author of *Grant Morrison: The Early Years* and editor of *Teenagers from the Future*, both from Sequart. He also writes for ComicBookResources.com and blogs about comics and pop culture at geniusboyfiremelon.blogspot.com.

Chuck Dixon is the proverbial lifelong comic-book fan who went on to live the fanboy dream, writing the actual comic stories. His list of DC writing credits is a testament to his imagination and professionalism, including work on *Detective Comics*, *Robin*, *Nightwing*, *Birds of Prey*, and *Green Arrow*. Chuck's a cornerstone of modern Batman history.

Robert Greenberger is one of the great fan-makes-good stories: as the founder of Starlog Press's late-lamented *Comics Scene* magazine, he parlayed his experience into a dream job as a DC Comics editor. Bob's been involved in a heck of a lot of incredible projects, including the legendary *Crisis on Infinite Earths*, *Who's Who in the DC Universe*, *Starman*, DC's *Star Trek* comics, and Dorling Kindersley's *DC Comics Encyclopedia*. He has since become an author of both novels and non-fiction about classic comics.

Michael D. Hamersky blogs at ComicBookCollectorsBlog.com and heads up Make It So Marketing, Inc., which specializes in comics and collectibles.

Michael Johnson has a degree in art, an interest in science and history, parents who are teachers, and a keen eye for the latest in technological advances. This is his first publication.

Paul Kupperberg has written just about everything. A comics fan who turned comics professional, he wrote an estimated 600 comic stories from the 1970s to the present, including what's considered the first comic-book mini-series, 1979's *World of Krypton*. He has also authored numerous novels, non-fiction, role-playing supplements, kids' books, magazines articles, newspapers pieces, comic strips, and blogs. Paul's also toiled as an editor with DC Comics from 1991 to 2006, and several other important journals, such as the late-lamented *Weekly World News*. Suffice it to say that he knows his pop culture and his comics.

Michael S. Miller has journalism in his blood. A consummate newsman, he's been the editor-in-chief of the Toledo Free Press since 2005. He's also an adamant follower of pop culture, especially music. Few others can pull musical references off the tops of their heads quite like Michael.

Will Murray may be *the* living expert on the pulp fiction genre. These days, it's hard to open up a reprint of a pulp novel or a history companion without finding one of Will's informative articles – he's the go-to guy for all things pulp. He's also a damn fine writer of fiction himself, having learned from some of the men who laid the groundwork for every single comic-book character and situation. Add to this his long involvement with films, TV, radio, and comics, and you've got a pop-culture giant of a man.

Jeff Rovin's list of credits would fill this entire book, so suffice it to say that he's the incredibly prolific writer of dozens of books in a multitude of genres. He's perhaps best known for his *New York Times* bestselling series of Tom Clancy's Op Center novels, his "How to Win" video game guides of the 1980s and '90s, and a set of encyclopedias covering comic-book and film subjects. On top of all this, Jeff was also an editor and writer for DC Comics, Warren Publications, and the infamous Atlas-Seaboard. But to me, all these accomplishments pale in comparison to authoring what I believe to be the finest licensed-character original novel ever written, *Return of the Wolf Man*. For that one, Jeff has my undying gratitude as well as that of Universal Monsters fans everywhere.

Peter Sanderson runs the gamut of knowledgeable professions: scholar, teacher, lecturer, historian. In the 1980s, he was hired by DC to read every single comic they had published since 1935 and make copious notes. That odyssey was used as a foundation for such weighty DC projects as the *Crisis on Infinite Earths* maxi-series and *Who's Who in the DC Universe*. Peter then scored the envious position of Marvel Comics' first archivist and soon became deeply entrenched in their long-running *Official Handbook of the Marvel Universe* series. Today, he continues to educate on comic books through online writings and books such as *The Marvel Vault*. His work has also appeared in Sequart's *Minutes to Midnight: Twelve Essays on Watchmen*.

Jennifer K. Stuller, a native of the San Francisco Bay area, makes her living as a professional writer, critic, and scholar, with regular contributions to such publications as *Geek Monthly*, *Bitch*, and *Washington CEO*. Her expertise lies in discussions of gender, sexuality, and diversity. In her own words she "strives to be the Joseph Campbell of modern myth – only much more feminist and much less crotchety." She is the author of *Ink-Stained Amazons and Cinematic Warriors: Superwomen in Modern Mythology*.

Bill Walko is a graphic designer and illustrator himself. If you're a fan of books about comics, you've probably seen his work. He's the designer of several guides to comics history from TwoMorrows. He also runs the engaging website titanstower.com.

Robert G. Weiner is the Associate Humanities Librarian at Texas Tech University and also their librarian for Art and Sequential Art. He is known for developing a distinct cataloging system for the graphic novel collection he helped the school amass.

Also from Sequart

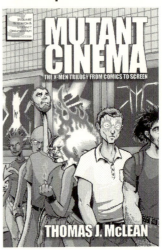

IMPROVING THE FOUNDATIONS: BATMAN BEGINS FROM COMICS TO SCREEN / by Julian Darius / 264p / $14.99

MUTANT CINEMA: THE X-MEN TRILOGY FROM COMICS TO SCREEN / by Thomas J. McLean / 296p / $15.95

TEENAGERS FROM THE FUTURE: ESSAYS ON THE LEGION OF SUPER-HEROES / edited by Timothy Callahan, foreword by Matt Fraction, afterword by Barry Lyga / 340p / $19.99

CLASSICS ON INFINITE EARTHS: THE JUSTICE LEAGUE AND DC CROSSOVER CANON / by Julian Darius / forthcoming

KEEPING THE WORLD STRANGE: A PLANETARY GUIDE / edited by Cody Walker / 180p / $11.99

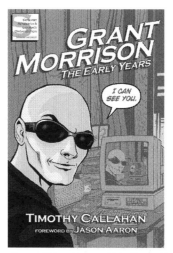

GRANT MORRISON: THE EARLY YEARS / by Timothy Callahan, foreword by Jason Aaron, Grant Morrison interview / 280p / $15.95

MINUTES TO MIDNIGHT: TWELVE ESSAYS ON WATCHMEN / edited by Richard Bensam / 180p / $11.99

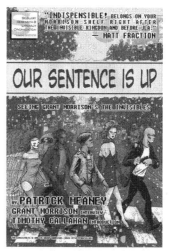

OUR SENTENCE IS UP: SEEING GRANT MORRISON'S THE INVISIBLES / by Patrick Meaney, introduction by Timothy Callahan, Grant Morrison interview / 356p / $19.99

For more information and for exclusive content, visit Sequart.org.

Made in the USA
Middletown, DE
14 April 2021

37674452R00177